Crazy *for* Casseroles

WITHDRAWN

Crazy *for* Casseroles

275 All-American Hot-Dish Classics

James Villas

THE HARVARD COMMON PRESS

Boston, Massachusetts

The Harvard Common Press
535 Albany Street
Boston, Massachusetts 02118
www.harvardcommonpress.com

Printed in the United States of America

Printed on acid-free paper

Library of Congress Cataloging-in-Publication Data

Villas, James.
    Crazy for casseroles : 275 all-American hot-dish classics / James
Villas.
        p. cm.
    Includes index.
        ISBN 1-55832-216-7 ((cl) : alk. paper) — ISBN 1-55832-217-5
((pbk) : alk. paper)
        1. Casserole cookery. I. Title.

TX693 .V53 2003
641.8'21—dc21   2002007436

Special bulk-order discounts are available on this and other Harvard Common Press books. Companies and organizations may purchase books for premiums or resale, or may arrange a custom edition, by contacting the Marketing Director at the address above.

10   9   8   7   6   5   4   3   2   1

Cover recipe: Chicago Shrimp, Spinach, and
Feta Cheese Casserole, page 199

Cover photographs by Alexandra Grablewski

Book design and illustration by Richard Oriolo

Contents

Acknowledgments

THIS IS MY FIFTH COOKBOOK edited by Pam Hoenig, and so involved has she been in its conception, execution, and overall design that she almost qualifies as co-author. Over the long haul, she has made numerous suggestions and important decisions, prepared heaven only knows how many of the dishes, edited the recipes with uncanny dexterity, and encouraged me far and beyond the call of duty. Pam is not only a highly professional and brilliant editor; she's also the most devoted and loyal friend an author could ever have.

No cookbook of this scope would have been possible without the cooperation and generosity of friends, family, colleagues, and utter strangers all over the country who champion authentic American cookery as much as I do and who've inspired and helped me over the years in ways they can't imagine. Many are acknowledged throughout the book, but to those whose names and faces have faded faster than the glorious aromas of their kitchens and the recipes jotted down in notebooks and on random slips of paper, I offer heartfelt thanks for nourishing my hungry body and soul.

I DON'T HESITATE A SECOND to insist that nothing typifies American cookery more than the sumptuous, highly varied casseroles that have been baked in ovens all over the country for the past century. Casseroles, in fact, not only define a major style of food on which millions of us were virtually weaned, but also illustrate like no other dishes what authentic regional cooking is all about. Just mention jambalaya and spoonbread to a Southerner, for instance, or baked beans and Indian pudding to a New Englander, or tamale pie to a Texan, or Dungeness crab and olive bake to a West Coaster, and watch the eyes light up. Over the decades, casseroles such as crabmeat Dewey, shrimp de Jonghe, chicken spaghetti, hog pot, country captain, and Sally Lunn have evolved into regional classics, and I dare say there's no honest soul anywhere who doesn't swoon over a luscious chicken pot pie, macaroni and cheese, lasagne, corn pudding, and apple brown betty.

Despite all the culinary innovations of recent years, not to mention the rampant snobbism that threatens the very integrity of our proud food traditions, casseroles remain one of

Introduction

The Romance of American Casseroles

America's greatest contributions to world gastronomy, an original, sound, and eminently simple method of cooking that deserves new attention and will undoubtedly still be around long after much of today's phony novelty has been burned to a crisp.

And, after all, why not? Whether prepared for casual family suppers, elegant formal buffets, potlucks, picnics, tailgate parties, or sick-ins, casseroles boast a versatility that is matched only by soups and stews. The ingredients are either carefully layered or mixed together; moistened with sauce, broth, milk, or a canned soup; and either baked alone or topped with all sorts of grated cheeses, bread crumbs and batters, shredded potatoes, or starchy flakes and meals to form a glorious crust. Numerous casseroles not only can but should be made in advance to allow flavors to develop and the cook to relax. Most can be divided into portions and frozen for future use. And since they're essentially oven-to-table dishes, they provide the ultimate solution to carefree entertaining.

So flexible is the structure, texture, consistency, and taste of a casserole that it can be made plain or complex, rich or bland, highly nutritional or low-cal, and when it comes to feeding large groups of people food that stays hot, requires no carving or manipulation, and involves minimum cleanup, there's simply nothing more sensible than a covered casserole that's as beautiful to look at as is great to eat. Children love casseroles as much as adults do and since the dishes rarely require any tricky cooking techniques, they are an ideal way to inspire youngsters to try their hands in the kitchen. Any way you look at it, the role of casseroles in American cooking is paramount, a convenient, economical, delicious, and downright fun method of preparing food that should be as important to us today as it was to our ancestors.

Just 40 or so years ago, there wasn't a cook in this country who didn't boast favorite casseroles intended to provide a practical, nutritious, and delicious way to feed both a small family and a large group of hungry friends. The ultimate holiday, wedding, or birthday gift was one of dozens of beautiful casserole dishes designed to enhance all sorts of baked components, and who could deny that anything was more mouthwatering (and easy to prepare) than a bubbly layered meat and vegetable casserole or a creamy poultry or seafood one crusted to a golden finish on top? It was an era without pretentions, when people gathered at the dining room or buffet table simply to share good food and enjoy one another's company, a time when cooking, far from being the complicated, contrived, and overwrought activity it often is today, was still a leisure affair, and when nothing satisfied and impressed more than a carefully prepared, attractive casserole, a fresh salad, a good loaf of bread, and an appropriate beverage.

The irony, of course, is that before casserole cookery became so popular during the first half of the twentieth century and gradually took on a distinctive American identity all its own, to prepare food *en casserole* in the European style was deemed the ultimate in culinary sophistication. (The actual origins of the French word "casserole" can be traced back to a Renaissance pot or crock called a *casse*.) French *cassoulet* and *coq au vin*, Spanish *paella*, Italian *lasagne*, Moroccan *tajine*, Greek *pastitsio*, Indian *pilau*, British hot pot—the names might have sounded exotic in those early days, but being no more than a combination of ingredients baked in and usually served directly from an earthenware, metal, or tempered glass vessel, the one-pot dishes were essentially no different from the simple casseroles that would become such an integral part of American cookery. Fannie Farmer did include a single casserole of meat and rice in her pioneering cookbook, but it was not till the first decade of the twentieth century that such influential authors as Marion Harland, Olive Hulse, and Marion Neil began to feature recipes for different types of casseroles. During World War I and the Depression, casseroles were promoted as a means to economize; Campbell's introduction of canned soups not long after as a substitute for elaborate sauces added a whole new dimension to casserole cookery; by 1943, *The Joy of Cooking* included almost two dozen sumptuous casseroles; and so popular were casseroles by the 1950s that James Beard devoted a whole cookbook to the subject.

Unfortunately, by the early 1970s some casseroles had been so abused by the use of canned luncheon meats and vegetables, dried parsley and garlic powder, Velveeta, bouillon cubes, MSG, crushed potato chips, and heaven knows what other "convenience" ingredients that the whole cooking concept gradually plunged into disrepute. No doubt many of these abominations got their just reward, but sadly and unfairly left behind in the carnage carried out by zealous food snobs was a veritable wealth of honest, intelligent, and delectable casseroles. They gradually disappeared from most leading cookbooks but remained as quietly and lovably indispensable to the home kitchen as they'd been 20 years earlier.

Since it appears today that every effort is finally being made to reclaim much of our culinary heritage (extending to everything from Tex-Mex and soul food to Shaker and Pennsylvania Dutch cookery to traditional Jewish desserts), my goal in this book is not only to restore old-fashioned, regional American casseroles—from appetizers to desserts—to their rightful status but also to demonstrate how our rich bounty of relatively new ingredients can be adapted to produce wondrous casseroles unimaginable in the past. Included are certainly old favorites like shrimp Creole, crabmeat Norfolk, turkey Divan, chicken Tetrazzini, scalloped potatoes, Iowa succotash, dilly casserole bread, and persimmon pudding, but here there is also an emphasis on casseroles made with fresh cheeses, ethnic sausages, lesser cuts of meat, root vegetables and new varieties of beans and wild mushrooms, fennel and celery root, baby leeks and sugar snap peas, interesting herbs and spices, oats and multigrain breads, and even a few exotic fruits.

To maintain the distinctive character of the American casserole, I by no means have any objections to the use of such traditional components as leftover cooked foods, canned broths, soups, and tomatoes, packaged bread stuffings, certain frozen vegetables, plain dried noodles, pimentos, and supermarket natural aged cheeses. On the other hand, nowhere in this book will you find canned meats and vegetables, frozen chives or dried parsley flakes, processed cheeses, liquid smoke, MSG, bouillon cubes, crushed potato chips, or, heaven forbid, canned fruit cocktail. As for all the delightfully quaint nomenclature associated with casseroles, there are indeed bakes, stratas, pots, scallops, divans, royales, supremes, and even fluffs.

There's nothing trendy about these casseroles, no weird, cutting-edge combinations, and, to be sure, no cooking techniques that even a teenager can't manage to master. This is food at its simplest and most appealing, the sort of no-nonsense, delicious fare that leaves lots of room for experimentation and variation and that the home cook can feel proud to serve at the humblest family gatherings or on the most elaborate buffet table any time of the year. This is the true cooking of America, and if there's ever been anyone (food elitists included) whose basic instincts and appetite couldn't be sparked by the sight, aroma, and taste of a great casserole, I've yet to meet such an individual.

I MUST OWN AT LEAST 20 different casseroles made of everything from enameled cast iron or steel to terra cotta to lined copper, and not one has the exact same dimensions, depth, or overall volume as another. Domestic and foreign casseroles come in every size, shape, and design imaginable. Some have lids and handles and some don't; some are suitable for stove-top, while others must be used only in the oven; and not all can be placed in microwaves for reheating or in freezers for storage. Yet I know the idiosyncrasies and distinct personalities of every casserole in my kitchen, and I love and respect each for the same reasons I treasure my collection of saucepans, skillets, and knives. So should you.

Since casserole dishes involve so many variables, the sizes called for in most recipes in this book should always be considered approximate. For a recipe indicating a 2-quart casserole, say, you might well use one that has a bit more volume. Likewise, depending on the bulk of a given dish (shredded chicken versus whole pieces, for example), you could probably get by with an off-size 1½-quart casserole instead of the

The Essentials of Modern Casserole Cookery

A Guide to Casserole Dishes

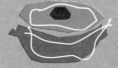

2-quart one specified. Remember, however, that generally a casserole dish that is too large can cause the food to dry out, while one that is too small risks the possibility of uneven cooking and messy spills. A good rule of thumb I try to maintain when judging the right size of any casserole is to allow about one inch between the ingredients and the rim of the vessel.

Unless a shallow casserole is specified, most of the recipes refer to a deep casserole with a lid. Soufflé or baking dishes and pans can often be substituted if you simply don't have the right casserole, in which case heavy aluminum foil can be used in place of a lid if the dish needs to be covered.

To determine the volume of any casserole, measure out quarts of water and fill the vessel to just shy of the rim.

Finally, when purchasing any casserole, look for both quality and beauty, and consider the vessel to be a sound investment that will not only provide years of dependable service but grace any dinner table or buffet.

GLAZED EARTHENWARE: Retains heat well; attractive for serving; not suitable for stove-top; easy cleaning; moderately priced. (Beware of inexpensive imported pottery, which might contain lead in the glaze and should not be used in food preparation.)

ENAMELED CAST IRON: Heavy, durable, cooks evenly, and retains heat well; nonreactive surface; suitable for stove-top; moderately easy cleaning; moderate to expensive.

HEAVY-GAUGE STAINLESS STEEL: Very durable but not a good heat conductor unless the bottom is reinforced with copper or heavy aluminum; suitable for stove-top; moderately easy cleaning; expensive.

LINED COPPER: Heavy, durable, and retains heat very well; beautiful for serving; suitable for stove-top; moderately easy cleaning; expensive to very expensive, depending on weight.

ANODIZED ALUMINUM: Moderately heavy, resists sticking, and retains heat well; suitable for acidic foods; suitable for stove-top; moderately easy cleaning; expensive.

OVENPROOF PORCELAIN (CERAMIC): Retains heat moderately well; suitable for acidic foods; not suitable for stove-top; subject to chipping and scratching; easy cleaning; inexpensive to moderately priced.

OVENPROOF GLASSWARE: Cooks evenly and retains heat well; suitable for acidic foods; not suitable for stove-top; some can go directly from freezer to oven to table; moderately fragile; not easy to clean; inexpensive.

Approximate Casserole/Baking Dish Equivalents

CASSEROLE SIZE	BAKING DISH EQUIVALENTS
1-Quart Casserole	8 x 6 x 1½-inch baking dish 6-inch soufflé dish
1½-Quart Casserole	8 x 8 x 1½-inch baking dish 7-inch soufflé dish
2-Quart Casserole	9 x 9 x 1½-inch baking dish 8-inch soufflé dish
2½-Quart Casserole	10 x 10 x 1½-inch baking dish 9-inch soufflé dish
3- to 4-Quart Casserole	13 x 9 x 2-inch baking dish 10 x 10 x 4-inch baking dish or pan
5-Quart Casserole	15 x 10 x 2-inch baking dish

Freezing Casseroles

ALTHOUGH MANY CASSEROLES CAN BE frozen before or after being baked for up to about three months, remember that the longer one is frozen, the more moisture is lost. I do not recommend freezing any baked casserole that contains potatoes, rice, or pasta, all of which will lose much of their texture. Casseroles that contain tomatoes or other acidic ingredients freeze particularly well. It's always better to freeze unbaked casseroles.

To freeze an unbaked casserole, line the casserole dish with enough heavy aluminum foil to come up over the top of the ingredients, assemble the casserole, cover, and freeze till solid. Remove from the dish, cover tightly with the foil, store in freezer paper, and label with the name of the dish and the date.

To bake, remove the freezer paper and foil, return the casserole to the appropriate cooking vessel, allow to thaw completely, and bake about 15 minutes longer than the time indicated in the recipe.

Freeze cooled, leftover casserole portions in tightly wrapped aluminum foil, freezer bags, or freezer paper, and remember to label with the name of the dish and date.

Some Useful Ingredient Equivalents

Onions

1 small = ¼ cup chopped

1 medium-size = ½ cup chopped

1 large = 1 cup chopped

Celery

1 small rib = ¼ to ⅓ cup chopped

1 large rib = ½ cup chopped

Bell Peppers

1 medium-size = ½ cup chopped

1 large = ¾ cup chopped

Potatoes

1 medium-size = 1 cup diced

1 large = 1½ cups diced

Tomatoes

1 medium-size = 1 cup chopped

Mushrooms

½ pound = 2½ cups chopped

Cheese

4 ounces = 1 cup grated or shredded

1 pound = 4 cups grated or shredded

4 ounces blue or feta = ½ cup crumbled

Herbs

1 tablespoon chopped fresh = 1 teaspoon dried

Meats and Poultry

1 pound cooked = about 3 cups cubed or diced

A Casserole Pantry of Basic Secondary Ingredients

All-purpose flour

All-purpose yellow onions

All-purpose russet potatoes

Carrots

Garlic bulbs

Lemons and oranges

Frozen vegetables *(peas, corn kernels, lima beans, green beans, and okra)*

Canned beans *(navy, pinto, black, and chick peas)*

Canned tomatoes *(whole and crushed)*

Canned tomato sauce

Canned tomato paste

Canned tuna *(chunk light and solid white)*

Canned fruits

Canned broth *(chicken and beef)*

Canned soup *(I always have on hand: Campbell's condensed cream of chicken, cream of mushroom, and cream of celery soups)*

Dried pastas

Dried wild mushrooms *(ceps, shiitakes, chanterelles)*

Dried beans *(Great Northern white, kidney, and pinto)*

Dry bread crumbs *(coarse and fine)*

Rice *(long-grain white or Carolina, short-grain brown, and wild)*

Cheese *(sharp aged cheddar, genuine Parmesan, Swiss Emmenthaler, Monterey Jack, and feta)*

Nuts *(pecans, walnuts, and almonds)*

Frozen shredded coconut

Bottled olives *(pimento-stuffed green and seedless black)*

Pimentos

Prepared horseradish

Dijon mustard

Hellmann's mayonnaise

Sour cream

Butter and margarine

Vegetable oil and virgin olive oil

Cream Sauce

¹/₄ cup (¹/₂ stick) butter

¹/₄ cup all-purpose flour

1 cup milk

1 cup half-and-half

Salt to taste

1. In a medium-size heavy saucepan, melt the butter over low heat, gradually add the flour, and whisk till the mixture is foamy, about 3 minutes.

2. Remove the pan from the heat and gradually add the milk and half-and-half, whisking constantly till smooth. Season with salt, return the pan to moderate heat, and cook, whisking constantly, till thickened, about 5 minutes. (For a thinner sauce, add a little more milk.)

Mushroom Cream Sauce: Melt 2 tablespoons butter in a small skillet over moderate heat, add 1 cup finely chopped mushrooms, and cook, stirring, till the mushroom liquid has evaporated, about 3 minutes. Add the mushrooms to the cream sauce before it has thickened, adding a little more milk before the final whisking.

MAKES 2 CUPS

Cheese Sauce

1 cup Cream Sauce (page 6)

1 cup shredded sharp or extra-sharp cheddar cheese

Dash of Worcestershire sauce

Dash of Tabasco sauce

Salt to taste

In a medium-size heavy saucepan, warm the cream sauce over moderately low heat, add the cheese, and stir till melted and well blended. Add the Worcestershire and Tabasco, season with salt, and stir till well blended and smooth. (For a thinner sauce, add a little warm milk.)

MAKES ABOUT 2 CUPS

Tomato Sauce

$^1/_2$ cup (1 stick) butter

1 medium-size onion, finely chopped

1 celery rib, finely chopped

$^1/_2$ small green bell pepper, seeded and finely chopped

2 garlic cloves, minced

3 cups canned crushed tomatoes

$^1/_2$ teaspoon sugar

Salt and black pepper to taste

In a medium-size heavy saucepan, melt the butter over moderate heat, add the onion, celery, bell pepper, and garlic, and stir till softened, about 5 minutes. Add the tomatoes and sugar, season with salt and pepper, stir well, and cook till the sauce is thickened, 10 to 15 minutes.

Marinara Sauce: Substitute olive oil for the butter and add about $^1/_2$ teaspoon crumbled dried oregano.

MAKES ABOUT 3 CUPS

Appetizer Casserole Dips, Quiches, and Ramekins

California Artichoke and Almond Casserole Dip

Maybe you don't care, but California produces 100 percent of the U. S. commercial crop of artichokes and one-half the world's crop of almonds, reason enough to peg this easy casserole dip as a West Coast original. Since genuine Parmigiano-Reggiano has such a distinctive punch, this is one time I don't object to using blander domestic Parmesan. Because both the mayonnaise and cheese are slightly salty, however, don't salt this dip—especially if the only almonds you have are salted. I serve this with toast rounds at cocktail parties or on a small buffet.

One 6-ounce jar artichoke hearts, drained

3/4 cup mayonnaise

2 teaspoons fresh lemon juice

1 cup freshly grated Parmesan cheese

Freshly ground black pepper to taste

1/2 cup slivered almonds

1. Preheat the oven to 350°F. Butter a 1-quart casserole or good-sized ramekin and set aside.

2. Place the artichoke hearts in a medium-size mixing bowl and mash well with a heavy fork. Add the mayonnaise, lemon juice, cheese, and pepper and continue mashing till the mixture is well blended and smooth.

3. Scrape the mixture into the prepared casserole or ramekin, sprinkle the almonds over the top, and bake till bubbly, about 20 minutes.

MAKES 6 TO 8 SERVINGS

Crusty Wild Mushroom Bake

2 tablespoons butter

8 scallions (white part only), finely chopped

1 garlic clove, minced

1 1/2 pounds wild mushrooms (shiitakes, chanterelles, or morels), stems removed or trimmed and caps cut into bite-size pieces

1/4 cup chopped fresh parsley

1 teaspoon chopped fresh thyme leaves or 1/4 teaspoon dried

1/2 cup half-and-half

1/4 cup dry white wine

Salt and freshly ground black pepper to taste

1/2 cup freshly grated Parmesan cheese

1. Preheat the oven to 350°F. Butter a shallow 1 1/2-quart casserole and set aside.

2. In a small skillet, melt the butter over moderate heat, add the scallions and garlic and cook, stirring, till softened, about 5 minutes.

3. Layer half the mushrooms in the prepared casserole, spoon half the scallions and garlic over the top, and sprinkle with half the parsley and half the thyme. Make another layer with the remaining mushrooms, scallions and garlic, parsley, and thyme.

4. In a small mixing bowl, beat together the half-and-half and wine and pour over the mushrooms. Season with salt and pepper and bake 15 minutes, covered.

5. Uncover, baste the mushrooms with the liquid, sprinkle the cheese evenly over the top, and bake till crusty, 10 to 15 minutes.

MAKES 6 SERVINGS

Just twenty years ago, the American home cook would have had to make this appetizer casserole with relatively bland button mushrooms or, heaven forbid, those awful canned ones. But with today's abundance of all sorts of fragrant wild mushrooms in markets, there's no reason not to make a dish that guests can really rave about. I like to serve this casserole at receptions with rounds of toasted French bread and let people spread on the mushrooms as they would a chunky pâté.

Savannah Quiche

Heaven only knows how and when this layered quiche became identified with Savannah, Georgia, but I've had it served to me both at private cocktail parties and in one restaurant there and find it addictive. One thing's for certain, according to locals: if the quiche does not contain tomatoes and provolone cheese, it's not a real Savannah quiche. Other herbs may be added and some cooks may top the pie with a mixture of Swiss cheese and grated Parmesan or all Parmesan, but the tomatoes and provolone—sliced and diced respectfully—are cardinal components. And nobody there blinks an eye at using commercial pie shells.

1 unbaked store-bought 9-inch pie shell

2 medium-size ripe tomatoes, peeled and sliced

Salt and freshly ground black pepper to taste

1 cup all-purpose flour

$1/4$ cup ($1/2$ stick) butter

2 medium-size onions, finely chopped

1 teaspoon dried oregano

$1/2$ cup diced provolone cheese

$3/4$ cup half-and-half

2 large eggs

1 cup shredded Swiss cheese

1. Preheat the oven to 350°F, then bake the pie shell till slightly browned, about 7 minutes, and set aside.

2. Season the tomatoes with salt and pepper and dip each slice in the flour to coat lightly on both sides. In a large skillet, melt 3 tablespoons of the butter over moderate heat, add the tomato slices in batches, cook about 1 minute on each side, and transfer to a plate. Add the remaining 1 tablespoon butter to the skillet, add the onions, stir about 2 minutes, and transfer to another plate.

3. Layer the tomatoes over the bottom of the prepared pie shell, spread the onions over the tomatoes, and sprinkle the oregano and provolone evenly over the onions.

4. In a medium-size mixing bowl, beat together the half-and-half and eggs and pour over the onions. Sprinkle the Swiss cheese evenly over the top and bake till golden, 35 to 40 minutes. Serve the quiche in small wedges hot or at room temperature.

MAKES ONE 9-INCH QUICHE; 6 TO 8 SERVINGS

Crazy for Casseroles

Cheesy Chicken Drumettes

1 cup freshly grated Parmesan cheese

2 tablespoons finely chopped fresh parsley leaves

2 tablespoons finely chopped fresh oregano leaves or 1 teaspoon dried

2 teaspoons sweet paprika

2 teaspoons salt

$^1/_4$ teaspoon black pepper

4 pounds chicken wing drumsticks (drumettes), wing tips cut off

$^1/_2$ cup (1 stick) butter, melted

1. Preheat the oven to 350°F.

2. On a large, flat dish, combine the cheese, parsley, oregano, paprika, salt, and pepper and mix well.

3. Dip each drumette in the melted butter, roll it in the cheese mixture to coat well, and arrange in a 2- to 2$^1/_2$-quart casserole. Drizzle any remaining butter over the top. Bake till the drumettes are lightly browned, about 1 hour, turning once. Serve at room temperature.

MAKES AT LEAST 8 SERVINGS

Chicken drumettes are no more than the sweet wing drumsticks (separated from the wing tips), and no part of the bird lends itself to easier casserole cookery. Bake them with a few herbs and a zesty grated cheese and both adults and children find them perfect for all sorts of informal parties and picnics. Just be sure to pass out plenty of paper napkins. I also love drumettes baked with a spicy barbecue sauce. This is one recipe in which you really should try to use genuine Italian Parmesan cheese, as well as fresh oregano.

Gingered Chicken Wings

Since the wings are the sweetest part of any chicken, I usually collect them in the freezer till there are enough to make any number of enticing appetizers for receptions, cocktail parties, and buffets. (Of course, you can buy packages of chicken wings in the supermarket, but, inexplicably, they are usually ridiculously expensive.) These gingered wings are particularly delectable and, since they almost have to be eaten with the fingers, I always provide a stack of small cocktail plates and plenty of napkins. Messy eating, to be sure, but I've yet to have a guest who objected to gnawing on the spicy critters.

1 cup honey

$^1/_4$ cup peanut oil

$^1/_4$ cup soy sauce

2 tablespoons ketchup

1 garlic clove, minced

Salt and black pepper to taste

18 chicken wings

2 scallions (white part and some of the green), finely chopped

2 tablespoons peeled and finely chopped fresh ginger

1. Preheat the oven to 375°F. Grease a shallow 1½-quart casserole and set aside.

2. In a 2-cup measuring cup, combine the honey, peanut oil, soy sauce, and ketchup and whisk till thoroughly blended. Add the garlic, season with salt and pepper, and stir.

3. Cut off and discard the wing tips of the chicken wings and cut the wings in two pieces at the joint. Arrange the pieces evenly in the prepared casserole, sprinkle the scallions and ginger over the pieces, pour the sauce evenly over the top, and bake till the chicken is well done and the sauce is caramelized, about 1 hour, basting from time to time to prevent burning. Serve directly from the casserole.

MAKES 6 TO 8 SERVINGS

Chicken Liver Casserole

6 strips lean bacon

3 tablespoons butter

1½ pounds chicken livers, trimmed of fat and membranes and cut in half

2 scallions (white part only), coarsely chopped

½ teaspoon dried summer savory

¼ teaspoon ground nutmeg

3 large eggs

¼ cup half-and-half

2 tablespoons port wine

Salt and freshly ground black pepper to taste

Toast rounds

1. Preheat the oven to 375°F. Line the inside of 1-quart casserole with the bacon and set aside.

2. In a large skillet, melt the butter over moderate heat, add the chicken livers, scallions, summer savory, and nutmeg, and stir till the livers lose their pink color, about 5 minutes.

3. Transfer the contents of the skillet to a food processor or blender, add the eggs, half-and-half, and wine, season with salt and pepper, and process until smooth.

4. Scrape the mixture into the prepared casserole, place the casserole in a baking pan, fill the pan with enough hot water to come about 1 inch up the sides of the casserole, and bake till firm, about 1 hour.

5. Remove the casserole from the water and let cool to room temperature. Serve with toast rounds.

MAKES AT LEAST 10 SERVINGS

Okay, so you never know what to do with all those chicken livers that collect in the freezer? The perfect solution is this simple but sublime casserole that chef Jeremiah Tower once told me how to prepare when he ran the wonderful restaurant Stars in San Francisco and would serve this to close friends with . . . Champagne! Of course, it's really a pâté of sorts (or a mousse), but whatever its pedigree, the casserole is ideal for cocktail parties and receptions, and even those who normally won't touch chicken livers always gobble it up.

Baked Spareribs with Apples and Prunes

If memory serves (and my only documentation are ingredients and notes scribbled on a scrap of paper), these are the ribs I proclaimed a winner some years ago while serving as a judge at a March of Dimes gourmet gala in Cleveland, Ohio. In any case, it's one of the best casseroles I've ever encountered, the apples and prunes giving an altogether new dimension to the pork ribs and the whole making for a memorable first course.

I loathe scrawny spareribs, so, when shopping, I look for ribs that are not only meaty between the bones but that also have a thin covering of meat over the bones. To leech out part of the fat and ensure the tenderest ribs possible, I always parboil any spareribs before baking them, and even after this initial preparation, if the ribs are not fork-tender after about $1^1/_4$ hours, for heaven's sake cook them till they are. Although the brown sugar and cinnamon add lots to this casserole's distinction, you can also bake the ribs with any good barbecue sauce.

4 pounds lean spareribs, cut into serving pieces

5 cooking apples (such as Granny Smith), peeled, cored, and thinly sliced

1 pound dried prunes, pitted

2 tablespoons firmly packed light brown sugar

1 teaspoon ground cinnamon

Salt and black pepper to taste

1. Place the ribs in a large pot with enough water to cover, bring to a simmer, cover, and cook for 30 minutes. Drain the ribs and set aside.

2. Meanwhile, place the apples in a large saucepan with enough water to cover, bring to a simmer, cook till soft, about 15 minutes, and drain. In another saucepan, cover the prunes with water, bring to a simmer, cook for 15 minutes, and drain.

3. Preheat the oven to 350°F. Grease a 2-quart casserole.

4. Arrange half the ribs snugly in the bottom of the prepared casserole. Arrange half the apples and half the prunes over the ribs, sprinkle with half the brown sugar and cinnamon, and season with salt and pepper. Repeat with another layer of the remaining ribs, apples, prunes, brown sugar, and cinnamon, season with salt and pepper, and bake, covered, till the ribs are fork-tender, about $1^1/_4$ hours. Serve directly from the casserole.

MAKES 6 SERVINGS

C A S S E R O L E   C H A T

As a rule, firm, tart, crisp apples such as Granny Smith, York Imperial, Rome Beauty, and Cortland are best for casserole cookery since they contain sufficient cellulose to hold their shape. Avoid eating-apple varieties like Golden Delicious and McIntosh, and always sprinkle with lemon juice any cut apple not used immediately to prevent it from turning brown.

Gratin of Leeks, Country Ham, and Cheese

6 to 8 medium-size leeks (white part and some of the green), rinsed thoroughly

3 scallions (white part and some of the green)

$1/4$ cup chicken broth

$1/4$ cup half-and-half

Salt and freshly ground black pepper to taste

2 ounces Parmesan cheese, grated

2 ounces cured country ham, diced

1 ounce Swiss cheese, shredded

2 tablespoons butter, cut into small bits

1. Preheat the oven to 350°F. Butter a shallow 2-quart casserole and set aside.

2. Cut each leek in half and place in a large pot with enough water to cover. Cut the scallions into small pieces and add to the pot. Bring to a boil, reduce the heat to moderate, cook till the leeks are just tender, about 10 minutes, and drain.

3. Arrange the leeks and scallions in the prepared casserole. In a small mixing bowl, combine the broth and half-and-half, pour over the leeks scallions, and season with salt and pepper. Scatter the Parmesan and ham over the top, sprinkle over the Swiss cheese, dot with the butter, and bake till bubbly and the top is golden, about 30 minutes.

MAKES 6 TO 8 SERVINGS

The second I tasted this gutsy appetizer casserole at Fearrington House outside Chapel Hill, North Carolina, I knew I couldn't leave the restaurant without getting the recipe (from the owner who, much to my delighted surprise, had been a high school classmate). Be sure to wash the leeks thoroughly under cold running water to remove any trace of dirt or grit and, for both additional flavor and color, do use part of the scallions' green tops. I suppose you could substitute regular leftover boiled ham for the cured country ham, but the dish won't be half as good. At the restaurant, they do garnish each serving with matchstick strips of roasted red bell pepper. Make sure you use genuine Parmigiano-Reggiano and Swiss Emmenthaler cheese.

Fingertip Ham, Asparagus, and Cheese Quiche

I call this a "fingertip" quiche for the simple reason that it's intended to be cut into small slivers and eaten with the fingers at cocktail parties. It's also a great knife-and-fork appetizer, in which case I sprinkle each serving with a few more chopped chives. To add even greater depth to the quiche, you might want to substitute cured country ham if you happen to have any on hand—which I always do. Be sure to use genuine Swiss Emmenthaler and Italian Parmigiano-Reggiano cheese if possible. And I think the quiche is just as good served at room temperature as hot.

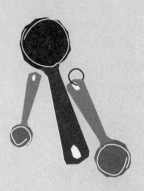

CASSEROLE PASTRY:

1 1/2 cups all purpose flour

1/2 cup (1 stick) butter, softened

1 large egg

2 tablespoons ice water

QUICHE:

6 to 8 stalks fresh asparagus, leaves and woody bottoms trimmed and stalks cut into 1-inch pieces

2 tablespoons butter

1/4 pound fresh mushrooms, sliced

1 cup shredded Swiss cheese

1 cup diced cooked ham

1/2 cup freshly grated Parmesan cheese

1 cup half-and-half

4 large eggs

3 tablespoons chopped fresh chives

Salt and cayenne pepper to taste

1. To make the pastry, combine the flour and butter in a medium-rise mixing bowl and cut with a pastry cutter or mix with your fingertips till the mixture is crumbly. In a small mixing bowl, beat the egg and water together till well blended. Gradually add this to the flour mixture and toss with a fork till the mixture is like soft crumbs, adding a little more flour if necessary. Using your fingertips, press the dough evenly against the bottom and sides of a shallow 1 1/2-quart casserole and chill for 30 minutes.

2. Preheat the oven to 400°F, bake the pastry for 10 minutes, and set the dish aside. Reduce the oven temperature to 350°F.

3. To make the quiche, place the asparagus pieces in a small pot of boiling water, reduce the heat to moderate, cook till just barely tender when pricked with a knife (about 5 minutes), pour into a colander, and drain on paper towels.

4. Meanwhile, melt the butter in a small skillet over moderate heat, add the mushrooms, and cook, stirring, till barely tender, about 8 minutes.

5. Sprinkle about half of the Swiss cheese over the bottom of the prebaked pastry, sprinkle the ham evenly over the cheese, arrange the asparagus pieces over the ham, and sprinkle over the remaining Swiss cheese plus the Parmesan.

6. In a medium-size mixing bowl, beat together the half-and-half, eggs, and chives till well blended, season with salt and cayenne, pour over the ingredients, and bake till the quiche is set, 30 to 35 minutes.

MAKES 6 TO 8 SERVINGS

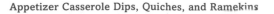

Sausage, Cheese, and Chile Casserole Dip

This zesty dip hails from the Mississippi delta, the creation of a friend who can munch on hot chile peppers the way others eat peanuts. When I told Ann that most of my cocktail guests would find the dip just too fiery with all the fresh bird's eye peppers she chopped with tomatoes, she looked at me in dismay and finally said, "Well, dear, if you must, I suppose those tomatoes and chiles marketed by Rotel might work halfway." Suffice it that I took her hesitant suggestion and have never seen an ounce of dip left over. Serve it with plenty of corn chips, or tortillas.

³/₄ pound bulk pork sausage

One 8-ounce package cream cheese, at room temperature

One 7-ounce can Rotel tomatoes and chiles (available in supermarkets)

¹/₄ pound extra-sharp cheddar cheese, shredded

1. In a large skillet, fry the sausage over moderate heat, breaking it up with a fork, till well cooked, then drain on paper towels.

2. Preheat the oven to 350°F. Grease a 1½-quart casserole and set aside.

3. In a large mixing bowl, combine the sausage, cream cheese, and tomatoes and chiles and mix till well blended

4. Scrape the mixture into the prepared casserole, sprinkle the cheese evenly over the top, and bake till bubbly and the cheese has melted completely, about 15 minutes. Serve hot.

MAKES 6 TO 8 SERVINGS

Hot Pecan Beef Casserole Dip

2 tablespoons butter

1 cup finely chopped pecans

One and a half 8-ounce packages cream cheese, at room temperature

$^1/_4$ cup milk

1 small onion, minced

One 3-ounce can dried beef, finely shredded

1 teaspoon garlic salt

Freshly ground black pepper to taste

$^3/_4$ cup sour cream

1. Preheat the oven to 350°F. Grease a 1-quart casserole and set aside.

2. In a small skillet, melt the butter, add the pecans, and toss over low heat just until fragrant, about 3 minutes. Remove from the heat.

3. In a medium-size mixing bowl, combine the cream cheese and milk and mash well with a heavy fork. Add one quarter of the hot pecans, the onion, dried beef, and garlic salt, season with pepper, and mix well. Add the sour cream and stir till well blended.

4. Scrape the mixture into the prepared casserole, top with the remaining pecans, and bake till golden, about 20 minutes. Serve the dip with small crackers or melba toast rounds.

MAKES 6 TO 8 SERVINGS

Dried beef was a popular kitchen staple back when I was growing up in the fifties and, as far as I'm concerned, it's high time the tasty commodity was given new respect. In the Midwest and South, cooks still use it in all sorts of informal dishes, and none is more appealing than this small casserole dip served with crackers at cocktail parties by a University of Missouri faculty housewife I know in Columbia. I advise that you not make the dip too far in advance since the pecans tend to get soggy— one of my mother's hints.

Hot Shrimp, Bacon, and Horseradish Casserole Dip

Shrimp seems to have a natural affinity with both bacon and horseradish, not only in composed salads, hot pies, and pilaus, but also in all sorts of clever casseroles. I first concocted this rather elegant dip years ago when, frankly, I wanted to get rid of some extra fresh shrimp I found on sale intended for a luncheon salad and needed something to serve with cocktails later that same evening. Guests raved over the dip, and it's been a staple ever since—almost as good at room temperature as piping hot.

$^{1}/_{2}$ pound medium-size fresh shrimp

6 strips lean bacon

One 8-ounce package cream cheese, at room temperature

1 cup mayonnaise

3 scallions (white part and some of the green), finely chopped

1 tablespoon prepared horseradish

$^{1}/_{2}$ cup slivered almonds

Cayenne pepper to taste

1. Place the shrimp in a saucepan with enough water to cover, bring to a boil, remove from the heat, and let stand 1 minute. Drain and, when cool enough to handle, shell and devein the shrimp, chop finely, and set aside.

2. In a medium-size skillet, fry the bacon over moderate heat till crisp, drain on paper towels, crumble, and set aside.

3. Preheat the oven to 350°F. Grease a shallow 1-quart casserole and set aside.

4. In a large mixing bowl, mash the cream cheese and mayonnaise together with a heavy fork till well blended. Add the shrimp, bacon, scallions, horseradish, almonds, and cayenne and mix till well blended.

5. Scrape the mixture into the prepared casserole and bake till bubbly and slightly browned, 20 to 25 minutes. Serve the dip with crackers or thin party rye bread.

MAKES 6 TO 8 SERVINGS

Chicago Shrimp de Jonghe

2 pounds medium-size fresh shrimp

$^1/_2$ cup (1 stick) butter, melted

$^1/_4$ cup dry sherry

2 garlic cloves, minced

2 tablespoons finely chopped fresh parsley leaves

1 tablespoon finely chopped fresh chives

Pinch of ground nutmeg

Salt and cayenne pepper to taste

1 cup dry bread crumbs

1. Place the shrimp in a large pot with enough water to cover, bring slowly to a boil, drain in a colander, and, when cool enough to handle, peel, devein, and set aside.

2. In a medium-size mixing bowl, combine the melted butter, sherry, garlic, parsley, chives, and nutmeg, season with salt and cayenne, and stir well. Add the bread crumbs and toss till the mixture is well blended and the crumbs are very buttery.

3. Preheat the oven to 350°F.

4. Butter a 1$^1/_2$-quart casserole and arrange half the shrimp over the bottom. Spread half the crumb mixture over the shrimp, add the remaining shrimp in another layer, and top with the remaining crumb mixture.

5. Bake, uncovered, till bubbly and slightly browned, about 30 minutes.

MAKES 6 TO 8 SERVINGS

Created in the late nineteenth century for the restaurant of a famous Chicago hotel owned by the Belgian Henri de Jonghe, this rich casserole has as many interpretations as the various seafood Newburgs. The version here is what I used to order religiously as an appetizer at Savoy Grill in Kansas City and can just as easily be prepared in small ramekins or baking shells. I often use additional fresh herbs such as chervil and tarragon, but the real secret to the dish is to have plenty of butter in the bread crumbs.

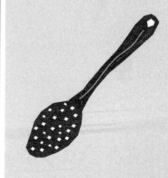

Shrimp Florentine Ramekins

I was introduced to these delightful ramekins at a very fancy private dinner party in Houston that included both Craig Claiborne and Pierre Franey as guests, and the first thought that came into my mind was what a glorious large casserole I could make for one of my buffets back home. Take your pick. If you really want to impress dinner guests, serve the individual ramekins; if you prefer something more informal and earthy, simply butter a 2-quart casserole, layer the ingredients in the same manner, and add plenty of buttered bread crumbs to the top before baking about 20 minutes.

2 pounds medium-size fresh shrimp

Two 10-ounce packages frozen chopped spinach, thawed

1/2 cup (1 stick) butter

1/3 cup all-purpose flour

2 1/2 cups half-and-half

Salt and black pepper to taste

2 scallions (white part only), minced

1/2 cup dry sherry

Juice of 1/2 lemon

1/2 cup freshly grated Parmesan cheese

1. Place the shrimp in a large saucepan with enough water to cover, bring to a boil, remove from the heat, and let stand for 1 minute. Drain in a colander, shell, devein, and set aside.

2. Cook the spinach according to package directions, drain in a colander, squeeze almost dry, and set aside.

3. In a medium-size heavy saucepan, melt 6 tablespoons of the butter over moderate heat, add the flour, and whisk constantly till very smooth, about 2 minutes. Add the half-and-half gradually, whisking till the sauce thickens, about 5 minutes. Season with salt and pepper, whisk, and remove from the heat.

4. Preheat the oven to 350°F. Butter six to eight 4-ounce ramekins and set aside.

5. In a small skillet, melt the remaining 2 tablespoons butter over moderate heat, add the scallions, and cook, stirring, for 1 minute. Add the sherry, cook till almost evaporated, and stir into the cream sauce. Add 1/2 cup of the sauce to the spinach, adding more sauce, if necessary, for a creamy but not soupy mixture.

6. Divide half the spinach among the prepared ramekins, layer equal amounts of shrimp over the spinach, sprinkle each with some of the lemon juice, and cover each with equal amounts of the remaining spinach. Sprinkle each with equal amounts of the cheese and bake on a heavy baking sheet till golden, about 10 minutes.

MAKES 6 TO 8 SERVINGS

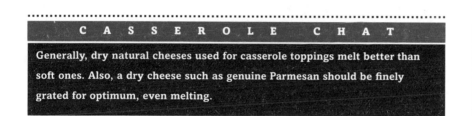

CASSEROLE CHAT

Generally, dry natural cheeses used for casserole toppings melt better than soft ones. Also, a dry cheese such as genuine Parmesan should be finely grated for optimum, even melting.

Shrimp and Crabmeat Newburg

Originally called "lobster a la Wenberg" after a certain sea captain who gave the recipe to the chef at New York's legendary Delmonico's restaurant in 1876, the dish was taken off the menu at one point when Wenberg and Charles Delmonico had a bad row, only to be restored by popular demand and renamed (with a reversal of the first three letters of the captain's name and a "u" substituted for the "e") "lobster a la Newburg."

Since those expansive days, the dish has undergone every transformation imaginable, the most important being the substitution of other shellfish for the lobster as in this delectable recipe. Although the original sauce contained heavy cream, I find that half-and-half produces quite enough richness. Served with no more than a salad and light bread, this casserole also makes a very stylish lunch.

1 pound medium-size fresh shrimp

6 tablespoons ($^3/_4$ stick) butter

$^1/_4$ pound fresh mushrooms, diced

3 tablespoons all-purpose flour

$1^3/_4$ cups half-and-half

4 large egg yolks, beaten

$^1/_4$ cup dry sherry

2 teaspoons Worcestershire sauce

2 teaspoons prepared horseradish

1 teaspoon dry mustard

Salt and cayenne pepper to taste

$^1/_2$ pound fresh lump crabmeat, picked over for shells and cartilage

1. Place the shrimp in a medium-size pot with enough water to cover, bring to a boil, and drain in a colander. When cool enough to handle, shell, devein, chop coarsely, and set aside.

2. In a small skillet, melt 1 tablespoon of the butter over moderate heat, add the mushrooms, cook for 5 minutes, stirring, and set aside.

3. Preheat the oven to 350°F. Butter a $1^1/_2$- to 2-quart casserole and set aside.

4. In a medium-size saucepan, melt the remaining 5 tablespoons butter over moderate heat, add the flour, and stir till well blended. Gradually add the half-and-half and stir till the sauce is thickened and smooth. Spoon a little of the hot sauce into the yolks, add the yolks to the saucepan, reduce the heat to low, stir exactly 1 minute, and remove the pan from the heat. Add the sherry, Worcestershire, horseradish, and mustard, season with salt and cayenne, and stir till well blended.

5. Scatter the shrimp over the bottom of the prepared casserole, scatter the mushrooms over the shrimp, then sprinkle the crabmeat over the mushrooms. Pour the sauce evenly over the top and bake, uncovered, till bubbly, about 30 minutes.

MAKES 6 TO 8 SERVINGS

C A S S E R O L E   C H A T

Although baked casseroles that are cooled, covered, and stored in the refrigerator a day or so before serving often improve in flavor, remember that moisture loss can produce a drier texture. The solution is to add a little extra cooking liquid when reheating.

Seafood Casserole Dip

The whole idea of this impressive casserole dip is to utilize any leftover seafood that might otherwise sit around too long in the fridge—boiled shrimp, part of a container of fresh crabmeat, a steamed lobster claw, even broiled fish fillets left on a buffet. Once you've prepared the sauce, use your imagination with whatever chopped or flaked seafood you prefer, and feel free also to add a little minced bell pepper, maybe a few snipped chives, and various herbs. The dip is great served with melba rounds at cocktail parties, but there's no reason why you can't include the casserole on a buffet or even spoon it out as a first course. If you really want to be elegant, serve the dip in a nice chafing dish.

$^1/_2$ cup (1 stick) butter

$^1/_2$ cup all-purpose flour

1 cup milk

$^1/_4$ cup evaporated milk

2 teaspoons sweet paprika

$^1/_2$ teaspoon black pepper

Salt to taste

2 tablespoons dry sherry

1 tablespoon Worcestershire sauce

Dash of cayenne pepper

$^1/_2$ pound fresh lump crabmeat, picked over for shells and cartilage

$^1/_2$ pound shelled and deveined cooked shrimp (page 220), chopped

$^1/_4$ pound fresh mushrooms, stems trimmed, sautéed in 1 tablespoon butter till tender, and finely chopped

1 cup finely chopped fresh parsley leaves

$^1/_4$ cup freshly grated Parmesan cheese

1. Preheat the oven to 350°F. Butter a shallow 1$^1/_2$-quart casserole.

2. In a medium-size heavy saucepan, melt the butter over moderate heat, add the flour, and whisk till well blended, about 1 minute. Gradually add the regular milk and evaporated milk, whisking constantly till the mixture is thickened and smooth. Add the paprika and black pepper, season with salt, and whisk till well blended.

3. Remove the pan from the heat, add the sherry, Worcestershire, and cayenne, and stir well. Fold in the crabmeat, shrimp, and mushrooms, mixing gently but well. Add the parsley, stir, and heat over low heat.

4. Transfer the mixture to the prepared casserole, sprinkle the cheese over the top, and bake till golden, about 20 minutes.

MAKES AT LEAST 8 SERVINGS

Crazy for Casseroles

Crabmeat Dewey

3 tablespoons butter

1 pound fresh mushrooms, finely chopped

1 medium-size green bell pepper, seeded and finely chopped

2 scallions (white part only), finely chopped

$^1/_2$ cup sweet sherry

3 tablespoons chopped pimentos

$1^1/_2$ cups half-and-half

Salt and black pepper to taste

$1^1/_2$ pounds lump crabmeat, picked over for shells and cartilage and flaked

1 cup freshly grated Parmesan cheese

1. Preheat the oven to 350°F. Butter a $1^1/_2$-quart casserole and set aside.

2. In a large skillet, melt the butter over moderate heat, add the mushrooms, bell pepper, and scallions and stir for 3 minutes. Add the sherry and simmer till the liquid is reduced by half, about 5 minutes. Add the pimentos, half-and-half, season with salt and pepper, and bring almost to a boil. Add the crabmeat, reduce the heat to low, and stir till well blended.

3. Scrape the mixture into the prepared casserole, sprinkle the cheese evenly over the top, and bake till lightly browned, about 20 minutes.

MAKES 6 SERVINGS

Crabmeat Dewey was created toward the end of the nineteenth century at a Maryland yacht club to commemorate Commodore George Dewey's victory at Manila Bay in the Spanish American War and I consider it one of the hallmarks of American gastronomy. Baked in ramekins or pastry shells, the crabmeat can certainly be served as a first course at any stylish meal, but I personally like to put the casserole out at cocktail receptions or on a buffet with melba toast rounds. The exact same casserole can also be made with $1^1/_2$ pounds of boiled, shelled, and deveined chopped fresh shrimp.

Cajun Crabmeat Casserole

I got this recipe years ago from Paul Prudhomme when he was chef at Commander's Palace in New Orleans, and while Paul prepares his crabmeat in individual 1/2-cup ramekins as a first course, I decided at some point to simply fix mine in a casserole and let guests help themselves. Paul uses fresh mayonnaise; I find that Hellmann's binds and browns better. He also includes chopped raw onion along with the scallions; for my taste, that's a bit of overkill. This crabmeat is equally delicious spread on toast points at cocktail parties—though it really should be kept as hot as possible.

2 1/2 tablespoons butter

1/3 cup finely chopped scallions (white part only)

1/3 cup finely chopped celery

1/3 cup seeded and finely chopped green bell pepper

1 small garlic clove, minced

6 tablespoons mayonnaise

1 tablespoon Creole or fine brown mustard

2 teaspoons finely chopped fresh parsley leaves

2 teaspoons Worcestershire sauce

1 teaspoon salt

1 teaspoon cayenne pepper

1 teaspoon Tabasco sauce

1 large egg

1 pound fresh lump crabmeat, picked over for shells and cartilage

1/2 cup heavy cream

Sweet paprika to taste

1. Preheat the oven to 350°F. Butter a 1 1/2-quart casserole and set aside.

2. In a medium-size saucepan, melt the butter over moderate heat, add the scallions, celery, bell pepper, and garlic and stir till the vegetables are just tender. Remove the pan from the heat, add 2 1/2 tablespoons of the mayonnaise, the mustard, parsley, Worcestershire, salt, cayenne, and Tabasco, and stir till well blended. Add the egg and whisk till the mixture is smooth. Add the crabmeat, toss gently, then scrape the mixture into the prepared casserole.

3. Pour the cream over the mixture, spread the remaining 3 1/2 tablespoons mayonnaise evenly over the top, sprinkle with paprika, and bake till bubbly and golden brown, about 20 minutes. Serve immediately.

MAKES 6 SERVINGS

Crazy for Casseroles

Commercial Shortenings, Oils, Sauces, and Condiments

Never are my culinary prejudices more pronounced than when it comes to certain commercial products necessary to cooking in general and casseroles in particular. I use nothing but Crisco vegetable shortening for deep frying, greasing casseroles, and baked goods, for example, having learned the hard way that cheaper brands usually spell disaster for one reason or another—due mostly to their high water content. When a casserole recipe calls for olive oil, I find that nothing suffices better than a good, moderately priced virgin Italian or Greek one—and certainly never one of those overpriced extra-virgin oils.

Worcestershire sauce, one of the greatest creations of all time, enhances any number of casseroles when used correctly. Too much can destroy a dish, too little is pointless. Ditto bottled hot pepper sauce. As for brands, I wouldn't have any Worcestershire sauce in my kitchen but the original Lea & Perrins, and if anyone ever tries to convince you that there's a hot pepper sauce that equals or surpasses Tabasco, ignore them politely. (One tip: to prevent Tabasco from turning dark and losing some of its distinctive savor, keep it in the refrigerator.)

Succinctly, standard American prepared yellow mustard (often called "ballpark mustard" or "hot dog mustard") has no place in my kitchen. I insist upon a good French Dijon mustard, but any Dijon-style domestic or imported product is better than that atrocious mess some people still spread on sandwiches and add to sauces without wincing. I also love a good Creole mustard, a pungent beige mixture lightly flecked with spices not unlike a fine brown mustard and available in specialty food shops and some supermarkets.

As for mayonnaise, I know one word and one word only: Hellmann's (or Best Western in the West).

Deviled Crabmeat Ramekins

Deviled crabmeat can be found all along the South-eastern coast in one guise or another, but never have I found a more delicious version than these ramekins prepared by the mother of an old friend in Baltimore. She serves hers strictly as an elegant first course—with tiny beaten biscuits—but I also like to increase the quantity of ingredients and produce a 1¹/₂- to 2-quart casserole for a spring buffet on the deck. Also, this is one crab dish in which much cheaper claw crabmeat is just as good as the lump backfin—so long, that is, as you don't mind picking it over very carefully for shells and cartilage.

1 pound lump or claw crabmeat, picked over for shells and cartilage

2 scallions (white part and some of the green), finely chopped

¹/₂ small green bell pepper, seeded and finely chopped

1 large hard-boiled egg, finely chopped

2 tablespoons chopped fresh parsley leaves

¹/₃ cup mayonnaise

1 teaspoon Dijon mustard

1 tablespoon fresh lemon juice

1 teaspoon Worcestershire sauce

Freshly ground black and cayenne pepper to taste

²/₃ cup fine dry bread crumbs

¹/₄ cup (¹/₂ stick) butter, melted

1. Preheat the oven to 350°F. Butter six to eight 4-ounce ramekins and set aside.

2. In a large mixing bowl, combine the crabmeat with all the remaining ingredients except the bread crumbs and butter and stir gently till well mixed. Divide the mixture evenly among the prepared ramekins, top each with equal amounts of the bread crumbs, drizzle equal amounts of the melted butter over each, and bake on a heavy baking sheet till slightly golden but still moist, about 10 minutes. Serve hot.

MAKES 6 TO 8 SERVINGS

Deviled Oysters and Bacon

6 strips lean bacon

1½ pints fresh shucked oysters, liquor included

1½ cups half-and-half

2½ cups crumbled soda crackers

¾ cup (1½ sticks) butter, melted

Salt and black pepper to taste

Tabasco sauce to taste

1. Preheat the oven to 350°F. Butter a 1½-quart casserole and set aside.

2. In a medium-size skillet, fry the bacon over moderate heat till almost crisp, drain on paper towels, and chop well or crumble.

3. Drain the oysters, saving about ½ cup of the liquor. In a medium-size mixing bowl, combine the liquor and half-and-half, stir well, and set aside. In another medium-size mixing bowl, combine the cracker crumbs and butter, season with salt and pepper and Tabasco, and set aside.

4. Sprinkle about a third of the cracker crumbs over the bottom of the prepared casserole, arrange half the oysters on top, sprinkle half the bacon over the oysters, and pour half the liquor mixture over the top. Add another third of the crumbs, arrange the remaining oysters on top, sprinkle on the remaining bacon, pour on the remaining liquor mixture, and top with the remaining crumbs. Bake till bubbly and lightly browned, about 35 minutes.

MAKES 6 SERVINGS

There's nothing my pal Jay and I love to do more than harvest blue point and Chincoteague oysters from the many bays and inlets of East Hampton and Montauk at the end of Long Island. We then serve them on the half-shell, roast them, or turn them into stews, and, when I want to begin an all-fresh seafood meal with something truly sensational, I can't imagine anything more appropriate than this luscious, smoky casserole served with . . . celery sticks. Also, a little dry sherry or rum spooned over the top before baking doesn't hurt.

Scalloped Scallops

When I was first served these unusual scallops at a friend's house on the island of Nantucket, I cringed at the idea of adding cheese and diced tomatoes to the sweet mollusks. After a single bite, however, I raved with delight and have served them ever since as an appetizer—either in a shallow casserole or in small baking shells. Don't make this dish with tiny bay scallops, which are just too delicate. Small fresh mussels can be substituted successfully, but the one time I tried making the dish with quahog clams, they turned out tough. But, then, I've never been great at cooking clams.

1 pound fresh sea scallops, drained and cut in half

$^{1}/_{4}$ cup ($^{1}/_{2}$ stick) butter, melted

$^{1}/_{2}$ cup all-purpose flour

2 tablespoons minced onion

2 tablespoons minced fresh parsley leaves

2 tablespoons freshly grated Parmesan cheese

2 tablespoons fresh lemon juice

1 teaspoon Worcestershire sauce

Salt and black pepper to taste

1 large ripe tomato, peeled, seeded, and finely diced

2 tablespoons minced fresh chives

1. Preheat the oven to 375°F. Butter a shallow 1$^{1}/_{2}$-quart casserole and set aside.

2. Dip the scallops into the melted butter, roll lightly in the flour, and arrange in the prepared casserole. Sprinkle the onion, parsley, and cheese over the top, add the lemon juice and Worcestershire, season with salt and pepper, and bake for 15 minutes.

3. Scatter the diced tomato and chives evenly over the top and continue to bake till bubbly, about another 10 minutes.

MAKES 6 SERVINGS

Finnan Haddie Delmonico

3 large red potatoes, peeled and diced

$^1/_4$ cup ($^1/_2$ stick) butter

1 large egg

Salt and black pepper to taste

2 pounds smoked haddock fillets, soaked $^1/_2$ hour in tepid water and drained

Milk as needed

3 large hard-boiled eggs, coarsely chopped

2 cups Cream Sauce (page 6)

1 cup freshly grated Parmesan cheese

2 tablespoons butter, melted

1. In a large saucepan, cover the potatoes with water, bring to a low boil, cook till very soft, about 20 minutes, and drain in a colander.

2. In a large mixing bowl, beat the potatoes with an electric mixer till smooth, add the butter and egg, season with salt and pepper, and beat till well blended and very smooth. Spoon the mashed potatoes into a pastry bag and set aside.

3. Preheat the oven to 350°F. Butter a 2-quart casserole and set aside.

4. Place the haddock in a pot with enough milk to cover, bring to a simmer, cook for 15 minutes, drain, and let the fish cool.

5. Flake the fish into a large mixing bowl, add the hard-boiled eggs and cream sauce, season with salt and pepper, and fold till well blended.

6. Transfer the mixture to the prepared casserole and sprinkle the cheese firmly over the top. Pipe the mashed potatoes around the edges, brush the potatoes with the melted butter, and bake till golden brown, 20 to 25 minutes.

MAKES 6 TO 8 SERVINGS

This rendition of the British classic was created around the turn of the twentieth century at the same Delmonico's restaurant in New York where lobster Newburg was first served. In England and Scotland, finnan haddie is no more than smoked haddock poached in milk with various seasonings and served at breakfast, but once it crossed the Atlantic, the dish was transformed into this sapid casserole that can be served with toast points either as an impressive first course or at receptions (with or without the potato piping). Filleted smoked haddock is now available at most seafood markets in the U. S., and the best variety of all, Arbroath Smokie, can often be found in specialty food shops. Any finnan haddie is super salty, so be sure to soak it about 30 minutes in water before baking.

Salmon and Potato Casserole Quiche

Thirty or forty years ago, this appetizer quiche would most likely have been made with canned salmon, but given the variety of beautiful fresh salmon in today's markets, it's almost a shame not to benefit from the superior flavor—especially since the fish is so easy to poach. (And, of course, a big slab of leftover grilled salmon could also be used.) On the other hand, I don't hesitate a second to use commercial pie shells for all my quiches, so long as they have some depth (and not all frozen pie shells are the same). Although I prefer to serve this type of quiche as a lovely first course, it also makes a great luncheon dish for four, served with a tangy mixed green or blanched vegetable salad, maybe some good rye or pumpernickel bread, and a nice dry white wine. Make sure to bake the quiche just till it's well set.

One 1/2-pound center-cut piece salmon fillet

1/2 pound small red potatoes, peeled and finely diced

2 tablespoons butter

2 scallions (white part only), minced

1 unbaked store-bought deep-dish 9-inch pie shell

3 tablespoons minced fresh dill

1/4 cup salmon poaching liquid or dry white wine

Salt and black pepper to taste

1 cup heavy cream

4 large eggs

1. Place the salmon in a medium-size skillet with enough water (or half water and half dry white wine) to cover, bring to a simmer, cover, and poach over low heat till flaky, about 30 minutes. Transfer the salmon to a plate, peel off the skin, remove any bones or darkened flesh, and flake. Reserve 1/4 cup of the poaching liquid.

2. Meanwhile, place the potatoes in a saucepan with water to cover, bring to a boil, reduce the heat to moderate, cook till tender, and drain.

3. In a small skillet, melt the butter over moderate heat, add the scallions, cook, stirring, for 2 minutes, and remove from the heat.

4. Preheat the oven to 350°F.

5. Scatter the potatoes over the bottom of the pie shell, then spoon the scallions evenly over the potatoes. In a medium-size mixing bowl, combine the flaked salmon, dill, and reserved poaching liquid, season with salt and pepper, mix well, and spoon evenly over the onions and potatoes. In another medium-size mixing bowl, whisk together the cream and eggs till well blended, pour over the top, and bake till set and golden, 35 to 40 minutes. Serve the quiche hot in wedges.

MAKES ONE 9-INCH QUICHE; 6 SERVINGS

Crazy for Casseroles

Breakfast and Brunch Casseroles, Stratas, and Scrambles

Bereavement Egg, Canadian Bacon, and Corn Soufflé

Bereavement brunches and lunches in the South are still as popular (and often downright festive) as half a century ago, the standard set-up being a large buffet filled with dishes donated by family friends of the departed. Since the whole idea is to serve food that requires little or no attention on the part of the hostess, small finger sandwiches, dips, cookies, and, above all, casseroles that can be popped and left in the oven are standard items. Heaven knows how many casseroles I've tasted at these midday social events over the years (there were no less than three on the table after my father's funeral), but one that stands out in my mind was this delectable creation with a biscuit-crumb topping prepared by an aunt known for her elaborate casseroles. Do try to use good-quality bread and fresh corn and, if you don't care to make biscuits (Southern cooks always tend to have leftover ones on hand), coarse dry bread crumbs will do. For the right texture, be sure to refrigerate this casserole at least 30 minutes before baking.

16 slices good sourdough or multigrain bread

8 thin slices Canadian bacon

8 slices sharp cheddar cheese

2 cups fresh or thawed frozen corn kernels

3 cups whole milk (not skim or lowfat)

6 large eggs, beaten

$1/4$ cup minced scallions (white part only)

$1/4$ cup seeded and minced green bell pepper

1 teaspoon dry mustard

Salt and black pepper to taste

Cayenne pepper to taste

1 cup biscuit or dry bread crumbs

$1/4$ cup ($1/2$ stick) butter, melted

1. Trim any crusts from the bread and cut 8 of the slices to fit snugly in the bottom of a buttered 2-quart casserole. Top each slice with a piece of Canadian bacon, then a slice of cheese, and distribute the corn evenly over the top. Fit the remaining bread slices snugly over the corn.

2. In a large mixing bowl, combine the milk, eggs, scallions, bell pepper, and mustard, season with salt, black, and cayenne pepper, and whisk till well blended. Pour the mixture over the casserole, cover with plastic wrap, and refrigerate overnight.

3. Remove the casserole from the refrigerator 30 minutes before baking. Preheat the oven to 325°F.

4. In a small mixing bowl, combine the bread crumbs and butter, mix well, spoon evenly over the casserole, and bake till browned on top, about 45 minutes.

MAKES 8 SERVINGS

Crazy for Casseroles

Baked Eggs and Chicken Livers

2 strips lean bacon

2 tablespoons butter

6 chicken livers, trimmed of fat and membranes and cut in half

6 tablespoons half-and-half

$^1/_2$ teaspoon dry mustard

$^1/_8$ teaspoon cayenne pepper

6 large eggs

Salt and black pepper to taste

1. Preheat the oven to 375°F. Butter six $^1/_2$-cup ramekins and set aside.

2. In a medium-size skillet, fry the bacon over moderate heat till crisp, drain on paper towels, and crumble. Pour off most of the fat from the skillet, melt the butter over moderate heat, add the livers, and cook, stirring, till there's no trace of pink, about 5 minutes. Place 2 liver halves in the bottom of each prepared ramekin.

3. In a small mixing bowl, combine the half-and-half, mustard, and cayenne and mix till well blended. Spoon 1 tablespoon of the cream mixture over the livers in each ramekin.

4. Break an egg over the top of each ramekin, season with salt and pepper, add equal amounts of crumbled bacon, and bake till the eggs are set, about 10 minutes.

MAKES 6 SERVINGS

Despite many people's strange aversion to chicken livers, I've yet to encounter a single soul who didn't exclaim over these ramekins I like to serve as something slightly different for a weekend breakfast— with, by the way, small bowls of fresh fruit compote and toasted English muffins. Remember, however, that if you overcook the livers, they'll be tough.

> ### C A S S E R O L E   C H A T
> Most casseroles can be assembled twenty-four hours before baking, tightly covered with plastic wrap and a lid, and refrigerated. Not only is this practice a big time-saver, it allows the flavors of the ingredients to meld.

Herbed Brunch Egg Casserole

This is a good, all-purpose brunch casserole that can be whipped up in no time with minimum effort and maximum guest satisfaction. If you do have fresh herbs, for heaven's sake use them (about 1 teaspoon each), and do feel free to experiment with various types, remembering that tarragon and chervil always complement most egg dishes. Also try different cheeses.

1 pound sliced lean bacon

$1/4$ cup ($1/2$ stick) butter

$1/4$ cup all-purpose flour

1 cup half-and-half

1 cup milk

$1/4$ teaspoon dried thyme

$1/4$ teaspoon dried tarragon

$1/4$ teaspoon dried chervil

$3/4$ pound blue cheese, crumbled

$1^1/2$ dozen hard-boiled eggs, thinly sliced

$1/4$ cup chopped fresh parsley leaves

$1/2$ cup dry bread crumbs

2 tablespoons butter, melted

1. In a large skillet, fry the bacon over moderate heat in batches till crisp, drain on paper towels, crumble, and set aside.

2. Preheat the oven to 350°F. Butter a $2^1/2$-quart casserole and set aside.

3. In a medium-size skillet, melt the butter over moderate heat, add the flour, and stir for 2 minutes. Gradually add the half-and-half and milk and whisk till the sauce is thickened and smooth. Add the herbs and cheese and cook till the cheese has softened or melted, without allowing the mixture to come to a boil.

4. Arrange one-third of the eggs over the bottom of the prepared casserole, sprinkle one-third of the crumbled bacon over the eggs, and sprinkle one-third of the parsley over the bacon. Repeat the layers twice more with the remaining eggs, bacon, and parsley and pour the cheese sauce evenly over the top.

5. In a small mixing bowl, combine the bread crumbs and melted butter, mix well, spoon evenly over the top of the casserole, and bake till crusty, about 30 minutes.

MAKES 8 TO 10 SERVINGS

C A S S E R O L E   C H A T

To hard-boil a perfect egg that has no green ring around the yolk, place the egg in a saucepan with enough cold water to cover, bring to a boil, turn off the heat, cover, and let stand for 20 minutes (or let cool completely before chilling).

Creole Breakfast Ham and Eggs

What makes this casserole so memorable when eaten in New Orleans and throughout most of Louisiana is the distinctive, highly spiced, smoked ham known as tasso used also in gumbos, jambalayas, and other local dishes. Unfortunately, tasso is rarely available outside the region, but I've found that well-cured, aged country ham at least approximates the savor. If that too is not easy to come by, regular smoked ham can always be used so long as it's enhanced by plenty of red pepper flakes and sage.

1 cup soda cracker crumbs

2 tablespoons butter, melted

8 large hard-boiled eggs, sliced

1 cup chopped cured country ham (such as Smithfield)

Salt and freshly ground black pepper to taste

Red pepper flakes to taste

Ground sage to taste

2 cups Cream Sauce (page 6)

1 cup Tomato Sauce (page 7)

1 cup grated sharp cheddar cheese

1. Preheat the oven to 350°F. Butter a 1½-quart casserole and set aside. In a small mixing bowl, combine the cracker crumbs and butter, toss well, and set aside.

2. Make alternate layers of eggs and ham in the prepared casserole, seasoning each layer with salt, black pepper, red pepper flakes, and sage.

3. In a medium-size mixing bowl, combine the two sauces, stir till well blended, and pour evenly over the top of the casserole. Sprinkle the cheese evenly over the top, spoon the buttered crumbs evenly over the cheese, and bake till bubbly and golden brown, about 20 minutes.

MAKES 6 SERVINGS

Weekend Egg and Feta Cheese Casserole

1¹/₂ cups Cream Sauce (page 6)

1 teaspoon Worcestershire sauce

1¹/₂ cups dry bread crumbs

¹/₄ cup (¹/₂ stick) butter, melted

8 large hard-boiled eggs, sliced

²/₃ cup crumbled feta cheese

Salt and black pepper to taste

Sweet paprika to taste

1. Preheat the oven to 350°F. Butter a 1¹/₂-quart casserole and set aside.

2. In a medium-size saucepan, combine the cream sauce and Worcestershire, mix well, bring to a simmer, and set aside.

3. In medium-size mixing bowl, toss the bread crumbs with the melted butter and set aside.

4. Spoon half the bread crumbs evenly over the bottom of the prepared casserole, arrange the egg slices over the bread crumbs, sprinkle the cheese over the eggs, and season with salt, pepper, and paprika. Spoon the hot cream sauce evenly over the top, spoon the remaining bread crumbs over the top, and bake till bubbly and golden brown, about 20 minutes.

MAKES 6 SERVINGS

Some years ago, when the original and legendary Coach House still existed in New York City, this is the casserole that Greek owner Leon Lianides would personally prepare from time to time when he knew I was coming down around midday to chat (the restaurant was always closed at lunch). After I told my Greek father about the dish, nothing would do but for me to get the exact recipe for my mother, after which it became almost a staple at weekend brunches she'd prepare for all our Greek friends in Charlotte, North Carolina. It does make all the difference in the world if you can find genuine Greek feta cheese in a food shop or deli (not that bland packaged stuff).

Patio Egg, Sausage, and Corn Scramble

Years ago, I and a friend were summer guests of an elderly lady on Cape Cod who served virtually every meal on her handsome brick patio overlooking the water, the most memorable being a few hearty breakfasts and brunches to which she'd also invite some of her charming cronies from nearby. Mrs. Elvira Birch was a real salty character, and when I asked her why this casserole that contained hard-boiled eggs was called a scramble, she simply fetched a small, tattered cookbook that must have been printed back in the '20s or '30s, turned to the recipe, and said, "Because this is what my bible calls it, that's why." At least Mrs. Birch did use fresh instead of canned corn, as directed in her "bible," and when I make this "scramble" for brunch, I might also add a little finely chopped green bell pepper.

1 pound bulk pork sausage

5 large hard-boiled eggs, sliced

$^1/_4$ cup ($^1/_2$ stick) butter

$^1/_4$ cup all-purpose flour

Salt and black pepper to taste

2 cups half-and-half

2 cups fresh or thawed frozen corn kernels

1 cup soft bread crumbs

2 tablespoons butter, melted

1. In a large skillet, break up the sausage, fry over moderate heat till well cooked and crumbly, and drain on paper towels.

2. Preheat the oven to 350°F. Butter a 1$^1/_2$-quart casserole and arrange half the egg slices over the bottom.

3. In a large heavy saucepan, melt the butter over moderate heat, add the flour, season with salt and pepper, and stir 1 minute. Add the half-and-half and whisk constantly till the sauce is bubbly and thickened. Stir the sausage and corn into the sauce, pour over the eggs in the casserole, and arrange the remaining egg slices over the top.

4. In a small mixing bowl, combine the bread crumbs and melted butter, spoon evenly over the top of the casserole, and bake till golden, about 30 minutes.

MAKES 6 SERVINGS

Roger's Anchovy Eggs in Tomato Sauce

1 dozen large hard-boiled eggs

4 teaspoons anchovy paste (available in tubes)

1 tablespoon cider vinegar

1 teaspoon dry mustard

$^1/_2$ teaspoon sugar

Black pepper to taste

$^1/_2$ pound fresh mushrooms, chopped

2 cups Cream Sauce (page 6)

3 tablespoons tomato paste

1. Preheat the oven to 350°F. Butter a shallow 2-quart casserole and set aside.

2. Cut the eggs in half lengthwise, remove the yolks, and press them through a sieve into a large mixing bowl. Add the anchovy paste, vinegar, mustard, and sugar, season with pepper, and stir till well blended and smooth.

3. Stuff each egg white with the yolk mixture, stick the eggs back together, arrange them snugly in the prepared casserole, and sprinkle the mushrooms evenly over the top.

4. In a heavy medium-size saucepan, heat the cream sauce over moderate heat, add the tomato paste, and stir till well blended. Pour the sauce evenly over the casserole and bake till bubbly, about 20 minutes.

MAKES 6 TO 8 SERVINGS

When I was teaching at the University of Missouri in Columbia, there was a colleague from St. Joseph who prided himself on nothing more than the unusual casseroles he'd concoct for Sunday brunches which could be pretty wild, all-afternoon affairs. Roger was not the most gifted cook on the planet, and, quite frankly, some of his casseroles turned out to be utter flops. This one, however, which he learned from his mother, worked beautifully, guests loved it served with his herbed sausage balls and very respectable homemade cheese rolls, and the only modification I've ever made is the substitution of a cream sauce for plain half-and-half.

Kedgeree

Although best known today as a staple on elaborate British breakfast buffets, kedgeree was actually an East Indian dish originally composed of rice, lentils, eggs, and spices that was brought to America three centuries ago by New England seamen who gradually added fish to the concoction. One of the best kedgerees I ever tasted was served at the colonial Griswold Inn in Essex, Connecticut, where cod was substituted for the more traditional smoked haddock. I personally love the savor of smoked fish, but if you don't, by all means use any firm white fish such as cod, scrod, plain haddock, or even snapper. I have found that, for most Americans, kedgeree is much more preferred as a midday brunch dish than at breakfast. I like to serve the hearty casserole with baked prunes or apricots and either herbed biscuits or whole wheat scones. If you want to be fancy, you can unmold the casserole onto a large plate and decorate the edges with parsley or watercress.

2 pounds smoked haddock or white fish fillets, soaked for $1/2$ hour in tepid water and drained

$2^1/_2$ cups milk

$1^1/_2$ cups water

2 thick strips lemon peel

1 bay leaf

2 teaspoons salt

$1/_2$ cup (1 stick) butter

1 medium-size onion, finely chopped

$1^1/_2$ cups long-grain rice

2 cups chicken broth

1 tablespoon mild curry powder

6 large hard-boiled eggs, chopped

1 cup sour cream

Salt and cayenne pepper to taste

1. Place the haddock in a shallow flameproof baking pan or dish and add the milk, water, lemon peel, bay leaf, and salt. Bring to a boil, reduce the heat to low, and simmer for 15 minutes. Let cool, then drain.

2. In a large saucepan, melt 2 tablespoons of the butter over moderate heat, add the onion, and stir for 2 minutes. Add the rice and stir till the grains are coated with butter. Add the broth, bring to a boil, reduce the heat to moderate, cover tightly, and cook the rice for exactly 17 minutes. Drain in a colander, rinse under cold running water, and transfer to a large mixing bowl.

3. In a small skillet, melt the remaining 6 tablespoons butter over moderate heat, add the curry powder, stir till fragrant, about 2 minutes, and set aside.

4. Preheat the oven to 350°F. Butter a 2-quart casserole and set aside.

5. Flake the haddock and add to the rice. Add the hot curried butter, the eggs, and sour cream, season with salt and cayenne, and fluff the ingredients thoroughly with a fork.

6. Pack the mixture into the prepared casserole and bake till slightly crusty, 15 to 20 minutes.

MAKES 8 SERVINGS

Tarragon Egg, Crabmeat, and Pea Casserole

Nothing enhances egg (and poultry) dishes like a little tarragon, and when you use the herb to add definition to an elegant summertime brunch casserole such as this, guests don't forget anytime soon. I simply don't make this dish unless I have fresh French tarragon in the garden (it's also available in small pots at most nurseries) and, believe me, tiny fresh peas make all the difference in the world. If you end up with too much stuffing for the eggs, just let it overflow into the casserole. Also, here's another time when I use only genuine Italian Parmigiano-Reggiano cheese for the top.

2 tablespoons butter

1 small onion, finely chopped

8 to 10 large hard-boiled eggs, cut in half lengthwise

1 cup small fresh or thawed frozen peas

2 teaspoons Dijon mustard

1 teaspoon Worcestershire sauce

1 teaspoon minced fresh tarragon leaves

2 cups Cheese Sauce (page 7)

Freshly ground black pepper to taste

3/4 pound fresh lump or claw crabmeat, picked over for shells and cartilage

1/2 cup freshly grated Parmesan cheese

1. Preheat the oven to 350°F. Butter a shallow 2-quart casserole and set aside.

2. In a small skillet, melt the butter over moderate heat, add the onion, stir for 2 minutes, and remove from the heat.

3. In a medium-size mixing bowl, mash the egg yolks finely with a fork, add the onion, peas, mustard, Worcestershire, tarragon, and 3 table-spoons of the cheese sauce, season with pepper, and mix till well blended. Add the crabmeat and mix till well blended.

4. Stuff each egg white half with equal amounts of the mixture and arrange the halves in the prepared casserole. Spoon the remaining cheese sauce over the eggs, sprinkle the top with the cheese, and bake till golden, about 30 minutes.

MAKES 6 SERVINGS

Corned Beef and Tomato Hash Bake

3 cups finely diced cooked corned beef

2 cups peeled and diced potatoes, cooked in water to cover until tender and drained

$1/4$ cup ($1/2$ stick) butter

1 medium-size onion, finely chopped

$1/2$ small green bell pepper, seeded and finely chopped

1 garlic clove, minced

1 tablespoon finely chopped fresh basil leaves or $1/2$ teaspoon dried

$1/2$ cup milk

Salt and black pepper to taste

2 medium-size ripe tomatoes, cut into $1/2$-inch-thick slices

Dijon mustard as needed

$1/2$ cup dry bread crumbs

2 tablespoons butter, melted

1. Preheat the oven to 350°F. Butter a 2-quart casserole and set aside.

2. In a large mixing bowl, combine the corned beef and potatoes, toss, and set aside.

3. In a medium-size skillet, melt the butter over moderate heat, add the onion, bell pepper, garlic, and basil, stir for 3 minutes, add to the corned beef and potatoes, and mix well. Add the milk, season with salt and pepper, mix well, and scrape the mixture into the prepared casserole. Spread the top of each tomato slice with mustard and arrange the slices evenly over the casserole.

4. In a small mixing bowl, combine the bread crumbs and melted butter, mix well, spoon evenly over the tomatoes, and bake till lightly browned, about 30 minutes.

MAKES 6 SERVINGS

If you love to serve traditional corned beef hash for breakfast or brunch, try transforming it into this crusty casserole for something new and really enticing. To make life easier, you can always resort to deli corned beef if you don't have leftovers, but, personally, I much prefer to buy a 2-pound slab on sale—flat or thin cut—and simmer it in water with various seasonings a few hours till fork-tender. Not only is the flavor so much better than the store-bought, but you'll probably have extra meat for sandwiches.

Wild Mushroom Brunch Casserole

This brunch casserole is one of the best ways I know to highlight the earthy distinction of wild mushrooms, and while I usually try to find the fresh varieties available today in so many markets, I don't hesitate a second to use about 2 ounces of dried ceps or shiitakes (exotic morels and chanterelles can be hideously expensive) soaked about 2 hours in 1/2 cup of cold water. (You can speed things up by soaking them only 30 minutes in warm water, but the flavor won't be as intense.) One advantage to using dried mushrooms, in fact, is that you can add the fragrant soaking water (strained to remove any grit) to the milk mixture for even more savor. Do check this casserole after about 30 minutes to make sure it doesn't get too dry.

8 strips lean bacon

3 tablespoons butter

$^3/_4$ pound fresh wild mushrooms (chanterelles, ceps, shiitakes, or morels), stems removed or trimmed and cut into bite-size pieces

4 scallions (white part only), chopped

1 small green bell pepper, seeded and chopped

10 slices multigrain bread

$1^1/_2$ cups shredded Monterey Jack cheese (preferably aged)

6 large eggs

$2^1/_2$ cups milk

1 teaspoon Dijon mustard

Salt and black pepper to taste

1 large ripe tomato, peeled, seeded, and diced

1. Preheat the oven to 350°F. Butter a $2^1/_2$-quart casserole and set aside.

2. In a large skillet, fry the bacon over moderate heat till crisp, drain on paper towels, crumble, and set aside.

3. Pour off the fat from the skillet, melt the butter over moderate heat, add the mushrooms, scallions, and bell pepper, cook, stirring, till soft, about 10 minutes, and remove from the heat.

4. Arrange 5 slices of the bread in the casserole, top with half the cheese, and spoon all the mushroom mixture over the cheese. Arrange the remaining bread slices over the mushrooms and top with the remaining cheese.

5. In a large mixing bowl, beat together the eggs, milk, and mustard, season with salt and pepper, and pour evenly over top of the casserole. Sprinkle the crumbled bacon and tomato over the top and bake till a knife inserted in the middle comes out almost clean, about 45 minutes.

MAKES 8 TO 10 SERVINGS

Crazy for Casseroles

Canadian Bacon and Cheese Strata

$^1/_4$ cup ($^1/_2$ stick) butter

1 small onion, finely chopped

1 pound Canadian bacon, casing discarded and meat thinly sliced

10 slices day-old bread, crusts removed

$^1/_2$ pound sharp cheddar cheese, cut into thin slices

2 cups milk

5 large eggs, beaten

1 teaspoon sweet paprika

$^1/_2$ teaspoon dry mustard

Salt and black pepper to taste

1. In a large skillet, melt 1 tablespoon of the butter over moderate heat, add the onion, cook, stirring, for 2 minutes, and transfer to a plate. Melt the remaining 3 tablespoons butter in the skillet over moderate heat, cook the Canadian bacon slices about 2 minutes on each side (in batches, if necessary), and transfer to the plate.

2. Preheat the oven to 350°F. Butter a 2-quart casserole.

3. Arrange half the bread slices over the bottom of the prepared casserole. Arrange half the bacon slices and the onion over the bread, then layer half the cheese slices on top. Repeat layering the remaining bread slices, bacon, and cheese slices.

4. In a large mixing bowl, beat together the milk, eggs, paprika, and mustard, season with salt and pepper, pour over the casserole, and bake till set and golden on top, about 30 minutes.

MAKES 6 SERVINGS

Also called "back bacon," Canadian bacon is the boneless, cured and smoked eye of the pork loin that is marketed presliced or in rolls. Why this glorious, lean meat is so rarely used these days is beyond me (maybe because it costs more than regular smoked ham), for it's not only ideal for eggs Benedict but for any number of classic casseroles like this one. Just be sure not to sauté the bacon too long, which toughens it. And do experiment with different aged cheeses for this strata.

The Cheese Kings: Cheddar and Parmesan

Perhaps no role in casserole cookery is more important than that played by the various cheeses that provide flavor, texture, and aroma while also serving to help bind the ingredients and form luscious toppings. And of all the cheeses that might be used (blue, mozzarella, Monterey Jack, Swiss Emmenthaler, feta, fontina, goat, and others), no two are more strategic than cheddar and Parmesan, each of which has distinctive character and melting properties that make them the ideal all-purpose casserole cheeses.

Of course, there's cheddar, then there's cheddar, and to compare that processed, pasteurized, plasticized supermarket abomination known generically as "American cheese" with the natural, aged cheddars of Great Britain, Canada, New York, Vermont, Oregon, and Wisconsin is like comparing Wonder Bread with true California sourdough. Superior domestic cheddars include Tillamook, Colby, Grafton, and some others made in California, Vermont, and New York, but in the final reckoning, there's still no cheddar on earth to equal those imported from England and Canada that are carefully aged at least two years (as opposed to six or less months for the bland imitations). Although I use a great deal of extra-sharp white Canadian cheddar, I'm certainly not adverse to natural cheddars found in supermarkets so long as they're aged at least a year. Sharp aged cheddar is suitable for most casseroles, but, personally, I always buy extra-sharp for its more complex and rounder flavor.

As for Parmesan cheese, which is so often grated to form the golden brown topping of a casserole, there is nothing to equal the rich, pungent, creamy flavor of imported Parmigiano-Reggiano, which has no more than about a half-inch of dry area next to the rind and displays a uniform straw-colored hue. Of course, the price of this noble cheese can be outrageous (up to $20 per pound in some areas of the country), but once you're addicted to its unique savor, it's difficult to substitute any of the anemic domestic products sold shredded or grated in cans and bottles and plastic packages. The irony is that a chunk of genuine Parmigiano-Reggiano might not only last longer but, in the long run, is basically less expensive than the commercial imitations. Also, few people realize that both imported Grana Padano and Pecorino Romano can serve as excellent substitutes for authentic Parmigiano-Reggiano at half its price.

In any case, although these hard grating cheeses have a longer shelf life than most natural cheeses, they will begin to dry out after a few weeks in the refrigerator, which is why I buy them in relatively small amounts and wrap each chunk tightly in plastic till I'm ready to grate what I need for a casserole. Never grate a chunk of Parmesan, Grana Padano, or Romano till you're ready to use it, and remember that freezing these or any other natural cheeses destroys both their texture and flavor.

Sunday Sausage, Apple, and Cheese Strata

Although I first had this strata when I was living in Missouri and being invited to lots of lavish weekend breakfasts and brunches in fine Midwestern style, it's a classic American concept that's as popular in Washington State as it is in New England and Georgia. Feel free to vary the styles of cheese, but, for heaven's sake, don't buy cheap, overly fatty sausage rolls for this casserole unless you want a greasy mess—even after frying and draining the meat. Fresh, lean sweet or hot Italian sausages (casings removed) can be substituted for standard breakfast sausage if you have any doubts about the quality of the packaged bulk style. The flavor of the casserole won't be the same, but its overall integrity will be better.

1 pound bulk pork sausage

4 slices white bread, crusts removed and cut into 1-inch cubes

2 medium-size apples (Granny Smith are ideal), peeled, cored, and cut into 1-inch cubes

$1/2$ pound Monterey Jack cheese, shredded

2 cups milk

6 large eggs, beaten

$1/4$ teaspoon ground sage

Salt and black pepper to taste

1. In a large heavy skillet, break up the sausage, fry over moderate heat till thoroughly cooked, and drain on paper towels.

2. Preheat the oven to 350°F. Butter a $1^1/2$- to 2-quart casserole.

3. Layer the bread cubes across the bottom of the prepared casserole. Scatter the sausage evenly over the bread, arrange the apples over the sausage, and sprinkle about three-quarters of the cheese over the apples.

4. In a large bowl, beat the milk, eggs, sage, and salt and pepper together till well blended, pour over the casserole, sprinkle the remaining cheese over the top, and bake till set and golden brown, about 30 minutes.

MAKES 6 SERVINGS

Country Ham, Spinach, and Mozzarella Strata

8 slices day-old white bread, crusts removed and torn into pieces

1 cup finely chopped or shredded mozzarella cheese (about 4 ounces)

1 cup diced cooked Smithfield ham (or other style cured country ham)

One 10-ounce package frozen chopped spinach, thawed and squeezed dry

3 tablespoons butter, melted

2 cups milk

6 large eggs

1 tablespoon Dijon mustard

Pinch of ground nutmeg

Freshly ground black pepper to taste

1. Preheat the oven to 350°F. Butter a 2-quart casserole.

2. Sprinkle half the bread pieces over the bottom of the prepared casserole. Top with half the cheese, sprinkle the ham evenly over the cheese, arrange the spinach evenly over the top, sprinkle on the remaining bread pieces, and drizzle the melted butter over the top.

3. In a large mixing bowl, whisk together the milk, eggs, mustard, nutmeg, and pepper till well blended and pour slowly over the casserole. Cover with plastic wrap and chill at least 30 minutes.

4. To bake, sprinkle the remaining cheese over the top and bake till a knife inserted in the center comes out clean, 45 to 50 minutes.

MAKES 6 SERVINGS

Prepared in the old style, this classic American strata would normally feature leftover baked ham and cheddar or Swiss cheese. I update it by substituting sweet Smithfield ham and tangy mozzarella, a combination that yields a truly sumptuous casserole worthy of the snazziest brunch. When I can find *mozzarella di bufala* (traditionally made in Italy from water buffaloes' milk), that's my ideal cheese for the dish, but given its scarcity, I do much prefer a ball of fresh mozzarella to that commercial stuff. The fresh is difficult to shred, but the flavor and texture are superior. The strata needs no extra salt, and it's one that really should be assembled a day ahead so that the flavors can meld.

Country Ham Spoonbread

For Southerners, spoonbread is the quintessential brunch dish and, when ingredients like assertive cheeses, nuts, bourbon, or diced country ham are added to the pudding, you can rest assured that not a morsel will be left in the casserole. There's lots of to-do made over whether white or yellow cornmeal should be used, not to mention whether sugar should be added, but, personally, I don't care. If genuine cured country ham (including Smithfield) is used, however, no salt is needed. Spoonbread also complements any hearty country breakfast, but nowhere does its elegance shine more than on a well-planned brunch buffet.

3 cups milk

1 1/2 cups white or yellow cornmeal

1/2 cup (1 stick) butter, softened and cut into pieces

2 teaspoons baking powder

5 large eggs, separated

1 cup diced cooked country ham

1. Preheat the oven to 350°F. Butter a 2-quart casserole and set aside.

2. In a large saucepan, bring the milk to a boil and gradually add the cornmeal, stirring rapidly with a spoon as you slowly pour it in. Reduce the heat to low and cook, stirring constantly, till the mixture is thick, about 10 minutes. Remove the pan from the heat, add the butter and baking powder, stir till the butter has melted, and set aside to cool.

3. In a small mixing bowl, beat the egg yolks with a fork till light, then stir them into the cooled cornmeal mixture. Add the ham and stir till well blended.

4. In a large mixing bowl, beat the egg whites with an electric mixer till stiff peaks form, then fold them into the mixture till all traces of white have disappeared.

5. Scrape the mixture into the prepared casserole and bake till a knife inserted in the center comes out clean, about 40 minutes. Serve hot.

MAKES 6 TO 8 SERVINGS

Plantation Grits and Cheddar Casserole

6 cups water

Salt to taste

1¹/₂ cups regular grits

³/₄ pound sharp cheddar cheese, shredded

2 large eggs, beaten

1 teaspoon Worcestershire sauce

¹/₂ teaspoon Tabasco sauce

Black pepper to taste

2 tablespoons butter

1 small onion, finely chopped

1 garlic clove, minced

1. In a large saucepan, bring the salted water to a boil and gradually add the grits, stirring constantly. Reduce the heat to low, cover, and cook till soft, about 25 minutes, stirring occasionally. Let cool slightly, then add 2¹/₂ cups of the cheese, the eggs, Worcestershire, and Tabasco, season with pepper, stir till the cheese has melted, and set aside.

2. Preheat the oven to 375°F. Butter a 1¹/₂-quart casserole and set aside.

3. In a small skillet, melt the butter over moderate heat, add the onion and garlic, stir for 2 minutes, and stir into the grits mixture. Scrape the mixture into the casserole, sprinkle the remaining cheese over the top, and bake till puffed and browned, 30 to 35 minutes. Serve hot.

MAKES 6 SERVINGS

C A S S E R O L E   C H A T

To minimize mold forming on store-bought aged cheddar cheese after opening, keep the cheese in its original package, secure with a rubber band, and store in an airtight plastic bag.

Grits cooked with various cheeses can be traced back to antebellum days throughout the South, and today this classic breakfast casserole is still just as popular in Louisiana as it is in Georgia households. You might be tempted to use instant grits, but be warned that the texture won't be right. Also, boiling grits correctly requires a bit of patience to prevent lumpiness. When added to the boiling water, they must be stirred constantly till they begin to absorb the water, and even after you've lowered the heat, it's a good idea to stir them regularly till they're perfectly soft. So long as sufficient salt has been added to the water (and nothing is more bland than unsalted grits), no further salt is needed in this casserole.

Baked Chicken and Vegetable Casserole Omelet

Never can you give more free rein to the imagination as in the preparation of a brunch casserole omelet such as this. Different fresh vegetables can be used, leftover cooked turkey, pork, ham, and even sweetbreads can be substituted for the chicken, and the seasonings can be varied. And, if you're really in a rush and don't care to take time layering the casserole, you can simply sauté all the major components together in the butter, scrape into the casserole, pour the beaten eggs over the top, and bake. Do try not to overcook this omelet—which can be touchy. It should be puffy but still slightly soft. Also, when I have on hand some light tomato salsa (fresh or bottled), I might heat it up to spoon over each wedge or serve it at room temperature on the side.

1 pound zucchini, cut into $1/4$-inch dice

Salt

$1/4$ cup ($1/2$ stick) butter

2 medium-size onions, finely chopped

1 garlic clove, minced

2 large ripe tomatoes, peeled, seeded, and chopped

$1^1/2$ cups minced cooked chicken

1 teaspoon chopped fresh tarragon leaves or $1/4$ teaspoon dried, crumbled

Black pepper to taste

8 large eggs

3 tablespoons chopped fresh parsley leaves (optional)

1. Place the zucchini in a colander, sprinkle salt over the top, toss, and let drain 30 minutes. Rinse, pat dry with paper towels, and set aside.

2. Preheat the oven to 350°F. Butter a 2-quart casserole and set aside.

3. In a large heavy skillet, melt about 2 tablespoons of the butter over moderate heat, add the zucchini, onions, and garlic, stir till the zucchini turns a bright green, about 5 minutes, and scrape the mixture into the prepared casserole in an even layer.

4. Melt another tablespoon of butter in the skillet, add the tomatoes, stir till most of the liquid has evaporated, about 5 minutes, and spoon evenly over the zucchini mixture. Melt the remaining butter in the skillet, add the chicken and tarragon, season with salt and pepper, stir for 5 minutes, and spoon evenly over the tomatoes.

5. In a large mixing bowl, beat the eggs well, pour over the casserole, and bake till puffy and golden, 25 to 30 minutes To serve, let rest about 5 minutes, cut into wedges, and sprinkle the parsley, if using.

MAKES 6 SERVINGS

Cold Turkey, Melon, Goat Cheese, and Fresh Vegetable Surprise

4 cups (about 1 pound) chopped fresh spinach

2 cups diced cooked turkey breast

2 cups seeded and diced ripe cantaloupe (1 medium-size melon)

1 cup fresh green peas, blanched in boiling water for 4 minutes and drained

1 cup fresh corn kernels, blanched in boiling water for 4 minutes and drained

2 scallions (white part and some of the green), minced

3 sprigs fresh parsley, stems removed and leaves chopped

1/2 cup plain yogurt

1 tablespoon red wine vinegar

Juice of 1 lemon

1 tablespoon capers, drained

Salt and freshly ground black pepper to taste

1/4 pound goat cheese (preferably aged), cut into dice or crumbled

1. In a large, decorative casserole, layer in order the spinach, turkey, cantaloupe, and peas and corn combined and sprinkle the scallions and parsley over the top.

2. In a small mixing bowl, whisk together the yogurt, vinegar, lemon juice, and capers, season with salt and pepper, and pour the dressing evenly over the top. Scatter the cheese evenly over the top, cover with plastic wrap, and chill till ready to serve.

3. To serve, toss the salad just enough to expose all the ingredients and coat lightly with the dressing.

MAKES AT LEAST 6 SERVINGS

The whole object of this chilled, layered, and extremely healthy casserole salad is not only to utilize any number of fresh summer vegetables but, frankly, to show off that beautiful casserole dish you either received as a gift or couldn't pass up in a shop. It's also a perfect way to use up part of a turkey breast you found on sale and roasted. (Two large, boneless, poached chicken breasts could just as easily be used.) If you can obtain an imported, tangy, aged goat cheese, all the better, but since most likely you'll have to settle for one of the many relatively bland, fresh cheeses that Americans seem to adore, at least try to find one with some distinctive flavor.

Bridge Casserole

I don't play much bridge anymore, but when I was an avid fan and responsible for cooking up something for a luncheon break in the game, this is the dish that friends begged for most—served (as my mother still does) with a light congealed salad, sesame bread sticks, and plenty of chilled chardonnay. I always made a larger casserole than was needed since I personally didn't eat that much during the middle of the day and knew there'd be leftovers to warm up for supper. In this casserole, I also sometimes like to scatter about 2 tablespoons of capers over the layered crabmeat.

3 tablespoons butter

$^1/_2$ pound fresh mushrooms, coarsely chopped

12 canned artichoke hearts, drained

1 pound fresh lump crabmeat, picked over for shells and cartilage

$1^1/_2$ cups Cream Sauce (page 6)

1 tablespoon Worcestershire sauce

$^1/_4$ cup medium dry sherry

Salt and black pepper to taste

$^1/_4$ cup freshly grated Parmesan cheese

Sweet paprika to taste

1. Preheat the oven to 350°F. Butter a $1^1/_2$- to 2-quart casserole and set aside.

2. In a medium-size skillet, melt the butter over moderate heat, add the mushrooms and cook, stirring, till golden, about 8 minutes, and set aside.

3. Arrange the artichoke hearts in the bottom of the prepared casserole, flake the crabmeat evenly over the top, and scatter the mushrooms over the crabmeat.

4. Season the cream sauce with the Worcestershire and sherry, stir, and pour over the mushrooms and season with salt and pepper. Sprinkle the cheese and paprika over the top and bake till bubbly and golden, 25 to 30 minutes.

MAKES 6 SERVINGS

San Francisco Shredded Crab and Olive Bake

1 1/2 cups soft bread crumbs

3 tablespoons butter, melted

1/4 cup mayonnaise

2 large eggs, beaten

1 teaspoon minced onion

1 teaspoon seeded and minced green bell pepper

1 tablespoon chopped fresh parsley leaves

1 tablespoon fresh lemon juice

1 tablespoon dry sherry

1/2 teaspoon Worcestershire sauce

1/8 teaspoon cayenne pepper

1 1/2 pounds fresh crabmeat (Dungeness, stone, or lump blue), picked over for shells and cartilage and shredded or flaked

1 cup black olives (not cured in brine), drained, pitted, and quartered

1. Preheat the oven to 350°F. Butter a 1 1/2-quart casserole and set aside.

2. In a small mixing bowl, toss the bread crumbs and butter together and set aside.

3. In a large mixing bowl, combine 1/2 cup of the bread crumbs and all the remaining ingredients except the crabmeat and olives and mix till thoroughly blended. Fold in the crabmeat gently, then scrape the mixture into the prepared casserole.

4. Scatter the olives evenly over the mixture, top with the remaining bread crumbs, and bake till golden, about 20 minutes. Serve hot.

MAKES 6 SERVINGS

I don't know whether Fournou's Ovens restaurant at the Stanford Court hotel in San Francisco still serves the delectable shells of baked Pacific Dungeness crab with California black olives that I relished for so many years, but when I want to recreate the sensuous experience and impress brunch guests, I prepare this very simple casserole I developed using the more readily available eastern blue or stone crabmeat. One of the secrets is that part of the bread crumbs are incorporated in the basic crabmeat mixture for a balanced texture, and I do take every precaution not to overseason the casserole. Nor would I dream of overwhelming the crabmeat by using Niçoise or any other highly cured black olive, though I have no objection to sometimes substituting about 3/4 cup of *rinsed*, chopped, pimento-stuffed green olives.

Portland Oyster and Bacon Pie

I call this a Portland pie (though technically it's not a pie at all) for the simple reason that none other than James Beard once prepared the casserole for brunch when I visited him and some local friends one summer in Oregon. Of course, Jim made his "pie" with those small, purplish, sublime Olympia oysters native to the West Coast and named after Washington State's Olympia Peninsula. (Actually, Olympias are harvested from Alaska down to Baja and, to add to the linguistic confusion, they're also called "California oysters.") Since Olympias are rarely available outside the region, I use whichever small oysters look freshest in the market. The Madeira does add distinct subtlety to the casserole, but I suppose a good semi-sweet port wine—or even sweet vermouth—could be substituted with interesting results. Sometimes I do scatter a few slivered almonds over the top before drizzling on the butter.

4 strips lean bacon

10 ounces oyster crackers, crushed

3 pints small fresh shucked oysters, liquor reserved

$1/2$ cup (1 stick) butter, melted

2 cups half-and-half

$1/2$ cup Madeira wine

2 teaspoons Worcestershire sauce

Salt and black pepper to taste

Tabasco sauce to taste

1. In a medium-size skillet, fry the bacon over moderate heat till crisp, drain on paper towels, and crumble.

2. Preheat the oven to 350°F. Butter a shallow 2-quart casserole.

3. Scatter half the oyster crackers over the bottom of the prepared casserole, arrange half the oysters over the crackers, sprinkle half the crumbled bacon over the oysters, and drizzle half of the melted butter over the top. Repeat with another layer of crackers (reserving $1/2$ cup of them), the remaining oysters, and bacon.

4. In a medium-size mixing bowl, combine the half-and-half, Madeira, and Worcestershire, season with salt and pepper and Tabasco, stir till well blended, and pour over the oysters. Sprinkle the reserved crackers over the top, drizzle the remaining butter over the crackers, and bake till slightly browned, 25 to 30 minutes.

MAKES 6 TO 8 SERVINGS

CASSEROLE CHAT

Since the transparency of glass allows radiant heat to pass directly through it, food baked in a glass casserole cooks more quickly than in an earthenware or metal one.

Crazy for Casseroles

Shrimp, Egg, Bacon, and Rice Pie

1 pound small fresh shrimp

6 strips lean bacon

3 large ripe tomatoes, peeled, seeded, and coarsely chopped
(juices included)

1 tablespoon Worcestershire sauce

Salt and black pepper to taste

1 cup cooked long-grain rice (not quick-cooking)

4 large hard-boiled eggs, sliced

1 cup dry bread crumbs

3 tablespoons butter, melted

1. Place the shrimp in a pot with enough water to cover, bring to a boil, and remove from the heat. When cool enough to handle, shell and devein the shrimp and set aside.

2. In a medium-size skillet, fry the bacon till crisp, drain on paper towels, and crumble.

3. Meanwhile, in a medium-size mixing bowl, combine the tomatoes with their juices and the Worcestershire, season with salt and pepper, mix well, and set aside.

4. Preheat the oven to 350°F. Butter a 2-quart casserole.

5. Spoon two-thirds of the tomatoes over the bottom of the prepared casserole. Arrange the shrimp evenly over the tomatoes, layer the rice over the tomatoes, layer the egg slices over the rice, sprinkle the crumbled bacon evenly over the eggs, and spoon the remaining tomatoes evenly over the top.

6. In a small mixing bowl, toss the bread crumbs with the butter, spoon evenly over the top of the casserole, and bake till golden brown, 20 to 25 minutes.

MAKES 6 TO 8 SERVINGS

A specialty of the coastal Carolina Low Country, this casserole pie is served as much at gracious weekend breakfasts as at more casual brunches. Around Charleston, cooks prefer to make the pie with tiny, local, sweet "breakfast" shrimp which require no cleaning. Most of us have to settle for the smallest (and, hopefully, sweetest) shrimp we can find, and if they're really undersized, I don't even bother to preboil them and simply remove the shells and any veins before adding them to the casserole. Also, fresh, well-picked claw crabmeat makes a wonderful substitution for the shrimp in this recipe. On the other hand, do not use quick-cooking rice in place of the regular. And here's the Low Country way to boil any long-grain white rice:

In a saucepan, combine one part rice with two parts *cold* water and bring to a boil. Reduce the heat to a low simmer, cover tightly, and cook exactly 13 minutes. Cut off the heat and let the rice stand 12 minutes before serving or using in cooking.

New England Cheddar, Onion, and Walnut Pie

This pie comes from one of Boston's most gifted chefs, Jasper White, and even if it doesn't fully qualify as a layered casserole, the dish is so incredibly luscious that I'm willing to fudge a little. Curiously enough, cheddar pie (slightly sweetened) was a favorite breakfast item in New England throughout the nineteenth century and, while I doubt it would be very appropriate these days as a way to start the morning, it is a perfect and unusual dish for any style of brunch.

Jasper prefers to use high-gluten bread flour for his pie shell, but I find that unbleached all-purpose makes a very respectable crust. This is one time when you really should buy the very best aged Vermont cheddar available (like Cabot); likewise, the walnuts should be as fresh as possible and not in the least rancid (if necessary, pecans can be substituted). Served in large wedges with a green or congealed salad, the pie also makes a great luncheon dish.

PIE SHELL:

1 cup unbleached all-purpose flour

¼ teaspoon salt

6 tablespoons cold lard, cut into small pieces

3 to 4 tablespoons ice water, as needed

FILLING:

⅓ cup half-and-half

4 large eggs

¾ pound aged cheddar cheese, grated

6 scallions (white part and some of the green), thinly sliced

Salt and freshly ground black pepper to taste

Tabasco sauce to taste

½ cup chopped walnuts

1. To make the pie shell, combine the flour and salt in a medium-size mixing bowl, add the lard, and work the mixture together with your fingertips till crumbly. Gradually add the water, stirring, using just enough to make the dough stick together. Transfer to a floured work surface and knead just till the dough begins to smooth out. Wrap in plastic wrap and refrigerate for 30 minutes. Preheat the oven to 350°F.

2. Line a shallow, round, 9-inch casserole with the chilled dough, pressing it down evenly with your fingers. Prick with a fork, bake for 20 minutes, and remove from the oven.

3. In a heavy saucepan, combine the half-and-half, eggs, cheese, and scallions and cook over low heat, stirring constantly, till creamy but not boiling. Season with salt and pepper and Tabasco, stir, and pour the mixture into the casserole. Bake for 10 minutes, sprinkle the walnuts over the top, and continue to bake till the filling is set and the top begins to brown, about 15 minutes. Let the pie cool slightly and serve warm in wedges.

MAKES ONE 9-INCH PIE; 4 TO 6 SERVINGS

Crazy for Casseroles

Curried Corn, Bell Pepper, and Cheese Soufflé

1/4 cup (1/2 stick) butter

3 tablespoons minced onion

3 tablespoons seeded and minced green bell pepper

3 tablespoons all-purpose flour

1 to 2 tablespoons mild curry powder, to your taste

1 1/2 cups half-and-half

Salt and black pepper to taste

6 large eggs, beaten

6 large ears fresh corn, kernels and milk scraped from cobs (see page 156), or about 2 cups frozen corn kernels, thawed

1/4 pound sharp cheddar cheese, grated

1/2 cup freshly grated Parmesan cheese

1. In a small skillet, melt 1 tablespoon of the butter over moderate heat, add the onion and bell pepper, stir for 2 minutes, and set aside.

2. Preheat the oven to 350°F. Butter a 1 1/2-quart casserole and set aside.

3. In a large heavy saucepan, melt the remaining 3 tablespoons butter over moderate heat, add the flour and curry powder, and stir till well blended and smooth, about 1 minute. Stirring rapidly, add the half-and-half and blend till thickened and smooth. Season with salt and pepper, then gradually add the eggs, stirring rapidly and constantly and never allowing the mixture to boil. Remove from the heat, add the onion and bell pepper, corn with its milk, and cheddar, and stir till the cheese melts.

4. Scrape the mixture into the prepared casserole, sprinkle the Parmesan evenly over the top, and bake till golden brown, about 25 minutes.

MAKES 6 SERVINGS

"Scrape out that milk, son, scrape out every drop of that milk." I can still hear my grandmother scolding as I cut the kernels off ears of fresh Silver Queen corn and carelessly forgot to scrape the precious milk off the cobs. What she was getting ready to bake was a corn casserole much like this one, minus the curry powder and grated Parmesan, and what I was getting was my very first lesson in how to clean an ear of corn properly. Of course, in those days the casserole would have been served for lunch with something like fried chicken or chopped pork barbecue, but today I find that my doctored version can just about stand on its own as a featured brunch dish—with maybe a few ham biscuits, pickled peaches, and fresh fruit compote. Truly fresh corn does make a difference, but if you have doubts about how old the ears are, you're better off using frozen kernels.

Macaroni, Cheese, and Tomato Soufflé

Who knows when the classic principles behind a genuine French soufflé were modified in America to accommodate any baked casserole containing eggs, and who can guess when the concept was stretched even further to include this sort of Italian-American brunch casserole that I was served more than once by an Italian colleague's wife when I was teaching in New Jersey at Rutgers? Do notice that the onions are not sautéed first for this dish, and do use Italian Parmigiano-Reggiano cheese if you want the casserole to really shine. Three or four canned Italian plum tomatoes can be substituted if you can't find ripe fresh ones.

1½ cups elbow macaroni

3 tablespoons butter

2 tablespoons all-purpose flour

Salt and black pepper to taste

2 cups milk

1 small onion, finely chopped

½ pound Parmesan cheese, grated

½ teaspoon dried oregano, crumbled

2 large eggs, beaten

2 medium-size ripe tomatoes, peeled, seeded, and chopped

1. In a large saucepan of boiling salted water, cook the macaroni according to package directions till tender and drain in a colander.

2. Preheat the oven to 350°F. Butter a 1½-quart casserole and set aside.

3. In a large heavy saucepan, melt the butter over moderate heat, add the flour, season with salt and pepper, and whisk till smooth, about 1 minute. Gradually add the milk, whisking, and cook till bubbly and thickened. Add the onion, cheese, and oregano, stir just till the cheese has melted, and remove the pan from the heat. Whisking constantly, stir a little of the hot cheese sauce into the eggs, then whisk the eggs back into the sauce till well blended.

4. In a large bowl, combine the macaroni and sauce, mix till blended, and scrape into the prepared casserole. Distribute the tomatoes evenly over the top and bake till the soufflé is firm but still moist, about 30 minutes.

MAKES 6 SERVINGS

C A S S E R O L E   C H A T

Do not rinse boiled pasta intended to be baked with a sauce in a casserole, since it's the starch that makes the sauce cling to the pasta.

Crazy for Casseroles

Monterey Celery, Almond, and Water Chestnut Bake

6 tablespoons (³/₄ stick) butter

¹/₄ pound mushrooms, sliced

6 large celery ribs, diced

Salt to taste

¹/₂ cup canned sliced water chestnuts, drained

¹/₄ cup slivered almonds

3 tablespoons all-purpose flour

1 cup chicken broth

³/₄ cup half-and-half

Black pepper to taste

¹/₂ cup soft bread crumbs

¹/₂ cup freshly grated Parmesan cheese

3 tablespoons butter, melted

1. In a small skillet, melt 2 tablespoons of the butter over moderate heat, add the mushrooms and cook, stirring, till soft, about 5 minutes.

2. In a medium-size saucepan, combine the celery with enough salted water to just cover, bring to a boil, cook for 5 minutes, and drain.

3. Preheat the oven to 350°F. Butter a 2-quart casserole and set aside.

4. In a medium-size mixing bowl, combine the mushrooms, celery, water chestnuts, and almonds, mix till blended, and scrape into the casserole.

5. In a medium-size heavy saucepan, melt the remaining 4 tablespoons butter over moderate heat, add the flour, and stir for 1 minute. Gradually add the broth and half-and-half and cook, stirring constantly, till the sauce is bubbly and thickened. Pour the sauce over the celery mixture.

6. In a small mixing bowl, combine the bread crumbs and cheese, sprinkle evenly over the casserole, drizzle the melted butter over the top, and bake till golden, about 30 minutes.

MAKES 6 TO 8 SERVINGS

Some years ago, after visiting the amazing aquarium in Monterey, California, I was stunned by a celery-and-nut casserole prepared by a friend of a friend at her home nearby and eventually developed my own brunch version to accompany cold poached chicken, fried shrimp, tiny crab cakes, and the like. And for something really unusual and modern, substitute about 3 cups diced fennel bulb (outer stalks and feathery tops discarded) for the celery, in which case you may want to feature the casserole as a main dish.

Vegetable and Two-Cheese Strata

I'm certainly no vegetarian and generally must have a little meat, poultry, or fish at any meal, but I must admit that, when summertime comes and the garden is abundant with fresh vegetables and herbs, I could eat nothing but this flavor-packed casserole and its variations three times a week. Serve it with cold fried chicken wing drumettes, herb biscuits, and chilled fresh berries and you'll have a simple but satisfying brunch to crow about. And do feel free to try different grated or shredded cheese combinations.

3 to 4 medium-size yellow squash (about 1 pound), ends removed and cut diagonally into 1/2-inch-thick slices

1 small eggplant (about 1 pound), stem removed, cut in half lengthwise, and cut into 1/2-inch-thick half-moons

Salt to taste

1/4 cup (1/2 stick) butter

3 medium-size onions, sliced

1 small green bell pepper, seeded and sliced

1 garlic clove, minced

1/4 pound slightly dry blue cheese, crumbled

1/4 pound provolone cheese (preferably sharp), shredded

2 large ripe tomatoes, chopped (juices included)

1 tablespoon chopped fresh oregano leaves or 1 teaspoon dried oregano, crumbled

Freshly ground black pepper to taste

1. Preheat the oven to 350°F. Butter a shallow 2-quart covered casserole and set aside.

2. In a large skillet, layer the squash and eggplant slices, add enough salted water to barely cover, and bring to a boil. Reduce the heat to low, cover, simmer for 10 minutes, drain, and set aside.

3. Wipe the same skillet dry, melt the butter in it over moderate heat, add the onions, bell pepper, and garlic and cook, stirring, till the vegetables are just tender, about 8 minutes, and remove from the heat.

4. In a medium-size mixing bowl, combine and toss the two cheeses.

5. In the bottom of the prepared casserole, layer half the onion mixture, then half the squash mixture and half the tomatoes. Sprinkle the oregano, pepper, and half the cheese mixture over the top. Repeat layering the remaining onions, squash, and tomatoes, sprinkle the remaining cheese over the top, cover, and bake for 20 minutes. Uncover and bake till golden, about 10 minutes longer.

MAKES 6 TO 8 SERVINGS

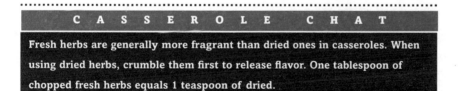

C A S S E R O L E   C H A T

Fresh herbs are generally more fragrant than dried ones in casseroles. When using dried herbs, crumble them first to release flavor. One tablespoon of chopped fresh herbs equals 1 teaspoon of dried.

Ranchero Green Chile, Cheese, and Tomato Casserole

Some of the earliest and greatest casseroles I've sampled have been in the American Southwest. I was served this style of casserole at an utterly unpretentious café-restaurant outside Sante Fe, New Mexico, guest of a very dapper New York restaurateur who had given up The Big Apple and who counted amongst his passions the genuine Mexican white cheese known as *queso fresco*. I, too, became addicted to the cream-colored, slightly acidic, crumbly cheese used in so many local dishes, and when it was combined with aged Monterey Jack and fiery chiles in the casserole I had, tears came to my eyes for more reasons than one. Good *queso fresco* can be found outside the area in the very best cheese shops and delis, but be warned that some can be rubbery and tasteless, in which case your best bet is to substitute aged *ricotta salata* (not fresh ricotta) sold in most Italian markets or use all Monterey Jack. For the right textural contrast, nothing works like the crumbled tacos.

1 pound aged Monterey Jack cheese, coarsely grated

1 pound Mexican white cheese (*queso fresco*), crumbled

Two 4-ounce cans green chiles, drained, seeded, and chopped

$^2/_3$ cup evaporated milk

4 large eggs

1 tablespoon yellow cornmeal

Salt and black pepper to taste

2 medium-size ripe tomatoes, coarsely chopped

1 cup crumbled taco shells

2 tablespoons corn oil

1. Preheat the oven to 350°F. Butter a shallow 2-quart casserole.

2. In a large mixing bowl, combine the two cheeses and the chiles, mix well, and scrape evenly into the prepared casserole.

3. In another large mixing bowl, whisk together the milk, eggs, and cornmeal, season with salt and pepper, and pour over the cheeses and chiles.

4. Spoon the tomatoes evenly over the top, scatter the tacos over the tomatoes, drizzle the oil over the tacos, and bake till a knife inserted into the middle comes out clean, 45 to 50 minutes.

MAKES 6 TO 8 SERVINGS

Hot Curried Fruit Casserole

One 16-ounce can pineapple rings

One 16-ounce can peach halves

One 16-ounce can pear halves

1 cup seedless golden raisins

One 14-ounce jar spiced apple rings

2 tablespoons all-purpose flour

$^1/_2$ cup firmly packed light brown sugar

1 tablespoon mild curry powder

1 cup dry vermouth

$^3/_4$ cup ($1^1/_2$ sticks) butter

1. Drain all the fruits and cut the pineapple rings in half. Butter a 2- to $2^1/_2$-quart casserole, arrange the fruits in alternating layers, saving the apple rings for the top, and set aside.

2. In a medium-size heavy saucepan, combine the flour, brown sugar, curry powder, vermouth, and butter over moderate heat and stir till the mixture is thickened and smooth, about 10 minutes. Pour the mixture over the fruit, cover with plastic wrap, and let stand in the refrigerator overnight.

3. Preheat the oven to 350°F. Place the casserole in the oven and bake till bubbly hot and slightly glazed on top, 20 to 30 minutes.

MAKES 8 TO 10 SERVINGS

CASSEROLE CHAT

Brown sugar, which contains molasses (a by-product of the cane sugar in refining process), adds distinctive flavor, aroma, and color to any number of casseroles, but it should be used in discreet quantities so as not to overwhelm the primary ingredients.

Baked hot fruits are as much a part of America's versatile casserole heritage as macaroni and cheese, and if ever a casserole lent itself to unlimited interpretation and experimentation, this is it. A fruit casserole can be sherried, curried, or minted; it can contain three or six different fruits; and it can be served not only at breakfasts and brunches as a side dish but also as a dessert. Because of the curry powder, this particular one is really most appropriate as a brunch dish on a fairly lavish buffet. Can you use fresh fruit instead of canned? All I can say is that I tried it once and, just as freshly made sauces cannot be substituted for canned soups in some casseroles, the results weren't right—the fruit seemed to turn mushy. In any case, do remember to let this casserole stand overnight—or at least a few hours—before baking so that the flavors will blend. Also, since the casserole can be reheated over and over, I always make it in large quantity.

Hot Sherried Fruit Casserole Deluxe

I can't swear to the exact fruits that were included in the hot sherried casserole at a very smart brunch reception I attended at the Drake Hotel in Chicago, but my approximation here is pretty close. I assume that the tag "Deluxe" noted on the identification card referred quaintly to the maraschino cherries fitted into each pineapple ring. For best results, don't forget to assemble this casserole in advance and let it stand in the refrigerator—preferably overnight—before baking. And, as with the Hot Curried Fruit Casserole, make this one in quantity so there will be some left over to reheat for another occasion.

$^1/_2$ cup (1 stick) butter

2 tablespoons all-purpose flour

$^1/_4$ cup granulated sugar

$^1/_4$ cup firmly packed light brown sugar

1 cup dry sherry

One 16-ounce can pitted purple plums, drained

One 16-ounce can pear halves, drained

One 16-ounce can apricot halves, drained

One 14-ounce jar spiced apple rings, drained

One 16-ounce can pineapple rings, drained

Maraschino cherries, stemmed

1. Butter a 2- to 2½-quart casserole and set aside.

2. In a medium-size heavy saucepan, melt the butter over moderate heat, add the flour, and stir for 1 minute. Add the two sugars and sherry, stir steadily till the sauce is thickened and smooth, about 10 minutes, and remove from the heat.

3. In the prepared casserole, arrange the fruit in alternating layers, saving enough pineapple rings for the top. Place a cherry in the center of each pineapple ring on top, pour the sauce over the fruit, cover with plastic wrap, and refrigerate overnight.

4. Preheat the oven to 350°F. Remove the casserole from the refrigerator 30 minutes before baking, then bake till bubbly and slightly glazed on top, about 20 minutes.

MAKES 8 TO 10 SERVINGS

Beef, Pork, Lamb, Veal, and Game Casseroles, Pots, and Pilafs

Mission Beef, Onion, and Olive Casserole

The Spaniards who settled in California's San Fernando and San Joaquin Valleys in the eighteenth century must have known how wonderfully olives complement beef when they introduced such olive varieties as the sevillano, manzanilla, and mission, and today the combination is as popular in that region of the country as it was over two hundred years ago. This casserole is great as it is, but if you want to give it real mystery, sprinkle about a tablespoon of grated orange rind over the layer of beef cubes.

3/4 cup all-purpose flour

Salt and black pepper to taste

2 pounds beef round, trimmed of excess fat and cut into 1 1/2-inch cubes

1/2 cup olive oil

2 medium-size onions, sliced

1 garlic clove, minced

1/2 teaspoon dried thyme, crumbled

20 to 25 large pitted green olives

1 cup dry red wine

1 cup water

1. On a plate, combine the flour and salt and pepper and dredge the beef cubes in the mixture, tapping off any excess.

2. Preheat the oven to 350°F. Grease a 2-quart casserole and set aside.

3. In a large heavy skillet, heat the olive oil over moderate heat, add the beef cubes, brown on all sides, and transfer to a plate. Add the onions, garlic, and thyme to the skillet, stir till softened, about 5 minutes, and transfer to another plate.

4. In a medium-size saucepan, combine the olives with enough water to cover, bring to a boil, cook for 2 minutes, drain in a colander, and cut in half.

5. Layer the beef cubes in the prepared casserole, spoon the onions evenly over the top, and layer the olives over the onions. Pour the wine and water over the top, cover, and bake for 1 hour. Uncover and continue to bake till the beef is fork-tender and the onions and olives slightly glazed, 15 to 20 minutes.

MAKES 6 SERVINGS

Crazy for Casseroles

Ranch Steak and Corn Casserole

$^1/_4$ cup all-purpose flour

Salt and black pepper to taste

2 pounds top-round (London broil) steak, trimmed of any fat and cut into $1^1/_2$-inch cubes

$^1/_4$ cup corn oil

2 medium-size onions, sliced

2 medium-size green bell peppers, seeded and chopped

1 celery rib, chopped

1 garlic clove, minced

One 10-ounce package frozen corn kernels, thawed

2 ripe tomatoes, peeled and chopped

$^2/_3$ cup beef broth, beer, or water

1. Preheat the oven to 325°F. Grease a 2-quart casserole and set aside.

2. On a plate, combine the flour and salt and pepper and dredge the steak pieces, tapping off any excess.

3. In a large heavy skillet, heat the corn oil over moderate heat, add the steak, brown on all sides, and transfer the pieces to the prepared casserole. Add the onions, bell peppers, celery, and garlic to the skillet, stir till the vegetables are softened, about 7 minutes, and spread the mixture evenly across the meat in the casserole. Layer the corn over the other vegetables, then layer the tomatoes over the corn and season again with salt and pepper. Add the broth, cover, and bake till the meat is fork-tender, $1^1/_2$ to 2 hours.

MAKES 6 SERVINGS

Here is the true flavor of the Old West, the type of casserole that a chuckwagon cook might have whipped up or a settler might have concocted using whatever meat and vegetables were on hand. Actually, my version is pretty fancy compared with what our predecessors probably produced, using chopped-up longhorn beef or hog seasoned with ground chile peppers and maybe a few wild herbs and moistened with beer or plain water. One time, in fact, trying to capture what I perceived to be a truly authentic ranch-style casserole, I simply layered all the raw ingredients in a big pot, added a little chili powder and a few herbs, and baked the dish at 300°F for about $3^1/_2$ hours. It was delicious.

Bourbon Beef and Oyster Pot

Created back in the 1970s by one of my most influential culinary mentors, Pearl Byrd Foster of Mr. & Mrs. Foster's restaurant in Manhattan, this luscious pot draws a fine line between a stew and a stovetop casserole, depending on the amount of liquid used to make the vegetable puree. In any case, the ideal vessel for preparing this is an enameled cast-iron pot, and be sure to cook the oysters just till they curl to prevent their being tough.

$^1/_4$ cup vegetable oil

2 tablespoons butter

One 3-pound bottom- or top-round beef roast, trimmed of all fat and cut into $1^1/_2$-inch cubes

3 ounces bourbon

2 cups beef broth

1 cup water

1 medium-size onion, chopped

1 celery rib, cut into 1-inch pieces

1 large carrot, scraped, halved lengthwise, and cut into 1-inch pieces

1 large russet potato, peeled and cut into cubes

2 tablespoons tomato paste

1 garlic clove, crushed

1 small bay leaf

2 cloves

$^1/_4$ teaspoon dried thyme, crumbled

Worcestershire and Tabasco sauces to taste

Salt and black pepper to taste

1 quart fresh shucked oysters, liquor included

$^1/_2$ cup peeled and freshly grated horseradish

1. In a flameproof, heavy 4-quart casserole or pot, heat the oil and butter together over moderate heat until the butter melts, then add the beef and brown on all sides. Pour off any excess fat, add the bourbon, ignite, and, when the flames die out, add the broth and water and scrape the bottom to loosen all the browned bits. Add the vegetables, tomato paste, garlic, bay leaf, cloves, and thyme, season with Worcestershire, Tabasco, and salt and pepper, and stir to blend well. Bring to a boil, reduce the heat to moderately low, cover, and simmer till the meat is very tender, about 2 hours.

Crazy for Casseroles

2. With a slotted spoon, transfer the meat to a platter, carefully pour the liquid and vegetables into a food processor or blender (in batches, if necessary), and reduce to a puree, adding a little more broth if the mixture is too thick. Return the meat and pureed vegetables to the casserole, arrange the oysters over the top, and pour the oyster liquor over the top. Bring to a simmer, cover, and cook just till the edges of the oysters curl, 7 to 8 minutes.

3. Serve the beef and oysters with a little horseradish on the side.

MAKES 8 SERVINGS

CASSEROLE CHAT

Flambéing the ingredients for a few casseroles burns off the alcohol of the spirit used while leaving its distinctive additional flavor. But be careful. To flambé, stand as far back from the casserole as possible and ignite just the edge with a match. Be careful of long hair and dangling shirt sleeves.

Yankee Corned Beef and Vegetable Pot

Talk about Yankee ingenuity! This luscious casserole is virtually fail-proof in that the corned beef can't be overcooked, the potatoes can be baked till just tender or almost crisp, and, if things dry out too quickly, all you do is add a little extra broth or water. When I'm planning to serve this casserole for a really relaxed, casual Saturday night dinner, I buy the biggest, flat- (or thin-) cut brisket I can find, so there'll be some left over for hash or sandwiches.

One 3 pound corned beef brisket (flat-cut)

1 cup beef broth

2 tablespoons all-purpose flour

2 medium-size onions, thinly sliced

2 celery ribs, halved lengthwise and cut into 2-inch pieces

2 carrots, scraped, halved lengthwise, and cut into 2-inch pieces

1 large ripe tomato, coarsely chopped

$^1/_2$ cup chopped fresh parsley leaves

$^1/_2$ teaspoon dried thyme, crumbled

Salt and black pepper to taste

3 medium-size russet potatoes, peeled and thinly sliced

1. Place the corned beef in a deep roasting pan with enough water to cover and bring to a boil, skimming off any scum on the surface. Reduce the heat to low, cover, and simmer till almost tender when stuck with a knife, about 2$^1/_2$ hours. Transfer the brisket to a cutting board, discard any fat, and cut the meat across the grain into thin slices.

2. Preheat the oven to 325°F. Grease a 2- to 2$^1/_2$-quart casserole.

3. In a small skillet, combine the beef broth and flour, bring to a simmer, whisk till well blended and smooth, and remove from the heat.

4. Layer the corned beef, then onions, celery, carrots, and tomatoes in the prepared casserole, sprinkling a little parsley between the layers and seasoning with the thyme and salt and pepper. Pour the broth over the top, cover, and bake till the beef is fork-tender, about 30 minutes.

5. Arrange the potato slices overlapping across the top of the casserole, baste them with a little of the juices, and continue to bake till the potatoes are tender and browned, about 30 minutes.

MAKES 6 SERVINGS

Country Short Ribs of Beef

6 meaty short ribs of beef

Salt and black pepper to taste

12 small onions, scored on the root ends

10 small red potatoes, peeled

One 16-ounce can whole tomatoes, undrained

Beef broth, if necessary

1. Place the short ribs in a large pot with enough water to cover and season with salt and pepper. Bring to a boil and skim off any scum that comes to the surface. Reduce the heat to low, cover, and simmer at least 3 hours, adding more water if necessary to cover. During the last hour of simmering, add the onions. During the last 30 minutes, add the potatoes.

2. Preheat the oven to 375°F.

3. With a slotted spoon, transfer the meat to a shallow 2- to 2½-quart casserole, place the onions and potatoes around the meat, and add the tomatoes with their juices. If the juice does not fill the casserole by about three quarters, add a little beef broth. Season with salt and pepper and bake till the top is slightly crusted, about 45 minutes.

MAKES 6 SERVINGS

C A S S E R O L E   C H A T

While alkali ingredients shorten the cooking process of any dish, highly acidic ones require longer simmering. Therefore, a casserole containing tomatoes must be baked longer than one without them.

If I were forced to name the one casserole I couldn't live without, it would have to be this one that's been in my Southern family for at least three generations and that I prepare at least once a month. Some people give the ribs a preliminary browning, simmer them in rich stock and wine with exotic vegetables, add everything to the pot from ginger to orange peel to chili paste, and take inordinate measures to degrease the casserole. That's all ridiculous. Simply follow my directions to the letter, and I'll guarantee you the most succulent, ungreasy short ribs and vegetables you'll ever eat—preferably served with a smooth squash casserole (page 302), hot biscuits, and either a modest red wine or beer. What matters most, of course, is the quality of the short ribs, which must be meaty and at least four inches wide and three inches thick. If all you can find are scrawny ribs, cook something else, and remember that beautiful ribs found on sale freeze very well.

Prairie Oxtail, Bean, and Vegetable Casserole

Still as highly prized in Texas and the Plains states as during pioneer expansion, oxtail, whether stewed, broiled, or braised as in this casserole, is one of the most succulent and inexpensive of all meats. I think I was first exposed to great oxtails about thirty years ago at a meat market called Snow's in Kansas City, Kansas, that raised and slaughtered its own prime beef, and ever since, I've just never understood why this full-flavored, gelatinous cut of meat has not been more popular in households and restaurants all over the country given its wide availability.

When shopping, look for oxtails with plenty of meat on the bones (one average disjointed tail should yield three or four servings), and if they do contain a good amount of fat, it's best to prepare the casserole a day in advance, chill it overnight, and degrease the surface before reheating.

I don't like the texture of canned beans for this casserole, so to avoid having to soak the

0 ounces (1¼ cups) dried Great Northern white beans, rinsed and picked over

3 pounds oxtail, disjointed

¼ cup all-purpose flour

¼ cup vegetable oil

2 medium-size onions, chopped

2 celery ribs, chopped

2 carrots, scraped and cut into small cubes

1 garlic clove, minced

½ teaspoon dried thyme, crumbled

Salt and black pepper to taste

1 cup dry red wine

1 cup beef broth

1. In a large mixing bowl, combine the beans with enough cold water to cover generously and let soak overnight.

2. Preheat the oven to 300°F. Grease a 3-quart casserole and set aside.

3. On a large plate, dust the oxtail in 3 tablespoons of the flour, tapping off any excess.

4. In a large heavy skillet, heat the oil over moderate heat, then add the oxtail pieces, brown till nutty in color on all sides, and arrange in the bottom of the prepared casserole. Add the onions, celery, carrots, garlic, and thyme to the skillet, season with salt and pepper, stir till the onions are slightly browned, about 10 minutes, and transfer to a plate. Stir the remaining 1 tablespoon flour into the juices left in the skillet, about 1 minute, then gradually add the wine and stir for about 3 minutes. Add broth, stir about 3 minutes, and remove the sauce from the heat.

5. Drain the beans, then distribute them evenly over the oxtails. Spoon the sautéed vegetables evenly over the beans, pour the sauce over the casserole, cover, and bake till the meat and beans are very tender, about 3 hours, skimming any fat from the top.

MAKES 6 SERVINGS

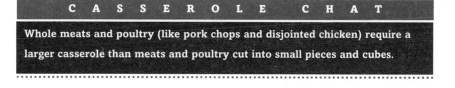

CASSEROLE CHAT

Whole meats and poultry (like pork chops and disjointed chicken) require a larger casserole than meats and poultry cut into small pieces and cubes.

dried ones overnight, simply bring them to a boil with enough water to cover for about 10 minutes, then let them soak two to three hours. Also, beer can be substituted for the wine and broth.

Chuckwagon Casserole

I found a rather crude version of this recipe in an old West Texas farm journal and immediately perceived it to be a first cousin—if not the ancestor—of chili con carne. Of course, I'm sure that chuckwagon cooks (and cowboys) would have used tough longhorn beef, beef suet, dried beans, and "rat cheese" (a type of cheddar) and made such a casserole in a heavy iron pot, and the inclusion of green olives might suggest that this type of casserole was just as popular as far west as California. In any case, although this is the most rudimentary of unlayered American casseroles, it's still an easy and delicious way to satisfy a hungry family or group of friends—served with a big tossed salad, biscuits or cornbread, and cold beer.

3 tablespoons corn oil

1 pound finely ground beef round

1 large onion, chopped

1 medium-size green bell pepper, seeded and chopped

1 garlic clove, minced

1 tablespoon chili powder

One 1-pound can Italian plum tomatoes, undrained

One 1-pound can kidney beans, undrained

$^1/_2$ cup chopped pitted green olives

1 tablespoon Worcestershire sauce

Pinch of ground cumin

Tabasco sauce to taste

Salt and black pepper to taste

$^3/_4$ cup shredded sharp cheddar cheese

1. Preheat the oven to 350°F. Grease a $1^1/_2$- to 2-quart casserole and set aside.

2. In a large heavy skillet, heat the oil over moderate heat, add the beef, and stir till lightly browned, about 8 minutes. Add the onion, bell pepper, garlic, and chili powder and stir till the vegetables soften, about 5 minutes.

3. Scrape the mixture into the prepared casserole, add the tomatoes, beans, olives, Worcestershire, and cumin, season with Tabasco, and salt and pepper, stir well, and bake for 30 minutes. Sprinkle the cheese over the top and continue to bake till golden brown on top, about 20 minutes.

MAKES 4 TO 6 SERVINGS

Stuffed Bell Pepper Casserole

6 large green or red bell peppers

2 strips lean bacon

1 medium-size onion, finely chopped

1 garlic clove, minced

$^1/_2$ teaspoon dried oregano, crumbled

Salt and black pepper to taste

1 cup soft fine bread crumbs

2 cups finely diced cooked beef, pork, or lamb

$^1/_4$ to $^1/_2$ cup shredded cheddar cheese, to your taste

1. With a sharp knife, cut a wide circle around the stems of the peppers and scoop out and discard all the seeds and white membranes. Arrange the peppers on their sides in a large kettle and add enough salted water to cover. Bring to a low boil, cover, and cook till crisp-tender, 6 to 8 minutes, then drain the peppers upside down on paper towels.

2. In a large skillet, fry the bacon over moderate heat till crisp, drain on paper towels, and crumble finely. Add the onion, garlic, and oregano to the skillet, season with salt and pepper, and stir till softened, about 5 minutes. Add the bread crumbs and stir till well blended. Add the crumbled bacon and other meat and stir till well blended.

3. Preheat the oven to 375°F.

4. Stuff the peppers with equal amounts of the meat mixture, stand them close together in a shallow 1$^1/_2$-quart casserole, and sprinkle the cheese over the tops. Pour about $^1/_4$ inch of hot water around the peppers and bake till tender, 35 to 45 minutes, adding a little more water if necessary.

5. Lift the peppers carefully from the water with a slotted spoon to a platter, pour any water from the casserole, and serve the peppers in the casserole.

MAKES 6 SERVINGS

What, in heaven's name, ever happened to the wonderful stuffed bell peppers that used to be almost a staple in American kitchens from coast to coast? They're simple to make, they're ideal for a casual supper, and, perhaps best of all, they're just as good served cold or at room temperature as they are piping hot. Bell peppers can be stuffed with every leftover meat from roast beef or pork to braised lamb to cooked hamburger, and what I really like about them is that they can be prepared well in advance. I'm aware that some people freeze stuffed bell peppers, but I never would since it does alter the texture of the peppers. Do feel free to try different cheese toppings for this casserole.

San Antonio Chili Casserole

"Honey, ain't nothing but baked chili," quipped the bored waitress serving us at a local café not far from the River Walk in San Antonio. There the casserole was made in a big black skillet and served in wedges like a loose quiche, but after I had serious words with the owner about exactly how it was concocted, it didn't take much imagination to come up with my own version prepared in a regular casserole dish. If you love chili con carne, you'll relish this fancified modification and agree it's considerably more than just "baked chili." The dish is perfect for a cold, bleak winter night served with a big green salad, hot cornbread or tortilla chips, and beer.

1 tablespoon corn oil

1 medium-size onion, chopped

1 medium-size green bell pepper, seeded and chopped

1 garlic clove, minced

1 pound lean ground beef chuck

1 tablespoon chili powder

One 8-ounce can tomato sauce

Salt and black pepper to taste

Two 16-ounce cans kidney beans, drained, reserving $^1/_2$ cup of the liquid

1 cup all-purpose flour

1 cup yellow cornmeal

2 teaspoons baking powder

1 teaspoon sugar

1 cup shredded sharp cheddar cheese

2 large eggs

$^1/_4$ cup ($^1/_2$ stick) butter, melted

1. Preheat the oven to 350°F. Grease a 2-quart casserole and set aside.

2. In a large skillet, heat the oil over moderate heat, add the onion, bell pepper, and garlic and stir till just softened. Add the beef, breaking it up with a fork, stir till browned, and pour off any excess fat. Add the chili powder, tomato sauce, and salt and pepper, and stir. Add the beans and reserved bean liquid, stir well, and scrape into the prepared casserole.

3. In a medium-size mixing bowl, combine the flour, cornmeal, baking powder, sugar, salt and pepper to taste, and cheese. In a small mixing bowl, beat together the eggs and butter, pour into the flour mixture, and stir till well blended and smooth. Spread the mixture evenly over the meat and beans and bake till the top is lightly browned, about 30 minutes.

MAKES 4 TO 6 SERVINGS

Texas Hash Casserole

1 pound ground beef chuck

2 large onions, sliced

2 medium-size green bell peppers, seeded and chopped

1 garlic clove, minced

2 large ripe tomatoes, chopped (juices included)

1 cup raw long-grain rice

2 teaspoons chili powder

Salt and black pepper to taste

1. Preheat the oven to 350°F. Grease a 1½- to 2-quart casserole and set aside.

2. In a large heavy skillet over moderate heat, break up the ground beef and cook, stirring, till the meat falls apart and loses most of its red color, about 8 minutes. Add the onions, bell peppers, and garlic and stir till the vegetables soften, about 8 minutes. Add the tomatoes plus their juices, the rice, and chili powder, season with salt and pepper, stir well, and cook about 5 minutes longer, stirring.

3. Scrape the mixture into the prepared casserole and bake till crusted on top, about 45 minutes.

MAKES 4 TO 6 SERVINGS

Mary Greenwood, who drove around in a Rolls-Royce and cursed like a sailor, was one of Houston's more glamorous and outrageous characters and a dear friend who could hold her own in the kitchen when necessity called for food to be on the table. Once, when we and another couple were kept waiting for our reserved table almost an hour in one of Houston's snazziest restaurants, Mary finally exploded at the head waiter, turned to us, and instructed, "Out! We're going back to the house and have some more booze while I whip up my hash casserole." I can still see Mary strapping on a bright red apron over her priceless dinner dress, plopping a few frozen hamburger patties in the frying pan, chopping vegetables, and, in almost no time, taking this simple but welcomed casserole out of the oven.

Graham's Anglo-American Shepherd's Pie

I like to think that this easy, thrifty casserole, once contrived by a close English chum while visiting me in East Hampton, is representative of the way so many British dishes were transformed and adapted to the American kitchen over the course of our history. The best thing about this casserole is that virtually any leftover cooked meat (beef, pork, lamb, ham, corned beef) can be used—as well as ground meat ($1^1/_2$ to 2 pounds) that is sautéed and drained of fat. Also, if I have any gravy left over from a roast, I might add a little of that and use only one or two eggs. Of course, there's nothing like freshly boiled mashed potatoes, but if you need to reconstitute leftover ones, simply beat in a little hot milk till they're fluffy. Do note that this pie can be assembled in advance, covered and chilled, and returned almost to room temperature when ready for baking. If, after thirty minutes, it's not browned to your liking, simply run it under the broiler for two to three minutes.

3 strips lean bacon

2 medium-size onions, finely chopped

1 medium-size green bell pepper, seeded and finely chopped

1 garlic clove, minced

3 cups finely chopped cooked beef or lamb

1 tablespoon Worcestershire sauce

Salt and black pepper to taste

3 large eggs, beaten

4 to 6 cups mashed potatoes

2 tablespoons butter, melted

1. Preheat the oven to 375°F. Grease a 2-quart casserole and set aside.

2. In a large heavy skillet over moderate heat, fry the bacon till crisp, drain on paper towels, and crumble finely. Add the onions, bell pepper, and garlic to the skillet and cook, stirring, till the onions are golden, about 10 minutes. Scrape the vegetables into a large mixing bowl, add the bacon, chopped meat, Worcestershire, salt and pepper, and eggs, mix till well blended, and set aside.

3. Spread half the mashed potatoes over the bottom of the prepared casserole, layer the meat-and-vegetable mixture over the top, and cover with the remaining potatoes, roughing them with a fork. Brush the top of the potatoes with the butter and bake till the top is puffy and golden brown, about 30 minutes.

MAKES 6 SERVINGS

86

3 tablespoons vegetable oil

1 medium-size onion, chopped

1 medium-size green bell pepper, seeded and chopped

$^1/_2$ pound ground beef round

$^1/_2$ pound ground veal or pork

$^1/_2$ pound fresh mushrooms, chopped

3 cups shell macaroni, boiled according to package directions (but no more than 6 minutes) and drained

Two 8-ounce cans tomato sauce

1 large (about 15 ounces) can cream-style corn

Salt and black pepper to taste

1 cup freshly grated Parmesan cheese

1. Butter a 1$^1/_2$-quart casserole and set aside.

2. In a large heavy skillet, heat the oil over moderate heat, add the onion and bell pepper, and stir for 3 minutes. Add the beef and veal or pork and stir, breaking up the meats with a fork, till browned. Pour off any fat from the skillet and remove from the heat.

3. Spoon half the meat mixture over the bottom of the prepared casserole, scatter the mushrooms over the top, and layer the macaroni over the mushrooms. Pour the tomato sauce evenly over the top, layer the corn evenly over the sauce, spoon the remaining meat mixture over the corn, and season with salt and pepper. Cover the casserole with plastic wrap and refrigerate for 1 hour.

4. When ready to bake, preheat the oven to 325°F, sprinkle the cheese evenly over the top, and bake till browned, about 45 minutes.

MAKES 6 SERVINGS

For years I thought that this layered casserole with the mysterious name was strictly Southern, then a lady I met not long ago in Chicago said she'd been making Greco for years—as did her mother from upstate Illinois. Whatever, the casserole is ideal when you have to produce a quick, tasty supper and don't feel like going to lots of trouble. With it, I usually serve some sort of salad or coleslaw, small dinner rolls, and a sturdy red wine.

Southwestern Chiles Relleños Casserole

This classic casserole is pre pared at least a dozen different ways throughout Texas, Arizona, and New Mexico, and in Idaho, I once even had it made with ground lamb seasoned with at least three wild herbs. To give the casserole even more regional flavor, I sometimes will also include a layer of about a cup or so of frozen corn kernels. The casserole should be baked just till it's set, so test it with a small knife or skewer after about 35 minutes to make sure it's fairly soft.

3 tablespoons corn oil

1/2 pound ground beef round

1/2 pound ground pork

1 medium-size onion, finely chopped

1 garlic clove, minced

1 1/2 teaspoons ground cumin

1 teaspoon dried oregano, crumbled

One 16-ounce can refried beans

Salt and black pepper to taste

Two 4-ounce cans green chiles, drained and chopped

8 ounces Monterey Jack cheese, shredded

1 1/2 cups milk

4 large eggs

1/4 cup cornmeal

Tabasco sauce to taste

1. Preheat the oven to 350°F. Grease a 1 1/2-quart casserole and set aside.

2. In a large heavy skillet, heat the oil over moderate heat, add the beef, pork, onion, garlic, cumin, and oregano and stir till the meats crumble and are no longer pink, about 10 minutes. Remove from the heat, add the refried beans, season with salt and pepper, stir, and set aside.

3. Spread half the chiles over bottom of the prepared casserole, spoon half the meat-and-bean mixture over the chiles, and sprinkle half the cheese over the top. Spread the remaining chiles over the top, then layer the remaining meat-and-bean mixture and the cheese.

4. In a medium-size mixing bowl, whisk together the milk, eggs, cornmeal, and Tabasco till well blended, pour over the casserole, and bake till set and golden, about 45 minutes. Let stand for 10 minutes; cut into squares.

MAKES 6 SERVINGS

Crazy for Casseroles

Pork Chop, Apple, and Wild Mushroom Strata

1/4 cup vegetable oil

6 boneless pork chops, each about 6 ounces, trimmed of excess fat

2 medium-size onions, chopped

2 celery ribs, chopped

1 garlic clove, minced

2 tablespoons all-purpose flour

1 tablespoon tomato puree

1/2 cup beef broth or bouillon

1/2 cup dry red wine

1/2 teaspoon crumbled dried sage

Salt and black pepper to taste

1/2 pound fresh wild mushrooms (morels, chanterelles, or shiitakes), stems removed and trimmed and caps coarsely chopped

3 cooking apples (such as Granny Smith), cored and cut into rings

1 tablespoon firmly packed light brown sugar

1. Preheat the oven to 350°F.

2. In a flameproof 2- to 2 1/2-quart casserole, heat the oil over moderate heat, add the pork chops, brown on both sides, and transfer to a plate. Add the onions, celery, and garlic and stir till soft, about 5 minutes. Sprinkle the flour over the vegetables and stir 1 minute longer. Add the tomato puree, broth, and wine and stir. Return the pork chops to the casserole, add the sage, season with salt and pepper, cover, and bake for 30 minutes.

3. Scatter the mushrooms over the top, arrange layers of apple rings over the mushrooms, sprinkle with the brown sugar, and bake for 30 minutes.

MAKES 6 SERVINGS

Pork chops are never so tender and succulent as in a slowly cooked casserole: mate them with racy wild mushrooms and apples, as in this strata, and you have something to really crow about. Since boneless pork chops can be terribly expensive in the supermarket, I always wait till loins are on sale and cut my own chops. Be careful that this casserole doesn't dry out; the apples should render the necessary extra liquid to keep it moist, but if not, simply add a little more wine toward the end. The strata is just as good with thinly sliced oranges substituted for the apples, and sometimes I sprinkle on a little freshly grated cinnamon instead of the brown sugar.

Maytag Stuffed Pork Chops

Iowa is known not only for its hogs and corn but for the superior Maytag blue cheese produced, yes, in Newton, almost right next to the plant that makes Maytag washing machines and dryers. Maytag Dairy Farms was founded back in 1920 by Frederick Maytag, and today the company produces annually around a quarter of a million pounds of the carefully aged cheese that has been favorably compared with the best of Europe.

I can't remember whether this utterly delectable recipe was given to me when I visited the Farms years ago or sent to me later on, but, whatever, it's a casserole that gives real pedigree to stuffed pork chops and never fails to impress guests. It's almost worth baking a pan of cornbread just to get the crumbs for this dish, and do try to use genuine Maytag cheese, available in most good markets around the country.

4 loin pork chops, about 1^1/2 inches thick, trimmed of excess fat

2 tablespoons butter

1 small onion, finely chopped

1 small celery rib, finely chopped

^{3}/4 cup leftover crumbled cornbread or soft bread crumbs

^{1}/2 cup fresh or thawed frozen corn kernels

^{1}/4 pound blue cheese (preferably Maytag), crumbled

1 large egg, beaten

Salt and black pepper to taste

^{1}/2 cup tomato ketchup

2 tablespoons firmly packed light brown sugar

2 teaspoons Dijon mustard

^{1}/2 teaspoon Worcestershire sauce

1. Using a sharp paring knife, make a 2-inch-long slash along the bone of each pork chop, then insert the knife in the opening and cut a pocket without cutting through the other side of the chop. Set aside.

2. Preheat the oven to 350°F. Butter a shallow 3-quart casserole and set aside.

3. In a small skillet, melt the butter over moderate heat, add the onion and celery, stir about 5 minutes, and scrape into a medium-size mixing bowl. Add the cornbread, corn, cheese, and egg, season with salt and pepper, and toss till well blended. Stuff equal amounts of the mixture into the pork chops and arrange the chops in a single layer in the prepared casserole.

4. In a small mixing bowl, combine the ketchup, brown sugar, mustard, and Worcestershire, and mix till well blended. Brush the mixture equally over the chops, cover, and bake till the chops are very tender, about 1 hour.

MAKES 4 SERVINGS

Old-Fashioned Pork Chop, Apple, and Sweet Potato Pot

$^1/_2$ cup all-purpose flour

Salt and black pepper to taste

6 loin pork chops, about 1 inch thick, trimmed of excess fat

$^1/_4$ cup vegetable oil

4 medium-size sweet potatoes, peeled and cut into $^1/_8$-inch-thick slices

$^1/_2$ cup firmly packed light brown sugar

3 medium-size cooking apples (such as Granny Smith), peeled, cored, and cut into $^1/_2$-inch-thick rings

$^1/_2$ cup apple cider

1. Preheat the oven to 350°F. Grease a 2- to 2$^1/_2$-quart casserole and set aside.

2. On a plate, combine the flour and salt and pepper and dredge the pork chops in the mixture, tapping off any excess. In a large heavy skillet, heat the oil over moderate heat, brown the chops on both sides, and arrange them in the prepared casserole.

3. Layer half the sweet potatoes over the chops, sprinkle a little brown sugar over the top, and season with salt and pepper to taste. Layer half the apples over the potatoes, sprinkle a little more brown sugar on top, then repeat layering the remaining potatoes, apples, and sugar. Pour the cider over the top, cover, and bake till the chops are tender, about 1$^1/_4$ hours. Uncover and continue to bake till slightly browned, about 15 minutes.

MAKES 6 SERVINGS

By virtue of the Midwestern pork, Yankee apples and apple cider, and Southern sweet potatoes, no casserole is more typically all-American with no regional boundaries than this old-fashioned one from the early years of the twentieth century. Cider and brown sugar yield a wonderful flavor when combined, but you can also moisten the casserole with beer, dry white wine or vermouth, or even . . . cola. Sometimes, I sprinkle the layers with a little powdered sage for even more flavor.

Baked Pork Chops with Hominy and Apples

Hominy, which is dried, hulled corn kernels, was one of the first foods that European settlers in America accepted readily from the natives. Although it is most closely associated today with Southern cooking (mainly in the form of grits), the cereal was actually introduced by northern tribes back in the seventeenth century and was popular throughout the Eastern states and developing Midwest well into the nineteenth century. This particular casserole, for example, hails from a Vermont country inn near Middlebury I once frequented, but it might just as easily be prepared by a Georgia housewife or Indiana farmer. In other words, it is consummately American, and one of the most delectable and unusual ways I know to deal with pork chops. Canned hominy is now available in virtually every supermarket in the country.

4 thick-cut pork chops

$^1/_2$ cup all-purpose flour

1 large onion, sliced

1 garlic clove, minced

2 cups canned hominy, drained

2 medium-size cooking apples, peeled, cored, and cut into $^1/_2$-inch-thick rings

1 tablespoon firmly packed light brown sugar

Salt and black pepper to taste

$^1/_4$ cup water

1. Preheat the oven to 350°F. Grease a shallow 2-quart casserole and set aside.

2. Trim the fat off the edges of the pork chops and render it over moderate heat in a large heavy skillet, discarding the rendered pieces. On a plate, dredge the chops in the flour, tapping off any excess, brown them on both sides in the hot fat, and transfer to a plate. Add the onion and garlic to the skillet, stir till softened, about 5 minutes, and remove from the heat.

3. Arrange the chops in the bottom of the prepared casserole, pour the hominy evenly over the chops, and layer the apples over the hominy. Sprinkle the brown sugar over the top and season with salt and pepper, add the water, cover, and bake till the chops are very tender, about 1$^1/_4$ hours.

MAKES 4 SERVINGS

Crazy for Casseroles

Pork Chop, Sweet Potato, and Orange Casserole

8 small sweet potatoes, peeled and cut into $1/4$-inch-thick slices

3 tablespoons butter, cut into small pieces

4 thick-cut pork loin chops, trimmed of excess fat

Salt and black pepper to taste

2 medium-size onions, sliced

2 oranges, peeled, seeded, and sliced

2 tablespoons firmly packed light brown sugar

1 cup beer

1. Preheat the oven to 325°F. Butter a 2-quart casserole.

2. Arrange the sweet potatoes in an overlapping layer across the bottom and dot evenly with the butter. Arrange the pork chops over the sweet potatoes and season with salt and pepper. Layer the onions evenly over the chops, layer the oranges over the onions, and sprinkle the brown sugar over the top. Pour the beer around the edges, cover, and bake 1 hour.

3. Uncover and continue to bake till the chops are very tender and the top glazed, about 20 minutes.

MAKES 4 SERVINGS

Here is still another pork casserole that reflects the German influence on so much of the cooking in the Midwest during the early days of settlement, the distinctively American element being the substitution of sweet potatoes for traditional white ones. Note also that, in the more Germanic style, all the major components are layered raw. A slightly sweet white wine can be used in place of the beer with equally sapid results.

Leah's Pork Chop and Cornbread Casserole

I've been going to Dooky Chase restaurant in New Orleans for as long as I can remember to eat Leah Chase's sublime Creole gumbo, shrimp Clemenceau, bread pudding with whiskey sauce, and any pork preparation, like this tangy casserole made with cornbread. This is soul food at its most "refined," still another example of how talented Southern black cooks can turn an otherwise bland, ordinary dish into a masterpiece of subtle flavors and textures.

6 tablespoons (3/4 stick) butter

8 pork chops, about 1/2 inch thick, trimmed of excess fat

1 medium-size onion, chopped

1 celery rib, chopped

1 small green bell pepper, seeded and chopped

1 garlic clove, minced

2 cups crumbled leftover cornbread

1 large egg, beaten

One 16-ounce can whole tomatoes, undrained, cut up

One 8-ounce can tomato sauce

1 teaspoon firmly packed light brown sugar

1/4 teaspoon chili powder

Salt and black pepper to taste

Tabasco sauce to taste

1. In a large heavy skillet, melt 3 tablespoons of the butter over moderate heat, then brown half the pork chops on both sides, and transfer to a plate. Repeat with the remaining chops. Melt the remaining 3 tablespoons butter in the skillet, then add the onion, celery, bell pepper, and garlic, stir about 5 minutes, and remove from the heat.

2. Preheat the oven to 350°F. Butter a 3- to 3½-quart casserole and set aside.

3. In a large mixing bowl, combine the cornbread, egg, and half the sautéed vegetable mixture till well blended and set aside.

4. Add the tomatoes, tomato sauce, brown sugar, and chili powder to the remaining vegetables in the skillet, season with salt, pepper, and Tabasco, mix well, and simmer till the sauce is nicely thickened, about 10 minutes. Remove from the heat.

Crazy for Casseroles

5. Arrange 4 of the pork chops in the prepared casserole and spread the cornbread mixture evenly over the top. Arrange the remaining chops over the top, scrape the sauce evenly over the chops, cover, and bake till the chops are very tender, about 1 hour.

MAKES 6 TO 8 SERVINGS

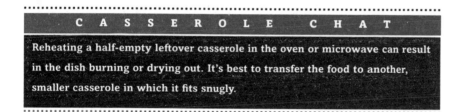

C A S S E R O L E   C H A T

Reheating a half-empty leftover casserole in the oven or microwave can result in the dish burning or drying out. It's best to transfer the food to another, smaller casserole in which it fits snugly.

Cincinnati Creamed Pork Cutlets, Potatoes, and Red Onions

Unbeknownst to many, Cincinnati, Ohio, was the major pork-packing center of America during the mid-nineteenth century, so much so that the city was often referred to as "Porkopolis." Later the industry moved to Chicago, but not before over ten thousand German settlers from Pennsylvania introduced ways of preparing pork that are as popular today in that city as 150 years ago. This particular casserole is purely German in concept, but if you'd like a better idea of how the immigrants might have transformed a classic into a German-American original, think of John Chapman (better known as Johnny Appleseed throughout Ohio) and add a layer of sliced apples over the cutlets before arranging the second layer of potatoes and onions.

3 tablespoons vegetable oil

4 to 6 pork cutlets, trimmed of excess fat and pounded lightly

3 medium-size russet potatoes, peeled and thinly sliced

2 medium-size red onions, thinly sliced

$^{1}/_{2}$ teaspoon caraway seeds

$^{1}/_{2}$ teaspoon ground sage

Salt and black pepper to taste

$1^{1}/_{2}$ cups sour cream

1. Preheat the oven to 350°F. Grease a 2-quart casserole and set aside.

2. In a large heavy skillet, heat the oil over moderate heat, add the pork cutlets, brown lightly on both sides, and remove from the heat.

3. Layer half the potatoes over the bottom of the prepared casserole and cover with half the onions. Season with half the caraway seeds and sage, and salt and pepper. Arrange the cutlets over the top, layer the remaining potatoes and onions over the cutlets, and season with the remaining caraway seeds and sage, and salt and pepper. Spoon the sour cream evenly over the top, cover, and bake till nicely glazed, about 40 minutes.

MAKES 4 TO 6 SERVINGS

Key West Pork and Pineapple Casserole

One 2-pound boneless pork loin, trimmed of excess fat
and cut into 1-inch-thick slices

2 scallions (white part and some of the green), finely chopped

6 tablespoons peanut oil

2 tablespoons fresh lime juice

2 tablespoons Worcestershire sauce

1 tablespoon peeled and minced fresh ginger

$1/2$ teaspoon dried sage, crumbled

$1/2$ teaspoon ground allspice

$1/2$ teaspoon red pepper flakes

1 medium-size onion, chopped

1 large green bell pepper, seeded and chopped

Salt and black pepper to taste

One 1-pound can pineapple chunks, undrained

1. In a large mixing bowl, combine the pork slices, scallions, 2 tablespoons of the peanut oil, the lime juice, Worcestershire, ginger, sage, allspice, and red pepper flakes, toss well, cover with plastic wrap, and let marinate at room temperature for about 30 minutes. Pick the pork out of the marinade, reserving the marinade, and pat dry with paper towels.

2. Preheat the oven to 350°F. Grease a shallow $2^{1}/_2$-quart casserole.

3. In a skillet, heat the remaining $1/4$ cup oil over moderate heat, add the pork, brown both sides, and transfer to a plate. Add the onion and bell pepper, season with salt and pepper, stir till softened, and remove from heat.

4. Arrange half the pork slices in the prepared casserole, layer half the sautéed vegetables over the pork, and top with half the pineapple chunks. Repeat, pour the pineapple juice and reserved marinade over the top, cover, and bake till the pork is tender, about 50 minutes.

MAKES 6 SERVINGS

Down in Key West, Florida, a friend took me to a crazy little Cuban place called El Cacique that served not only some of the best conch chowder and grilled red snapper anywhere but also a few remarkable pork dishes. I really don't know what this particular pork and fresh pineapple combination was called, but it was so delicious that I wasted no time when I got home trying to reproduce the spicy casserole using canned pineapple and seasonings that seemed appropriate. Yes, fresh pineapple is better if you can find a perfectly ripe one (mine sometimes take literally two weeks to ripen) and don't mind the hassle of cleaning it, but this modified version of the dish is nonetheless mighty good. This is still another casserole I like to make when I find whole boneless pork loins on sale and can roast the other half for another occasion.

Pork, Apple, and Pine Nut Soufflé

As illustrated by this classic recipe discovered in an old community cookbook from Pella, Iowa, soufflé casseroles, (i.e., any savory casserole that contains eggs) are not unique to the South and have been popular throughout the Midwest and West for at least the past one hundred years. What is old-fashioned about this particular casserole is that the meat and vegetables are not browned or sautéed before being layered, a method that might deprive the dish of a little flavor but produces a more interesting texture. Pine nuts are sold shelled and blanched in most specialty food shops and large supermarkets and have a delightfully earthy savor. Do note that, like pecans, they are oilier than other nuts and must be kept refrigerated. If you can't find them, substitute chopped pecans, hazelnuts, or filberts, and, for optimum flavor, toast them on an ungreased baking pan in a preheated 300°F oven until lightly colored, about 20 minutes, stirring from time to time.

¹/₄ cup (¹/₂ stick) butter

¹/₄ cup all-purpose flour

1¹/₂ cups milk

4 large eggs, beaten

2 pounds boneless pork shoulder, trimmed of excess fat and cut into medium-size dice

1 large onion, chopped

1 medium-size green bell pepper, seeded and chopped

2 cooking apples (such as Granny Smith), peeled, cored, and diced

1 cup pine nuts

Salt and black pepper to taste

1. Preheat the oven to 325°F. Grease a 2- to 2¹/₂-quart casserole and set aside.

2. In a large heavy saucepan, melt the butter over moderate heat, then add the flour and whisk for 1 minute. Gradually add the milk and whisk till thickened, about 5 minutes. Whisk a few tablespoons of the hot sauce into the beaten eggs, then whisk the egg mixture back into the sauce and remove from the heat.

3. Layer half the pork in the prepared casserole, then make separate layers of half the onion, bell pepper, apples, and pine nuts over the pork, and season with salt and pepper. Repeat the layering with the remaining pork, onion, bell pepper, apples, and pine nuts and season again with salt and pepper. Pour the hot sauce over the top, cover, and bake for 1 hour.

4. Uncover and continue to bake till the pork is very tender and the top is slightly crusty, about 20 minutes.

MAKES 6 SERVINGS

Crazy for Casseroles

Curried Pork and Squash Casserole

2$^1/_2$ pounds boneless pork shoulder, trimmed of excess fat
and cut into 1$^1/_2$-inch pieces

$^1/_2$ cup all-purpose flour

$^1/_4$ cup vegetable oil

2 medium-size onions, chopped

2 garlic cloves, minced

1 tablespoon mild curry powder

1 teaspoon minced fresh sage leaves or $^1/_2$ teaspoon dried, crumbled

Salt and black pepper to taste

1$^1/_2$ pounds (about 4 medium-size) yellow squash, ends trimmed
and cut into $^1/_2$-inch-thick rounds

1$^1/_2$ to 2 cups chicken broth, as needed

1. Dredge the pork pieces lightly in the flour, tapping off any excess. In a large heavy skillet, heat the oil over moderate heat, add the pork, and brown it on all sides. Add the onions, garlic, curry powder, and sage, season with salt and pepper, stir till the onions are softened, about 7 minutes, and transfer the pork and onions to a platter.

2. Preheat the oven to 325°F. Grease a 2- to 2$^1/_2$-quart casserole.

3. Arrange half the pork and onions on the bottom of the prepared casserole, then half the squash in a layer on top and continue layering the remaining pork and onions and squash. Pour 1$^1/_2$ cups of the broth over the top, cover the casserole, and bake for 1 hour.

4. Uncover and continue to bake till the pork is very tender, about 20 minutes, adding the remaining $^1/_2$ cup broth if the casserole seems too dry.

MAKES 6 SERVINGS

I love curried pork in any shape or style, and layer it with onions and summer squash in a casserole and you have a truly unusual dish with American overtones all its own. This casserole should not be at all soupy, so add extra broth during the last twenty minutes of baking only if the ingredients appear to be really dry (a lot depends on how fresh the squash is and the amount of liquid it yields).

Michigan Pork and Sauerkraut

Typical of the many German American casseroles that followed early settlers in the upper Midwest during the nineteenth century, this one can be made with virtually any cut of pork you might find on sale, trimmed of excess fat. When, for example, I see a whole, boneless pork loin priced at $1.99 a pound, I might well use half to make this type of casserole and roast the other half for another occasion. If you like, you can also stir about a tablespoon of grainy brown mustard into the pork and vegetables and add a few caraway seeds to the sauerkraut.

2 pounds sauerkraut, drained

Salt to taste

8 strips lean bacon, diced

1 pound boneless lean pork, trimmed of excess fat and cut into small cubes

1 large onion, finely chopped

$1/2$ medium-size green bell pepper, seeded and finely chopped

2 garlic cloves, minced

2 medium-size ripe tomatoes, peeled and chopped

$1/2$ pound smoked pork sausage (such as kielbasa), thinly sliced

$1^1/_2$ cups sour cream

Black pepper to taste

Medium hot paprika to taste

1. In a large pot, cover the sauerkraut with salted water. Bring to a boil, reduce heat to low, cover, and cook for 20 minutes. Drain and set aside.

2. Preheat the oven to 350°F. Grease a 3-quart casserole and set aside.

3. In a large heavy skillet, fry the bacon over moderate heat till almost crisp and drain on paper towels. Add the pork to the skillet and brown slightly on all sides. Add the onion, bell pepper, garlic, and tomatoes, stir till softened, about 8 minutes, and remove from the heat.

4. Arrange one third of the sauerkraut over the bottom of the prepared casserole, then the bacon and half the sausage slices over the sauerkraut. Layer another third of the sauerkraut, then the remaining sausage, and spoon about half the sour cream over the top. Layer the pork-and-vegetable mixture on top, cover with the remaining sauerkraut, and spoon the remaining sour cream over the top. Sprinkle with salt, pepper, and paprika, cover, and bake till bubbly, about 45 minutes.

MAKES 6 SERVINGS

Southern Hog Pot

2 pigs' feet, cleaned

2 pigs' ears, cleaned

$1/4$ pound lean salt pork

$1/4$ cup vegetable oil

1 pound boneless lean pork, trimmed of excess fat and cut into 1-inch cubes

1 large onion, chopped

1 celery rib, chopped

1 carrot, scraped and chopped

Salt and black pepper to taste

1 medium-size head green cabbage, discolored leaves discarded, cored, quartered, and coarsely chopped

$1/2$ pound smoked pork sausage (such as kielbasa), sliced

1 cup dry white wine

1 cup water

1. Place the pigs' feet in a large heavy pot with enough water to cover, bring to a simmer, skimming off any scum from the surface, cover, and cook for 2 hours. Add the ears and salt pork to the pot, add more water to cover if necessary, return to a simmer, and cook till the feet and ears are tender, 1 to $1\frac{1}{2}$ hours. Drain and, when cool enough to handle, remove any loose bones from the feet, cut the ears and salt pork into thin strips, and set aside.

2. Preheat the oven to 350°F. Grease a 3- to 4-quart casserole and set aside.

3. In a large heavy skillet, heat the oil over moderate heat, then brown the pork cubes on all sides and transfer to a plate. Add the onion, celery, and carrot to the skillet, season with salt and pepper, stir till the vegetables soften, about 5 minutes, and remove from the heat.

Because of the public's current obsession with cholesterol, you don't see as many hog pots in the South as in the good old days, but there are still church suppers, political cookouts, and big weekend family dinners where nothing is more loved and appreciated than a hefty casserole featuring at least four types of pork. If you live in the South or Midwest, chances are you'll have no trouble finding packaged pigs' feet and perfectly cleaned pigs' ears in better supermarkets, and elsewhere, any good butcher should be happy to fill your order and prepare the cuts for cooking. In any case, if you've never eaten these products, you don't know what you've been missing. The ears have a wonderful texture, and while the feet (or trotters) are usually bony and full of gristle and tendons, after long cooking they become delectably gelatinous and tender. For additional flavor, feel free to add any herbs and spices to the simmering feet, ears, and salt pork, and do try to find sausage that is good and smoky. If you use pork shoulder (which has the best flavor) in this casserole, trim off as much excess fat as possible before browning the cubes. It just might add an extra hour to your life.

4. Arrange the pigs' feet, ears, salt pork, and pork cubes in the prepared casserole, spoon the sautéed vegetables evenly over the top, scatter the cabbage over the top, and arrange the sausage slices over the cabbage. Season with salt and pepper, pour the wine and water over the top, cover, and bake till the pork cubes are tender and the cabbage very soft, about 1 hour.

MAKES 6 TO 8 SERVINGS

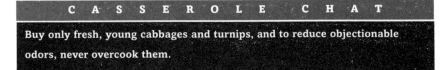

C A S S E R O L E   C H A T

Buy only fresh, young cabbages and turnips, and to reduce objectionable odors, never overcook them.

Pork and Bell Pepper Moussaka

1/4 cup olive oil

2 medium-size green bell peppers, seeded and cut into thin strips

2 medium-size red bell peppers, seeded and cut into thin strips

2 medium-size onions, thinly sliced

Salt and black pepper to taste

2 pounds ground pork

1 garlic clove, minced

1 tablespoon tomato paste

1/2 teaspoon dried sage, crumbled

1/2 teaspoon dried oregano, crumbled

1 cup freshly grated Parmesan cheese

1/4 cup (1/2 stick) butter

1/4 cup all-purpose flour

3 cups milk

2 large eggs, beaten

2 cups cooked long-grain rice

1. In a large heavy skillet, heat 2 tablespoons of the oil over moderate heat, add all the bell peppers and the onions, season with salt and pepper, stir till the vegetables are quite soft, about 8 minutes, and transfer to a medium-size mixing bowl. Heat the remaining 2 tablespoons oil in the skillet, add the pork and garlic, and stir till the pork loses its pink color, about 10 minutes. Add the tomato paste, herbs, 1/2 cup of the cheese, and salt and pepper, stir till well blended, and remove from the heat.

2. Preheat the oven to 350°F. Grease a 2- to 2 1/2-quart casserole and set aside.

3. In a large saucepan, melt the butter over moderate heat, then add the flour and whisk for 3 minutes. Gradually add the milk, whisking steadily

Traditional Greek and Turkish moussaka is actually a very complicated casserole made with lamb, eggplant, and all types of seasonings, but once it crossed the Atlantic with immigrants in the late nineteenth century, the dish underwent every transformation imaginable. What makes this modified version distinctive is not just the ground pork but the substitution of rice for bread crumbs and bell peppers for eggplant.

till the sauce is thickened and smooth, about 5 minutes, and remove from the heat. Whisk a few tablespoons of the sauce into the beaten eggs, then add the eggs to the sauce, whisking to combine well, and set aside.

4. Spoon the rice evenly over the bottom of the prepared casserole, then spoon a few tablespoons of sauce over the rice. Layer the bell pepper-and-onion mixture over the rice, layer the pork mixture over that, and spoon the remaining sauce evenly over the top. Sprinkle the remaining $1/2$ cup cheese over the top and bake till puffy and golden brown, 45 minutes to 1 hour.

MAKES 6 SERVINGS

Deviled Ham and Mushroom Strata

4 to 5 slices white bread, crusts removed

2 tablespoons butter

$^1/_2$ pound fresh mushrooms, finely chopped

1 medium-size onion, finely chopped

3 cups diced cooked ham (about 1 pound)

2 teaspoons Dijon mustard

1 cup finely shredded Swiss cheese

2 cups half-and-half

3 large eggs, beaten

1 teaspoon Worcestershire sauce

Salt and black pepper to taste

Tabasco sauce to taste

Here is a good all-purpose strata that is actually better when layered in advance and allowed to meld a couple of hours in the fridge before baking. Furthermore, it can be baked about 30 minutes, then set aside till ready to be reheated and served. For variations, you can substitute diced cooked pork, Canadian bacon, a pound of fried and drained bulk sausage, or even broiled sweetbreads for the ham.

1. Butter a 2- to 2$^1/_2$-quart casserole, arrange the bread slices across the bottom in a single layer, trimming the bread to fit when necessary, and set aside.

2. In a large skillet, melt the butter over moderate heat, then add the mushrooms and onion and stir till very soft, about 8 minutes. Add the ham and mustard and stir till well blended. Spoon the mixture evenly over the bread slices and sprinkle the cheese over the top.

3. In a medium-size mixing bowl, whisk together the half-and-half, eggs, and Worcestershire, season with salt, pepper, and Tabasco, and pour over the cheese. Cover the strata with plastic wrap and refrigerate for at least 2 hours.

4. Preheat the oven to 350°F. Bake the strata till just set, about 30 minutes. When ready to serve, bake an additional 15 to 20 minutes.

MAKES 6 SERVINGS

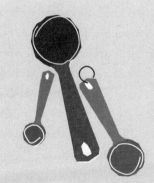

Ham and Turkey Tetrazzini

rguments rage over whether chicken Tetrazzini was created in Charleston, South Carolina, or San Francisco for the famous coloratura soprano Luisa Tetrazzini when she toured America in the early years of the twentieth century. Whatever the truth might be, a great American casserole was developed and has not only stood the test of time but lent itself to multiple interpretations, such as this one that I love to make with leftover turkey and ham during the Thanksgiving or Christmas holidays—or, in fact, any time I have leftover meat and want to fix a quick supper for friends. Note that no Tetrazzini is ever layered like most casseroles, and note also that the tossed dish can either be refrigerated overnight before baking or frozen till ready to be thawed and baked.

6 tablespoons ($^3/_4$ stick) butter

$^1/_4$ pound fresh mushrooms, chopped

$^1/_4$ cup all-purpose flour

1 teaspoon salt

Black pepper to taste

$^1/_4$ teaspoon ground nutmeg

1 cup chicken broth

1 cup milk

1 pound cooked ham, cubed (about 3 cups)

1 pound cooked turkey, cubed (about 3 cups)

1 cup black olives, drained, pitted, and chopped

$^1/_2$ cup slivered almonds

$^1/_2$ cup freshly grated Parmesan cheese

1 large egg yolk, beaten

7 ounces spaghetti, cooked according to package directions (but not more than 8 minutes) and drained

1. Preheat the oven to 350°F. Butter a 2- to 2$^1/_2$-quart casserole.

2. In a small skillet melt 2 tablespoons of the butter over moderate heat, add the mushrooms, stir for 5 minutes, and remove from the heat.

3. In a large heavy pot over moderate heat, melt the remaining $^1/_4$ cup butter, add the flour, salt, pepper, and nutmeg, and stir for 1 minute. Gradually add the broth and milk and stir till the sauce begins to thicken, 5 to 7 minutes. Remove the pot from the heat, add the ham, turkey, olives, almonds, cheese, and egg yolk, and stir till well blended.

4. Place the spaghetti in the casserole, pour the meat mixture over the top, toss to mix well, and bake till crusty, 25 to 30 minutes.

MAKES 6 SERVINGS

Crazy for Casseroles

Mamie's Country Ham and Black-Eyed Pea Supper

$^1/_4$ cup peanut oil

4 medium-size onions, sliced

$^1/_2$ medium-size green bell pepper, seeded and chopped

One 10-ounce package frozen black-eyed peas, thawed

1 teaspoon salt

$^1/_2$ teaspoon sugar

Pinch of cayenne pepper

Black pepper to taste

2 cups diced cured country ham

3 medium-size ripe tomatoes, peeled and sliced

$^1/_2$ cup freshly grated Parmesan cheese

1. Preheat the oven to 350°F. Grease a 2-quart casserole and set aside.

2. In a large heavy skillet or saucepan, heat the oil over moderate heat, add the onions and bell pepper, and stir till the onions brown slightly, about 10 minutes. Add the peas, salt, sugar, and cayenne, season with black pepper, stir for 3 minutes, and remove from the heat.

3. Layer the ham in the prepared casserole and cover with the pea mixture. Arrange the tomatoes evenly over the top, sprinkle with the cheese, and bake till golden brown, 30 to 35 minutes.

MAKES 6 SERVINGS

In Memphis, Tennessee, I usually spend most of my time searching for "wet" ribs that fall off the bones, but when I once heard about a place called Mamie's that served a casserole of real country ham and black-eyed peas (as well as one of cinnamon-flavored potatoes), I wasted no time getting there for lunch. Notice that the only liquid used in this recipe is the juice rendered from the tomatoes, producing a crusty, slightly dry casserole. At the restaurant, they used fresh boiled black-eyed peas, but frozen ones are just as good. (Dried peas can also be used, but they have to be soaked overnight, then boiled till almost tender.) I suppose you could substitute ordinary baked ham for the cured, but the casserole won't be as succulent and distinctive.

Ham and Zucchini Soufflé

The safflower oil and eggs make this all-purpose soufflé casserole delightfully light even with the ham and cheese, so much so that I serve it (cut in wedges) as much at casual lunches as at last-minute dinners. And so versatile is the basic idea that you can easily substitute yellow squash, broccoli or cauliflower florets, chopped eggplant, or even shredded celeriac for the zucchini. Also experiment with various assertive firm cheeses.

3 medium-size zucchini, shredded

1 large onion, finely chopped

1/2 pound cooked ham, cut into small cubes

1/2 pound sharp cheddar cheese, shredded

1 1/2 cups self-rising flour

1 cup safflower oil

5 large eggs, beaten

Salt and black pepper to taste

1. Preheat the oven to 375°F. Grease a shallow 2-quart casserole and set aside.

2. In a large mixing bowl, combine the zucchini, onion, ham, cheese, and flour and toss till well blended. Add the oil and eggs, season with salt and pepper, and stir till well blended and smooth.

3. Scrape the mixture into the prepared casserole and bake till golden brown but still moist, about 45 minutes.

MAKES 4 TO 6 SERVINGS

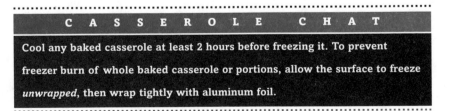

C A S S E R O L E   C H A T

Cool any baked casserole at least 2 hours before freezing it. To prevent freezer burn of whole baked casserole or portions, allow the surface to freeze *unwrapped*, then wrap tightly with aluminum foil.

Sausage and Lentil Pot

2 cups dried lentils (1 pound), rinsed and picked over

1 tablespoon salt

1 medium-size onion, studded with 2 cloves

1 bay leaf

$1/2$ teaspoon dried thyme or rosemary, crumbled

10 to 12 sweet or hot Italian sausages

2 tablespoons butter

1 large onion, chopped

Black pepper to taste

1 cup dry red wine

1. In a large heavy pot, combine the lentils, salt, studded onion, and thyme with enough water to cover. Bring to a boil, reduce the heat to low, cover, and simmer till the lentils are tender but not mushy, about 45 minutes, stirring occasionally to prevent sticking. Drain in a colander.

2. Preheat the over to 350°F. Grease a $2 1/2$-quart casserole and set aside.

3. Just before lentils have finished cooking, arrange the sausages in a large heavy skillet or a baking pan, prick well with a fork, and add enough water to cover. Bring to a low boil, poach for 5 minutes, and transfer to a plate.

4. In a medium-size skillet, melt the butter over moderate heat, then add the chopped onion, stir for about 5 minutes, and remove from the heat.

5. Arrange half the sausages in the bottom of the prepared casserole, scatter half the lentils over the sausages, spoon half the onion over the top, and season with salt and pepper. Layer the remaining lentils over the onion, arrange the remaining sausages on top, pour on the wine, and bake till the sausages are nicely browned, about 30 minutes.

MAKES 6 TO 8 SERVINGS

James Beard introduced me to this remarkable casserole one cold evening at his New York townhouse, and I remember discussing with him how small braised lamb chops, roast duck or pork cut up into chunks, or even leftover pieces of baked ham could be substituted for the sausages. Since the lentils might stick once they've absorbed most of the water, do watch them carefully. If you don't have a bottle of red wine in the house, chicken broth can be used with equally good results.

Herbed Lamb and White Bean Bake

The combination of lamb and white beans is one of the great marriages of gastronomy, and although this noble casserole takes quite a while to make, take my word that it's worth every minute of effort. To shorten prep time for the beans, you can simply bring them to a boil in enough water to cover, let them stand off the heat for an hour, then simmer them till tender, about 1½ hours. I like to use lamb shoulder for this casserole, and if I have a can of crushed tomatoes, I might layer a cup or so over the lamb and vegetables before adding the sauce and bread crumbs.

1 cup dried Great Northern white or navy beans, rinsed and picked over

¼ cup minced fresh parsley leaves

¼ cup olive oil

2 pounds boneless lean lamb, trimmed of excess fat and cut into 1½-inch cubes

1 large onion, chopped

1 celery rib, chopped

1 carrot, scraped and chopped

2 garlic cloves, minced

½ teaspoon dried rosemary, crumbled

½ teaspoon dried sage, crumbled

Salt and black pepper to taste

1 cup dry white wine

½ cup (1 stick) butter

3 tablespoons all-purpose flour

2 cups milk

1 tablespoon cider vinegar

½ cup dry bread crumbs

1. Place the beans in a large heavy saucepan, add enough cold water to cover by 3 inches, and let soak overnight.

2. Drain the beans, add more fresh water to cover, bring to a low simmer, cover, and cook till tender, about 1 hour.

3. Grease a 2- to 2½-quart casserole and set aside.

4. Drain the beans in a colander, rinse under cold running water, and transfer to a medium-size mixing bowl. Add the parsley, toss, spread over the bottom of the prepared casserole, and set aside.

5. In a large heavy pot, heat the oil over moderate heat, then add the lamb, onion, celery, carrot, garlic, and herbs, season with salt and pepper, and stir till the lamb is lightly browned, about 8 minutes. Add the wine, bring to a boil, reduce the heat to low, cover, and simmer till the lamb is tender, about 1½ hours. Spoon the lamb, vegetables, and ½ cup of the cooking liquid over the beans and set aside.

6. Preheat the oven to 350°F.

7. In a medium-size saucepan, melt 3 tablespoons of the butter over moderate heat, then add the flour and whisk for 3 minutes. Gradually add the milk, whisking, till the mixture boils, reduce the heat to low, and stir till the sauce thickens, about 5 minutes. Add the vinegar, stir well, and pour the sauce evenly over the lamb in the casserole.

8. In a small saucepan, melt the remaining 5 tablespoons butter. Combine the melted butter and bread crumbs in a small mixing bowl, then spoon over the top of the casserole and bake till golden brown, about 30 minutes.

MAKES 6 SERVINGS

Scalloped Sausage and Potatoes

This hearty Sunday-night casserole comes from a Hungarian lady who left Budapest in the early 1970s to become librarian at the College of Human Ecology at Michigan State University in East Lansing. Suzanne used to complain that American potatoes just didn't have the flavor of those she left behind in Hungary, and she remained appalled that we didn't have a wider variety of really spicy smoked sausages. She adapted, however, and once guests tasted this casserole, they wondered what the complaining was all about. Be warned that genuine Hungarian paprika is considerably more fiery than other styles found in our markets.

¹/₂ cup (1 stick) butter or margarine, melted

1 cup soft bread crumbs

8 medium-size red potatoes, boiled in their skins in water to cover till almost for tender, drained, and thinly sliced

³/₄ pound smoked sausage (such as kielbasa), thinly sliced

8 large hard-boiled eggs, sliced

Salt and black pepper to taste

1 cup sour cream

Medium-hot imported paprika to taste

1. Preheat the oven to 350°F.

2. Spoon about 3 teaspoons of the melted butter into a 2-quart casserole and sprinkle with about 3 teaspoons of the bread crumbs. Arrange a layer of sliced potatoes evenly over the crumbs, then a layer of the sausage, and finally a layer of the eggs. Season with salt and pepper, then spoon about 4 teaspoons of the crumbs and 4 teaspoons of the butter over the eggs. Continue to layer the remaining ingredients, ending with crumbs and butter, spread the sour cream evenly over the top, sprinkle with paprika, and bake till golden brown, about 1 hour.

MAKES 6 SERVINGS

Spiced Lamb Chops and Radicchio Casserole

3 tablespoons vegetable oil

10 loin lamb chops, trimmed of excess fat

Pinch of ground mace

Pinch of ground cinnamon

Pinch of ground cardamom

$^1/_4$ cup chopped radicchio

1 teaspoon sugar

Salt and black pepper to taste

One 12-ounce bottle beer or ale

1. Preheat the oven to 350°F. Grease a 3-quart casserole and set aside.

2. In a large heavy skillet, heat the oil over moderate heat, add the lamb chops, brown about 2 minutes on each side, and arrange in the prepared casserole. Sprinkle the spices evenly over the top, scatter the radicchio over the chops, sprinkle the sugar over the top, and season with salt and pepper. Pour the beer around the sides, cover the casserole, and bake till the chops are very tender, about 40 minutes.

MAKES 6 SERVINGS

This modern casserole is delightful not only in the unusual combination of lamb and radicchio but in the way sugar and certain spices cleverly tame the slight bitterness of the radicchio. Used extensively in Scandinavian breads and British casseroles, gingery cardamom seeds are available in most markets and can either be crushed in a mortar and pestle or pulverized between two heavy spoons fitted together.

Lamb and Savoy Cabbage Cobbler

Crinkly, green Savoy cabbage (grown extensively in Europe for centuries) is the finest of cabbages, with a distinctive flavor and texture all its own, and now that it's available in most of our markets, it's a shame we don't utilize it more. The heads range from about one to four pounds and, when shopping, look for those with loose, crisp, deep green leaves. It does speed things up here if you have a heavy iron casserole that can be used on top of the stove, but, if not, just use a large skillet for the browning and sautéing before layering the ingredients in a greased casserole intended for the oven. To keep the potatoes rather soft but crusty (like the fruit in many sweet cobblers), simply press them down with a spatula a couple of times during the last hour of baking. (For a delicious variation on this casserole, substitute a basic cream sauce (page 6) for the broth and wine and sprinkle about $^1/_2$ cup grated sharp cheddar cheese over the top for the final thirty minutes of baking.)

$^1/_4$ cup vegetable oil

4 to 6 loin lamb chops, 5 to 6 ounces each, trimmed of excess fat

2 large onions, sliced

One $^1/_2$-pound head Savoy cabbage, cored and shredded

$^1/_2$ teaspoon dried rosemary, crumbled

$^1/_4$ teaspoon caraway seeds, crushed

Salt and black pepper to taste

4 medium-size russet potatoes, peeled and thinly sliced

2 cups beef broth

$^1/_2$ cup dry red wine

$^1/_4$ cup ($^1/_2$ stick) butter, melted

$^1/_4$ cup chopped fresh parsley leaves

1. Preheat the oven to 350°F.

2. In a heavy flameproof 2- to $2^1/_2$-quart casserole, heat the oil over moderate heat, brown the chops in the hot oil about 2 minutes on each side, and transfer to a plate. Add the onions, cabbage, rosemary, and caraway seeds to the casserole, season with salt and pepper, reduce the heat to low, and cook till soft, about 10 minutes, stirring a few times.

3. Transfer half the vegetables to a plate, arrange the chops over the vegetables remaining in the casserole, layer half the potatoes on top, and pour the broth and wine over everything. Layer the remaining vegetables over the potatoes, layer the remaining potatoes over the vegetables, brush the potatoes with half the melted butter, and bake for 20 minutes.

4. Press down on the potatoes with a metal spatula, brush again with the remaining butter, season with salt and pepper, and continue to bake till the lamb is tender and the top is golden brown and slightly crusty, about 1 hour. Garnish the top with the chopped parsley before serving.

MAKES 4 TO 6 SERVINGS

Crazy for Casseroles

3 large russet potatoes, peeled and cut into medium-size dice

2 pounds boneless lamb shoulder, chops, or neck, trimmed
of excess fat and cut into 1-inch cubes

2 large onions, diced

2 carrots, scraped and thinly sliced

1 celery rib, thinly sliced

2 large ripe tomatoes, peeled and coarsely chopped (juices included)

1 tablespoon chopped fresh rosemary leaves or $1/2$ teaspoon dried,
crumbled

Salt and black pepper to taste

1 cup beef broth

1. Preheat the oven to 325°F. Grease a 2-quart casserole.

2. Layer the bottom of the prepared casserole with the potatoes. Layer the lamb over the potatoes, then layer in the onions, carrots, celery, and tomatoes and sprinkle with the rosemary and salt and pepper. Add the broth, cover, and bake till the lamb is tender, about $1^{1}/_{2}$ hours.

3. Uncover and continue to bake till browned on top, 20 to 30 minutes.

MAKES 6 SERVINGS

I'm sure that the origins of this layered casserole can be traced back to the English and Irish settlers of New England, possibly an ideal way to utilize leftover mutton—which, believe me, I'd try if I could find some. Unfortunately, most of our leftover lamb these days usually comes from the leg, which tends to be dry, so unless you have some extra braised lamb shanks or baked shoulder chops on hand (which would reduce the cooking time by at least half), I strongly suggest you start from scratch with boneless lamb shoulder trimmed of excess fat, chops, shank, or even neck. Even using fresh meat, this hot pot is ridiculously simple to make, yet is perfect on a handsome buffet.

CASSEROLE CHAT

Never freeze casseroles that contain potatoes, rice, or pasta, since all will become mushy.

Colorado Lamb and Lima Bean Bake

Ever since ranching began in western Colorado during the late nineteenth century, the state has been the nation's leading producer of Rocky Mountain lamb—though the notion of "spring lamb" is far-fetched, given the fact that most animals are slaughtered in early fall. You could make this casserole with a large can of Great Northern white beans (in the French style), but I love it with baby limas—often enhanced by a few pine nuts sprinkled between the layers. This casserole can also be made with lean beef chuck or pork shoulder.

¹/₄ cup all-purpose flour

Salt and black pepper to taste

2 pounds boneless lamb shoulder, trimmed of excess fat
and cut into 1-inch cubes

¹/₄ cup vegetable oil

1 large onion, chopped

2 garlic cloves, minced

1 carrot, scraped and chopped

¹/₄ pound fresh mushrooms, chopped

¹/₄ teaspoon dried thyme, crumbled

¹/₄ teaspoon dried rosemary, crumbled

1¹/₂ cups beef broth

One 10-ounce package baby lima beans, parboiled
about 10 minutes and drained

1. Preheat the oven to 350°F. Grease a 2- to 2¹/₂-quart casserole.

2. On a plate, combine the flour and salt and pepper and dredge the lamb cubes in the mixture, tapping off any excess. In a large heavy skillet, heat the oil over moderate heat, add the lamb, brown on all sides, and transfer to a plate. Add the onion, garlic, carrot, mushrooms, thyme, and rosemary to the skillet, stir till the vegetables soften, about 8 minutes, and transfer to another plate. Add the broth to the skillet, scrape up browned bits from the bottom, and remove from heat.

3. Layer half the lamb in the casserole, then half the limas. Spoon half the vegetable mixture over the limas and season with salt and pepper. Repeat layering the remaining lamb, limas, and vegetable mixture, pour the hot broth over the top, cover, and bake till the lamb is tender, about 1 hour. Uncover and bake till the top is crusty, about 10 minutes longer.

MAKES 6 SERVINGS

Lamb and Eggplant Pilaf

1 large eggplant, peeled and cut into $1/4$-inch-thick rounds

Salt

2 tablespoons olive oil

2 medium-size onions, finely chopped

1 garlic clove, minced

One 16-ounce can Italian plum tomatoes, undrained

$1/2$ cup seedless dark raisins

Black pepper to taste

1 tablespoon finely chopped fresh mint leaves

1 cup raw long-grain rice

$2^1/2$ to 3 cups diced cooked lamb

1. Place the eggplant rounds in a colander, sprinkle with salt, and let stand to drain about 30 minutes. Rinse the rounds, pat dry, and set aside.

2. In a heavy, flameproof 2- to $2^1/2$-quart casserole, heat the oil over moderate heat, add the onions and garlic, and stir till softened, about 7 minutes. Layer the eggplant over the vegetables, mixing slightly, add the tomatoes and their juices, the raisins, pepper, and mint, bring to a simmer, cover, and cook for 30 minutes over moderately low to low heat.

3. Preheat the oven to 325°F.

4. Sprinkle the rice evenly over the casserole and stir slightly. Layer the lamb over the top, stir slightly, cover, and bake till bubbly, about 20 minutes.

MAKES 6 SERVINGS

Lamb and eggplant always make a nice marriage, and never so much so as in this minty casserole that can be cooked just as easily on top of the stove as in the oven. If you don't have any leftover lamb, simply buy about two pounds of lamb shoulder, dice it, then brown it in olive oil before sautéing the vegetables. In any lamb casserole, I often also add a little chopped fresh or dried crumbled rosemary to taste.

Last-Minute Lamb and Spinach Casserole

Leftover rare leg of lamb, a couple of packages of frozen spinach in the freezer, a carton of tangy feta cheese in the fridge—that's about all I needed to produce a quick casserole for a few friends stranded at my house one night by a ferocious snow storm. I could just as easily have used leftover pork, beef, chicken, or even duck; I would most likely have substituted sour cream for the mayo if I'd had any on hand; and maybe I would have reached for a different dried herb (or herbs). Even when the meat is not ideal (I would have much preferred some leftover lamb shanks or shoulder chops), who says that casseroles are not the most flexible and often life-saving devices of the entire kitchen repertory?

2 cups cubed cooked lamb

Two 10-ounce packages frozen chopped spinach, thawed and squeezed almost dry

$^1/_4$ cup mayonnaise or sour cream

$^1/_4$ cup ($^1/_2$ stick) butter, melted

$^1/_2$ cup dry sherry

$^1/_2$ teaspoon dried rosemary, crumbled

Salt and black pepper to taste

$^1/_2$ cup crumbled feta cheese

1. Preheat the oven to 350°F. Butter a 1$^1/_2$-quart casserole and set aside.

2. In a large mixing bowl, combine the lamb and spinach and toss well. Add the mayonnaise, butter, sherry, and rosemary, season with salt and pepper, mix till well blended, and scrape into the prepared casserole. Sprinkle the cheese evenly over the top and bake till bubbly and golden, about 30 minutes.

MAKES 4 SERVINGS

Crazy for Casseroles

Minnesota Liver, Rice, and Apple Casserole

1/2 cup water

1/2 cup raw long-grain rice

1/4 cup (1/2 stick) butter

2 medium-size red onions, finely chopped

2 cooking apples, peeled, cored, and finely chopped

12 ounces lamb's liver, trimmed of fat and membranes and minced

1 cup beef broth

1 large egg, beaten

2 tablespoons sour cream

Pinch of ground cloves

Salt and black pepper to taste

6 strips lean bacon

1/2 cup chopped fresh parsley leaves

1. In a medium-size saucepan, bring the water to a boil, add the rice, cook for 10 minutes, and drain.

2. Preheat the oven to 325°F. Grease a 1 1/2-quart casserole and set aside.

3. In a medium-size skillet, melt the butter over moderate heat, then add the onions and apples and stir till softened, about 7 minutes. Scrape into a large mixing bowl, add the drained rice, liver, broth, egg, sour cream, and cloves, season with salt and pepper, and mix till well blended. Scrape into the prepared casserole, cover, and bake for 45 minutes.

4. Meanwhile, fry the bacon over moderate heat till crisp, drain on paper towels, and crumble. In a small bowl, combine the bacon and parsley.

5. Uncover the casserole and continue to bake till slightly crusted on top, about 15 minutes. To serve, sprinkle the bacon mixture over the top.

MAKES 4 SERVINGS

Given the wide ethnic diversity of Minnesota's immigrant heritage (British, Germans, Scandinavians, Finns, and Slavs), it's hard to determine which group might have originated this type of lusty casserole that's as popular in rural areas today as it was in the nineteenth century. My guess is that it's German or Swedish, the only question being why the casserole is not traditionally made with the region's indigenous wild rice that has grown in shallow lakes for centuries. In any case, this is perhaps the best way I know to prepare lamb's liver, which is redder and slightly stronger than calf's liver and lends itself well to slow baking. Do remember that all liver is highly perishable and should be cooked within 24 hours of purchase.

Veal Parmigiano

A classic Italian-American veal parmigiano is one of the greatest casseroles of all time, so long, that is, as the ingredients are top-notch and certain precautions are taken. To counteract the acidity of the tomatoes in the sauce, for instance, a little sugar must be added, and the sauce itself should be watched carefully to make sure it's not too thin or too thick. Also, if you overbrown the veal slices, they'll be rubbery and tough. As for the cheeses, I wouldn't dream of using anything but fresh mozzarella and genuine Parmigiano-Reggiano. Veal scaloppine can be hideously expensive, which is why I don't hesitate sometimes to substitute thinly sliced chicken or turkey breast when I want to economize and don't have to worry about trying to impress anyone other than family or close friends. Contrary to what some people think, fine veal does indeed have a distinctive flavor and texture, but I've learned that the other white meats (including pork loin) can produce nice results if handled carefully.

³/₄ cup olive oil

1 medium-size onion, finely chopped

1 garlic clove, minced

One 16-ounce can Italian plum tomatoes, undrained

2 teaspoons sugar

¹/₂ teaspoon dried oregano, crumbled

¹/₄ teaspoon dried sage, crumbled

Salt and black pepper to taste

1 pound thin veal scaloppine

2 large eggs, beaten

1 cup dry bread crumbs

¹/₂ pound mozzarella cheese, thinly sliced

¹/₂ cup freshly grated Parmesan cheese

1. In a large heavy saucepan, heat about 2 tablespoons of the oil over moderate heat, add the onion and garlic, and stir for 3 minutes. Add the tomatoes, sugar, oregano, and sage, season with salt and pepper, and mash the tomatoes with a fork to break them up. Bring to a boil, reduce the heat to low, cover, and simmer till the sauce is thickened, about 10 minutes. Set aside.

2. Preheat the oven to 350°F. Grease a 1¹/₂- to 2-quart casserole and set aside.

3. In a large heavy skillet, heat the remaining 10 tablespoons oil over moderate heat. Dip the veal slices in the egg, then in the bread crumbs, coating them evenly, brown slightly in the hot olive oil in batches, 2 to 3 minutes on each side, and arrange the slices in the prepared casserole in a single or slightly overlapping layer.

Crucial Crumbs

Both soft and dry bread crumbs, as well as various types of cracker crumbs, are indispensable by themselves or as components in all sorts of casserole toppings intended to produce golden or browned crusts. Although I personally eat nothing but freshly baked breads on a daily basis, I'm the first to recommend standard, inexpensive commercial white and whole wheat loaves for making soft or dry bread crumbs. (Since I bake lots of biscuits and cornbreads, I also often crumb these leftovers for certain casserole toppings.) Since I find that commercial dry bread crumbs usually have a strange off-flavor, I keep a can only for dire emergencies. For cracker crumbs, frankly I buy the cheapest soda crackers, wheat crackers, oyster crackers, and croutons (never any sweetened cracker) I can find in the supermarket. I store all dry bread crumbs in tightly sealed jars and simply crumble crackers and croutons by hand as I need them.

To make soft bread crumbs, trim the edges off standard bread slices, tear the bread into small pieces or cut into small cubes and, for coarse crumbs, either buzz for 5 to 10 seconds in a blender or pulse 5 or 6 times in a food processor fitted with a metal blade. Buzz or pulse longer for fine crumbs. One slice of bread yields about ½ cup coarse or fine crumbs.

To make dry bread crumbs, trim the edges off standard bread slices, toast the slices in a toaster or oven, tear the bread into small pieces, and either buzz the pieces in a blender or pulse in a food processor to the desired texture. (Crumbs from stale, dry bread are produced in the same manner.) One slice of bread yields about ½ cup coarse or fine crumbs.

4. Spoon half the tomato sauce over the veal, layer half the mozzarella over the sauce, and sprinkle half the Parmesan over the top. Repeat with the remaining sauce, mozzarella, and Parmesan, cover, and bake till bubbly and golden, about 30 minutes.

MAKES 4 TO 6 SERVINGS

Country Club Veal, Carrot, and Olive Casserole

In the 1940s, veal consumption in the United States was about ten pounds per capita annually, compared with no more than a pound today, one reason being the ever-increasing exorbitant price of veal. Once was the time when a veal casserole such as this was the highlight of any country club buffet, and all you have to do is flip through the pages of old church and community cookbooks to see how popular veal casseroles were with housewives who wanted to impress guests with something deemed "elegant." Fortunately, you can hold the cost down today by using veal shoulder or flank, both of which are often seen in better supermarkets and always available in butcher shops. (The cheapest cut often on sale is veal breast, but I gave up long ago trying to get enough meat off the bones to make it worth all the trouble.) If the sauce for this casserole appears too thin, simply mix 1 tablespoon of flour with 1 tablespoon of softened butter and thicken the sauce with the paste before pouring over the veal.

2 pounds veal shoulder, trimmed of excess fat and cut into 1-inch cubes

2 tablespoons all-purpose flour

1/4 cup (1/2 stick) butter

2 medium-size onions, chopped

4 carrots, scraped and thinly sliced

1 garlic clove, minced

2 cups chicken broth

1/2 cup heavy cream

1/2 teaspoon dried tarragon, crumbled

Salt and black pepper to taste

20 to 25 pimento-stuffed green olives

1. Preheat the oven to 350°F. Butter a 2-quart casserole and set aside.

2. On a large plate, dredge the veal in the flour, tapping off any excess. In a large heavy skillet, melt the butter over moderate heat, then add the veal, brown on all sides, and transfer to the prepared casserole. Add the onions, carrots, and garlic to the skillet and stir till softened, about 5 minutes. Add the broth, heavy cream, and tarragon, season with salt and pepper, stir about 5 minutes, and remove from the heat.

3. Scatter the olives evenly over the veal, pour the sauce over the top, cover, and bake for 45 minutes. Uncover and to bake till slightly crusted, about 15 minutes.

MAKES 6 SERVINGS

Crazy for Casseroles

Sweetbread, Ham, and Olive Strata

6 frozen veal sweetbreads, thawed

3 cups water

3 tablespoons cider vinegar or fresh lemon juice

1 teaspoon salt

3 tablespoons butter

6 scallions (white part and some of the green), chopped

2 medium-size ripe tomatoes, peeled, seeded, and chopped

1 medium-size carrot, scraped and grated

1½ cups chicken broth

1 cup diced cooked ham

1 cup pimento-stuffed green olives, drained

Black pepper to taste

1. In a large saucepan, combine the sweetbreads with the water, vinegar, and salt, bring to a low simmer, cook till tender, 35 to 40 minutes, and drain. Cut the sweetbreads in half and remove and discard any tubes or membranes.

2. Preheat the oven to 350°F. Butter a 2-quart casserole and set aside.

3. In a medium-size skillet, melt the butter over moderate heat, then add the scallions and stir for 3 minutes. Add the tomatoes, carrot, and broth, cook till the mixture is slightly thickened, and remove from the heat.

4. Layer the sweetbreads over the bottom of the prepared casserole, sprinkle the ham evenly over them, then distribute the olives evenly over the ham. Season with the pepper, scrape the tomato mixture evenly over the top, and bake till slightly crusty, 25 to 30 minutes.

MAKES 6 SERVINGS

When prepared with care, sweetbreads (the thymus gland of young animals) are one of the most delectable vituals imaginable—flavorful, tender, rich, and, alas, as expensive as prime beef. The finest are fresh veal sweetbreads, but since they are very fragile and perishable (they cannot be kept safely more than one day), I always buy the frozen ones available in better markets. Do check even frozen-sweetbreads for membranes and tubes, which must be removed and discarded, and, to keep the organs white and firm while simmering, always add either a little vinegar or lemon juice to the water. The ham and olives complement the sweetbreads beautifully in this distinctive strata, and while it's basically a simple dish to prepare, it's also a very elegant one.

Veal Kidney, White Onion, and Mushroom Casserole

Veal kidneys, which are much more delicate and tender than beef or pork ones, are ideal simmered in a casserole with any number of vegetables and seasonings. When shopping, remember that ³/₄ pound of kidneys generally makes two servings, and note that it's much easier to clean away the knobs of interior fat if the kidneys are first halved.

¹/₃ cup (about ³/₄ stick) butter

1³/₄ pounds (3 to 4) fresh veal kidneys, trimmed of fat and membranes and cut in half

¹/₂ pound fresh mushrooms, sliced

Salt and black pepper to taste

1 cup dry white wine

1 tablespoon Dijon mustard

1¹/₂ cups beef broth

¹/₂ cup half-and-half

³/₄ pound tiny white boiling onions, peeled

2 tablespoons chopped fresh parsley leaves

1. Preheat the oven to 350°F. Butter a 1¹/₂- to 2-quart casserole and set aside.

2. In a large heavy skillet, melt about half the butter over moderate heat, then add the kidneys, brown quickly on both sides, about 2 minutes, and transfer to a plate. Add the mushrooms to the skillet, stir for about 3 minutes, and transfer to another plate. Melt the remaining butter in the skillet, then add the wine and mustard, stir well, and cook till the liquid is almost evaporated, about 8 minutes. Add the broth and half-and-half, continue to cook till the sauce thickens, 8 to 10 minutes, and remove from the heat.

3. Layer the kidneys over the bottom of the prepared casserole, layer the onions over the kidneys, layer the mushrooms over the onions, and season with salt and pepper. Pour the sauce over the casserole, cover, and bake for 30 minutes.

4. To serve, sprinkle the parsley over the top.

MAKES 5 TO 6 SERVINGS

Crazy for Casseroles

Smothered Calf's Liver and Vegetables

5 strips lean bacon

$1/4$ cup all-purpose flour

Salt and black pepper to taste

1 to $1^1/_2$ pounds calf's liver, trimmed of excess fat and membranes and cut into serving pieces

4 to 5 medium-size onions, to your taste, thinly sliced

$1/2$ medium-size green bell pepper, seeded and thinly sliced

$1/4$ pound fresh mushrooms, sliced

$1^1/_2$ to 2 cups Cream Sauce (page 6), to your taste

1 tablespoon fresh lemon juice

2 teaspoons Worcestershire sauce

1. In a large heavy skillet, fry the bacon over moderate heat till crisp, drain on paper towels, and crumble.

2. Preheat the oven to 350°F. Grease a 2-quart casserole and set aside.

3. On a plate, combine the flour and salt and pepper and dredge the liver pieces in the mixture, tapping off any excess. Brown the liver lightly on both sides in the hot bacon fat, then arrange the pieces in the prepared casserole. Add the onions, bell pepper, and mushrooms to the skillet and stir till softened, about 7 minutes, then scatter the vegetables over the liver and scatter the crumbled bacon over the vegetables.

4. Heat the sauce, add the lemon juice and Worcestershire, and stir well. Pour the sauce evenly over the casserole, cover, and bake till bubbly, about 30 minutes.

MAKES 4 TO 6 SERVINGS

Calf's liver smothered with various vegetables was almost a staple at family restaurants, cafeterias, and diners all across America during the first half of the twentieth century, and I wish we could still find the preparation more often these days. If you want to modernize the casserole, you might substitute slightly sweeter yellow bell pepper and any fresh wild mushroom, as well as add various herbs (sage especially complements the liver). One or two tablespoons of port wine added to the sauce also gives the casserole new dimension. While lamb's liver could be used here, I do find beef liver much too strong.

Fall Venison, Parsnip, and Mushroom Bake

The only thing better in the chilly fall months than a good venison stew is a layered venison casserole with any variety of earthy root vegetables and mushrooms (cultivated or wild). The Romans were so fond of plump, sweet parsnips that cooks treated them with utter reverence, and even in Tudor England, the vegetable was still prized enough to be used to make special breads. Thereafter, and for whatever reasons, parsnips fell out of favor throughout most of the world and still don't command the respect they deserve—boiled with a little brown sugar and mashed, roasted, French-fried, or, best of all, slowly baked with full-flavored meats. Large parsnips can have woody cores, so look for medium-sized ones that are clean, firm, and evenly shaped. I like to serve this casserole with wild rice and a good, sturdy Zinfandel.

$2^1/_2$ pounds boneless venison shoulder, trimmed of excess fat and cut into $1^1/_2$-inch pieces

1 cup all-purpose flour

Salt and black pepper to taste

Cayenne pepper to taste

$^1/_4$ cup vegetable oil

1 cup sweet vermouth

2 cups beef broth

2 medium-size onions, chopped

2 celery ribs, chopped

$^1/_2$ teaspoon dried thyme, crumbled

$^1/_2$ teaspoon dried rosemary, crumbled

3 cloves

4 medium-size parsnips, peeled and sliced

$^1/_2$ pound fresh mushrooms, sliced

1. Rinse the venison pieces briefly under cold running water, then pat dry well with paper towels. On a plate, combine the flour, salt, black pepper, and cayenne and dredge the venison in the mixture, tapping off any excess. Heat the oil over moderate heat in a flameproof, heavy $2^1/_2$- to 3-quart casserole, add the venison, and brown on all sides. Add the vermouth and stir to scrape up any browned bits off the bottom of the casserole. Add the broth, onions, celery, thyme, rosemary, and cloves, bring to a simmer, cover, and cook for 1 hour.

2. Preheat the oven to 325°F.

3. Arrange half the parsnips in a layer over the venison and vegetables, arrange half the mushrooms in a layer over the parsnips, and repeat the layering with the remaining parsnips and mushrooms. With a large spoon, baste the parsnips and mushrooms with a little of the cooking liquid, then bake till the meat and vegetables are very tender and the top is slightly crusted, about 1 hour longer, basting once more.

MAKES 6 SERVINGS

Ann Arbor Venison and Wild Mushroom Bake

If there's a way to prepare venison, my venison expert, who lives in Ann Arbor, Michigan, knows about it. Over the years, Bill has turned out stews, roasts, chilis, steaks, and even burgers and sausages, but no preparation has been as memorable as this creamy casserole chock-full of equally earthy wild mushrooms. Living where he does, Bill has little trouble finding plenty of fresh venison (or fresh wild mushrooms), which has inimitable flavor but can require lengthy marination unless it's been aged long enough to allow its natural enzymes to partially tenderize the meat. Fresh, legally inspected venison sold in better markets these days is usually fairly young and tender, but if there's any question, I don't hesitate a moment to use the frozen product (often available cut up in packages), especially since the long baking itself is enough to produce succulent meat. Any combination of wild mushrooms can be used in this bake—fresh or dried. Two ounces of soaked dried mushrooms equals about one pound

1 ounce dried cep mushrooms

1 ounce dried shiitake mushrooms

2 pounds boneless venison shoulder, trimmed of excess fat

1/2 cup all-purpose flour

3 tablespoons vegetable oil

6 scallions (white part and some of the green), finely chopped

2 carrots, scraped and finely chopped

1/2 teaspoon ground sage

Salt and black pepper to taste

1/2 cup gin

1 cup heavy cream

1. In a small mixing bowl, combine the mushrooms with enough warm water to cover and soak for 30 minutes. Transfer the mushrooms to a cutting surface and chop coarsely. Strain the soaking liquid through cheesecloth or a paper towel into another small bowl and reserve.

2. Cut the venison into 1 1/2-inch cubes and dust in the flour, tapping off any excess. In a large heavy skillet, heat the oil over moderate heat, brown the venison on all sides, and transfer to a plate. Add the scallions, carrots, and sage to the skillet, season with salt and pepper, stir for about 3 minutes, and transfer to another plate. Add the gin to the skillet and deglaze, scraping up any browned bits and pieces clinging to the bottom of the pan. Add about 1/4 cup of the reserved mushroom soaking liquid and stir. Add the heavy cream, bring to a simmer, stirring, and remove the sauce from the heat.

Crazy for Casseroles

3. Preheat the oven to 350°F. Grease a 2- to 2½-quart casserole, then layer the venison across the bottom and season with salt and pepper. Spread half the chopped mushrooms over the venison, cover with all the vegetables, and top with the remaining mushrooms. Pour the sauce evenly over the top, cover, and bake till the venison is very tender, about 2 hours.

MAKES 6 SERVINGS

of fresh, but remember that if you use the fresh, you won't have the highly aromatic soaking liquid to add to the sauce.

C A S S E R O L E   C H A T

Store dried wild mushrooms in tightly sealed jars and, when handling them, always use dry hands to prevent possible mold and spoilage.

Braised Rabbit, Mushrooms, and Tomatoes

Lean, light, delicate, high in protein, and available frozen in most supermarkets today, rabbit is the most popular furred game in the U. S. and an ideal meat for all sorts of casseroles. Large, mature rabbits (at least three months old) are really best for braising, and you have to look carefully when shopping to make sure the rabbit is not too small and bony. If you don't have much choice, remember that a meaty 3½-pound rabbit is usually enough for at least four persons, whereas if the rabbit appears bony, the safest bet is to buy two. This exact same recipe, by the way, can also be used for a 3½-pound chicken.

¼ cup (½ stick) butter

One 3½-pound rabbit, dressed and cut into serving pieces

1 large onion, chopped

1 garlic clove, minced

½ pound fresh mushrooms, sliced

1 cup dry white wine

3 large ripe tomatoes, peeled, seeded, and chopped

1½ cups beef broth

2 teaspoons chopped fresh tarragon leaves or ½ teaspoon dried, crumbled

1 teaspoon chopped fresh chervil leaves or ¼ teaspoon dried, crumbled

Salt and black pepper to taste

1. Preheat the oven to 350°F. Butter a 2- to 2½-quart casserole and set aside.

2. In a large heavy skillet, melt the butter over moderate heat, then add the rabbit pieces (in batches, if necessary), brown on all sides, and transfer to a plate. Add the onion, garlic, and mushrooms to the skillet and stir for 5 minutes. Add the wine and continue to cook till most of the liquid has evaporated, about 5 minutes. Add the tomatoes, broth, tarragon, and chervil, season with salt and pepper, bring to a boil, and allow to boil till the sauce begins to thicken, 5 to 7 minutes. Remove from the heat.

3. Arrange the rabbit pieces in the prepared casserole, pour the sauce over the top, cover, and bake till the rabbit is fork-tender and the sauce nicely thickened, 30 to 35 minutes.

MAKES 4 TO 6 SERVINGS

Poultry Pies, Perloos, Surprises, and Suppers

All-American Chicken Pot Pie

What makes this classic chicken pot pie different from most others is the layer of pastry strips within the pie itself, a technique that not only yields a firmer pie but provides an interesting contrast between the soft interior pastry and the crispy top crust. Don't make this pie unless you're willing to make the pastry from scratch—actually a very simple procedure. To give the pie a slightly racy and more modern flavor, think about adding about $1/2$ cup of sliced or chopped fresh shiitake or cep mushrooms to the first layer of carrots and peas.

One $3^1/_2$-pound chicken, cut into serving pieces

1 medium-size onion, quartered

2 celery ribs (leaves included), each broken into 3 pieces

Salt and black pepper to taste

2 cups all-purpose flour

$2/_3$ cup vegetable shortening

$1/_4$ cup ice water

2 medium-size carrots, scraped, cut into thin rounds, blanched for 5 minutes in boiling water, and drained

1 cup fresh or thawed frozen green peas

2 tablespoons butter, melted

1. Place the chicken pieces in a large pot, add the onion and celery, and season with salt and pepper. Add enough water to cover, bring to a boil, reduce the heat to low, cover, and simmer for 30 minutes. With a slotted spoon, transfer the chicken to a cutting board and, when cool enough to handle, bone, cut the meat into bite-size pieces, and set aside. Strain the broth into a bowl and set aside.

2. While the chicken is cooking, combine the flour and $1/_4$ teaspoon salt in a large mixing bowl, then cut in the shortening with a pastry cutter or 2 knives till the mixture resembles coarse meal. Stirring with a spoon, gradually add the ice water till a ball of dough is formed. On a lightly floured work surface, roll out half the dough about $1/_8$ inch thick and line the bottom and sides of a greased $1^1/_2$-quart casserole with it, tucking the crust into the corners. Roll out the remaining dough about $1/_8$ inch thick and cut half of it into 1-inch-wide strips, reserving the remainder for the top of the pie.

3. Preheat the oven to 350°F. Spread a piece of heavy aluminum foil over the bottom rack in the oven to catch any drips.

Crazy for Casseroles

4. Arrange half the chicken pieces over the bottom of the casserole, half the carrots and peas over the chicken, and top with the pastry strips. Arrange the remaining chicken, carrots, and peas on top of the strips, season with salt and pepper, and pour in enough reserved chicken broth to almost cover the top layer.

5. Fit the remaining pastry over the top of the pie, pressing down the edges and trimming off the excess. Brush the top with the melted butter, cut a couple of vent holes in the pastry with a knife, and bake till the top is golden brown, 30 to 40 minutes.

MAKES 6 SERVINGS

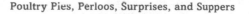

Chicken Spectacular

If ever a chicken dish harked back to the golden age of casseroles in the 1940s and '50s when economy and minimum prep time were the major cooking virtues, this is it. Every regional cookbook put out by churches and junior leagues has had at least one Chicken Spectacular, and if the casseroles were not necessarily "spectacular," they were at least simple to prepare and, for the most part, satisfying to eat. Do note that because of the condensed soup and cheese, this casserole needs no extra salt.

3 cups diced cooked chicken

1½ cups fresh or thawed frozen green peas

½ cup coarsely chopped almonds

One 4-ounce jar pimentos, drained and chopped

One 10¾-ounce can Campbell's condensed cream of mushroom soup

Freshly ground black pepper to taste

One 5-ounce can water chestnuts, drained and sliced

1 cup grated sharp cheddar cheese

1. Preheat the oven to 350°F.

2. Grease a 1½-quart casserole and layer half the chicken over the bottom. Layer half the peas over the chicken, then half the almonds over the peas, then half the pimentos over the almonds, and pour half the soup over the top. Season with pepper and scatter the water chestnuts evenly over the top. Repeat the layering, then sprinkle the cheese evenly over the top and bake till golden brown, about 35 minutes.

MAKES 4 SERVINGS

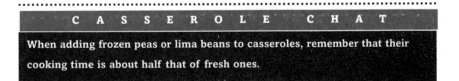

CASSEROLE CHAT

When adding frozen peas or lima beans to casseroles, remember that their cooking time is about half that of fresh ones.

Hawaiian Chicken and Pineapple Casserole

$^{1}/_{4}$ cup vegetable oil

One 3- to 3$^{1}/_{2}$-pound chicken, cut into serving pieces

1 large onion, thinly sliced

1 medium-size green bell pepper, seeded and cut into thin strips

1 medium-size red bell pepper, seeded and cut into thin strips

12 fresh mushrooms, sliced

Salt and black pepper to taste

$^{1}/_{2}$ fresh pineapple, peeled, cored, and cut into small chunks

$^{1}/_{4}$ cup soy sauce

1 tablespoon honey

$^{1}/_{2}$ cup pineapple juice

$^{1}/_{2}$ cup semisweet white wine

1. Preheat the oven to 350°F. Grease a 2- to 2$^{1}/_{2}$-quart casserole and set aside.

2. In a large heavy skillet, heat the oil over moderate heat, add the chicken, brown lightly on all sides, and transfer to a plate. Add the onion, both bell peppers, and mushrooms, season with salt and pepper, and stir till softened, about 5 minutes. Remove from heat.

3. Layer half the vegetables and half the pineapple chunks over the bottom of the prepared casserole, removing the other half of the vegetables from the heat. Arrange the chicken pieces over the vegetables and pineapple. Mix the soy sauce and honey together in a small bowl and brush the pieces with the mixture. Layer the remaining vegetables and pineapple over the chicken. Mix the pineapple juice and wine together in a small mixing bowl, pour evenly over the top, cover, and bake till the chicken is tender, about 1 hour.

MAKES 4 TO 6 SERVINGS

One of my most exciting ventures was a visit to a pineapple field on the Hawaiian island of Oahu, which is still the center of the industry. Traditionally, shoots are planted by hand in holes punched through vast sheets of tar paper used to raise the soil temperature and conserve moisture, a laborious procedure but one that produces some 700,000 tons of pineapple annually. And if you ever wonder why fresh pineapples are so expensive, remember that it takes a plant twenty months to bear a single fruit.

This casserole couldn't be more typical of the dishes found in the restaurants and hotels of Oahu, and it's almost obligatory that you use fresh pineapple. Cleaning a truly ripe pineapple should produce the $^{1}/_{2}$ cup of juice needed, but, if not, use canned juice. Also, if you find fresh shiitake or enoki mushrooms, you might consider substituting them for the cultivated ones since they yield more flavor.

Poppy Seed Chicken

If I had to pinpoint the one casserole that the women in my Southern family—mother, sister, aunt, or niece—prepare at least once a month for all sorts of informal occasions, it would have to be Poppy Seed Chicken. Given the nature of the dish, I suspect its origins go back at least to the 1940s, when cooking with canned soups, sour cream, and Ritz crackers was so fashionable. Whatever, it's not only a reliable casserole made in the traditional manner, but also one that can be easily prepared unbaked in disposable aluminum pans and taken to sick friends, shut-ins, or bereavements to be popped into the oven and cooked with no worry about the container having to be returned.

6 whole chicken breasts, cut in half

One 10³/₄-ounce can Campbell's condensed cream of chicken soup

1 cup sour cream

2 tablespoons fresh lemon juice

2 tablespoons poppy seeds, plus extra for topping

Salt and black pepper to taste

¹/₂ pound (1 sleeve) Ritz crackers, crushed

¹/₂ cup (1 stick) butter or margarine, melted

1. Place the chicken breasts in a pot with enough water to cover, bring to a boil, reduce the heat to low, and cook till tender, about 20 minutes. With a slotted spoon, transfer the chicken to a plate and, when cool enough to handle, bone and skin the chicken, cut into bite-size pieces, and place a large mixing bowl.

2. Preheat the oven to 325°F. Butter a 2¹/₂-quart casserole and set aside.

3. Add the soup, sour cream, lemon juice, and poppy seeds to the chicken and mix till well blended. Transfer the mixture to the prepared casserole and spread the crushed crackers evenly over the top. Drizzle the melted butter over the crackers, sprinkle poppy seeds liberally on top, and bake till bubbly and browned, about 30 minutes.

MAKES 6 TO 8 SERVINGS

Paper Bag Chicken Creole

²/₃ cup all-purpose flour

1 tablespoon chili powder

¹/₂ teaspoon salt

2 whole chicken breasts (about 1 pound each), cut in half

¹/₂ cup vegetable oil

1 large onion, minced

¹/₂ medium-size green bell pepper, seeded and cut into thin strips

1 garlic clove, minced

²/₃ cup raw long-grain rice

One 28-ounce can crushed tomatoes

1 tablespoon finely chopped fresh basil leaves

Black pepper to taste

1. Preheat the oven to 350°F. Grease a 1¹/₂-quart casserole and set aside.

2. In a brown paper bag, combine the flour, chili powder, and salt and shake. Add the chicken breasts one at a time to the bag, shake till well coated, tap off any excess flour, and place on a plate.

3. In a large heavy skillet, heat the oil over moderate heat, add the breasts, brown slightly on both sides, and transfer to a plate. Add the onion, bell pepper, garlic, and rice to the skillet and stir for 5 minutes. Add the tomatoes and basil, season with salt and pepper, stir about 2 minutes, and remove from the heat.

4. Arrange the chicken breasts in the bottom of the prepared casserole, spoon the tomato mixture evenly over the top, cover with aluminum foil, and bake till the chicken is tender, about 1 hour.

MAKES 4 SERVINGS

Since Chicken Creole found in old community cookbooks from Georgia to Montana calls for shaking the chicken with seasoned flour in a paper bag, I've always wondered what's so "Creole" about the technique. (I've used paper bags for preparing Southern fried chicken my whole life.) No matter, the casserole has become a classic all around the country, and when time is short and there are hungry mouths to feed without going too much effort, this always fills the bill. Chicken breasts always seem to be used in the recipes, but for more flavor (and less cost), you might consider substituting thighs.

Buckeye Chicken and Chestnut Casserole

Ohio, the Buckeye State, is nicknamed appropriately after the buckeye chestnuts that once flourished there before a blight destroyed all the trees in the early twentieth century. The trees may be sadly gone, but still nobody in the country appreciates and loves to cook with imported chestnuts more than a real Buckeye. In this recipe, just be sure not to let the nuts brown when tossing them in the butter since this can destroy their subtle texture. If you don't want the tedious job of shelling and peeling fresh chestnuts, remember that some specialty food shops now carry shelled and peeled frozen European chestnuts—at a hefty price.

10 to 12 chestnuts

4 strips lean bacon, diced

1 medium-size onion, chopped

1 garlic clove, minced

$^1/_4$ pound fresh mushrooms, sliced

$^1/_2$ teaspoon dried thyme, crumbled

$^1/_2$ teaspoon dried tarragon, crumbled

Salt and black pepper to taste

One 3- to $3^1/_2$-pound chicken, cut into serving pieces

$^3/_4$ cup chicken broth

$^1/_4$ cup medium-sweet sherry

2 tablespoons butter

1. To prepare the chestnuts, cut a deep X on each flat side with a sharp knife, place them in a medium-size saucepan with water to cover, bring to a low boil, cook 10 minutes, and drain. When cool enough to handle, remove and discard the outer shells and skins, halve the nuts, and set aside.

2. Preheat the oven to 350°F. Grease a 2-quart casserole and set aside.

3. In a large skillet over moderately high heat, fry the bacon for 5 minutes. Add the onion, garlic, mushrooms, thyme, and tarragon, season with salt and pepper, stir till softened, about 5 minutes, and transfer to a plate. Add the chicken to the skillet, brown on all sides, and arrange the pieces in the casserole. Spoon the mushroom mixture evenly over the top. Combine the broth and sherry, pour over the chicken, and bake for 30 minutes.

4. Melt the butter in a small skillet over low heat, add the chestnuts, and toss 2 to 3 minutes; do not brown. Add to the chicken, cover, and continue to bake till both are very tender, about 30 minutes.

MAKES 4 TO 6 SERVINGS

Crazy for Casseroles

Luigi's Chicken Cacciatore

1 cup all-purpose flour

$^1/_2$ teaspoon dried thyme, crumbled

$^1/_2$ teaspoon dried oregano, crumbled

Salt and black pepper to taste

One 3-pound chicken, cut into serving pieces

2 tablespoons butter or margarine

2 tablespoons olive oil

2 medium-size leeks (white part only), washed well and chopped

1 small green bell pepper, seeded and chopped

2 garlic cloves, minced

$^1/_2$ pound fresh mushrooms, sliced

One 16-ounce can Italian plum tomatoes, undrained, chopped

2 teaspoons tomato paste

$^1/_2$ teaspoon sugar

1 bay leaf

1. Preheat the oven to 350°F. Grease a 2-quart casserole and set aside.

2. In a paper or plastic bag, shake together the flour, thyme, oregano, and salt and pepper, add the chicken pieces, shake, tapping off any excess and set on a plate.

3. In a large heavy skillet, heat the butter and oil together over moderate heat till the butter melts, then add the chicken, brown on all sides, and arrange the pieces in the prepared casserole. Add the leeks, bell pepper, garlic, and mushrooms to the skillet and stir till softened, about 5 minutes. Add the tomatoes plus their juices, tomato paste, sugar, and bay leaf and stir till well blended. Pour the vegetables and sauce over the chicken, cover, and bake till the chicken is very tender, about 1$^1/_2$ hours.

MAKES 4 SERVINGS

When I was a young boy visiting relatives with my parents in New York City, I looked forward to nothing more than going to a small West Side Italian restaurant called Luigi's and ordering chicken cacciatore. Of course, we had no idea that the dish was totally unknown in Italy and had simply evolved as still another Italian-American creation after World War II. To us, it was a quintessential Italian specialty, and eventually my mother went so far as to ask Luigi himself for the sacred recipe. To this day, she and I both still make the casserole just the way she did almost half a century ago, the only variations being the substitution of leeks for onions and perhaps wild mushrooms for the button ones. Also, when I find turkey breast on sale, bake or roast it, and have plenty of leftovers, I might cut the meat into 1-inch strips and use them in place of the browned chicken pieces to make an unorthodox cacciatore. Whatever, don't forget to add the sugar to tame the acidity of the tomatoes.

Virginia Country Captain

Who knows where the name of this curried Virginia classic comes from, and who really cares? Most likely the term captain evolved as a distortion of the word "capon," but what's much more important to remember is that an authentic country captain is not a quick fricassee, like that found in many restaurants, but a casserole baked slowly enough to allow all the varied flavors to meld. Personally, I like the chicken in my country captain almost falling off the bones and might well bake it up to 50 minutes before sprinkling the top with the almonds.

¹/₄ cup all-purpose flour

Salt and freshly ground black pepper to taste

Pinch of ground allspice

One 3- to 3¹/₂-pound chicken, cut into serving pieces

2 tablespoons butter

1 tablespoon peanut oil

2 medium-size onions, finely chopped

1 small green bell pepper, seeded and finely chopped

1 garlic clove, minced

2 teaspoons medium-hot curry powder

4 medium-size ripe tomatoes, chopped (juices included)

3 tablespoons seedless golden raisins

1 cup chicken broth

1 cup sliced blanched almonds

1. Preheat the oven to 350°F. Butter a 2- to 2¹/₂-quart casserole and set aside.

2. In a paper or plastic bag, combine the flour, salt and pepper, and allspice, add the chicken pieces, shake, tapping off any excess and set on a plate.

3. In a large heavy skillet, heat the butter and oil together over moderate heat till the butter melts, then brown the chicken pieces on all sides and transfer back to the plate. Add the onions, bell pepper, garlic, and curry powder to the skillet and stir till the vegetables are softened, about 5 minutes. Add the tomatoes plus their juices and the raisins, stir till slightly thickened, and remove from the heat.

4. Arrange half the chicken pieces in the prepared casserole and spoon half the vegetables evenly over the top. Repeat with the remaining

chicken and vegetables, add any remaining juices from the skillet plus the broth, cover, and bake for 30 minutes.

5. Uncover, sprinkle the almonds evenly over the top, and bake, uncovered, till the chicken is tender and the almonds browned, about 30 minutes.

MAKES 4 TO 6 SERVINGS

Georgia Chicken and Peanut Bake

Prepared with both peanuts and peanut butter, this simple casserole has been in my mother's Georgia family since she was a child in Montecello. Traditionally, it is always served with rice and, while Georgia crackers would deem it nothing less than heresy, I did once substitute cracked cashews for the chopped peanuts with slightly sweeter but very tasty results. I do like a few good shots of Tabasco in this casserole.

$1/4$ cup peanut oil

3 pounds chicken thighs and legs, separated if joined

2 medium-size onions, chopped

1 small green bell pepper, seeded and chopped

1 cup coarsely chopped salted peanuts

2 cups chicken broth

$1/2$ cup crunchy peanut butter

One 6-ounce can tomato paste

Salt and black pepper to taste

Tabasco sauce to taste

1. Preheat the oven to 350°F. Grease a 2- to 2$1/2$-quart casserole and set aside.

2. In a large heavy skillet, heat the oil over moderate heat, brown the chicken pieces on all sides, and arrange in the prepared casserole. Add the onions and bell pepper to the skillet, stir till softened, about 5 minutes, and spoon evenly over the chicken. Scatter the peanuts over the vegetables.

3. In a medium-size mixing bowl, combine the broth, peanut butter, and tomato paste and season with salt, pepper, and Tabasco. Stir vigorously till well blended and smooth and pour over the top of the casserole. Cover and bake till the chicken is tender, about 1 hour.

MAKES 4 TO 6 SERVINGS

Crunchy Chicken, Mushroom, and Green Pea Casserole

6 tablespoons (³/₄ stick) butter

1 pound boneless, skinless chicken breasts, cubed

1 medium-size leek (white part and some of the green), washed well, patted dry, and cut into pieces

1 pound fresh mushrooms, sliced

1 cup frozen green peas

2 cups sour cream

2 teaspoons Dijon mustard

Salt and black pepper to taste

¹/₂ cup all-purpose flour

¹/₂ cup rolled oats

1 cup soft bread crumbs

¹/₄ cup freshly grated Parmesan cheese

1 teaspoon dried tarragon, crumbled

1. Preheat the oven to 350°F.

2. In a flameproof 1¹/₂-quart casserole, melt 2 tablespoons of the butter over moderate heat, then add the chicken and brown till just golden on all sides, 5 to 6 minutes. Add the leek and stir till softened, about 5 minutes. Add the mushrooms and peas and stir till the peas have thawed, about 3 minutes. Add the sour cream and mustard, season with salt and pepper, stir well, and remove from the heat.

3. In a medium-size mixing bowl, combine the flour, oats, and the remaining ¹/₄ cup butter and work with a fork till the mixture is mealy. Add the bread crumbs, cheese, and tarragon, stir till well blended, spoon evenly over top of the chicken, and bake till golden brown, 35 to 40 minutes.

MAKES 4 SERVINGS

Nothing in cookery produces a crunchier baked topping than rolled oats, and what is so sublime about this easy and quick casserole is the contrast between the creamy interior and crusted exterior. Since boneless and skinless chicken breasts are inordinately expensive in supermarkets, it's foolish (and just lazy) not to buy three good-sized half-breasts and bone them yourself. Also, if you're watching calories (which I never do), plain yogurt makes a much better substitute for the real sour cream than that ghastly "lite" sour cream product.

Baked Chicken Salad Casserole

When Diane Phillips's off-beat but intelligent *The Soup Mix Gourmet* was published recently, illustrating numerous sensible ways of cooking with canned soup and soup mixes, I was intrigued by a casserole of baked chicken salad and immediately set about to prepare it. Suffice it that I and my guests raved about the unusual dish, proving once again that there are certain casseroles that can only be made with canned soup if they're to turn out right. (Another good example is my mother's broccoli casserole—page 303.) My only objection was to the crushed potato chips called for as a topping, so I've deleted them altogether and doubled the amount of almonds. I'm addicted to potato chips with burgers and hot dogs, but rarely do I find them justified in casserole cookery. To give this dish more exotic character, you might add about 2 teaspoons of curry powder to the soup mixture and a cup of mixed chopped apples and seedless golden raisins to the chicken mixture. This casserole needs no salt.

Two 10 ¾ ounce cans Campbell's condensed cream of chicken soup

½ cup mayonnaise

2 tablespoons fresh lemon juice

3 medium-size whole chicken breasts, cooked, boned, skinned, and cut into 1-inch dice

3 celery ribs, finely chopped

4 scallions (white part and some of the green), finely chopped

6 large hard-boiled eggs, coarsely chopped

Black pepper to taste

1 cup slivered almonds

1. Preheat the oven to 350°F. Butter a 2½-quart casserole and set aside.

2. In a medium-size mixing bowl, combine the soup, mayonnaise, and lemon juice and stir till well blended.

3. In a large mixing bowl, combine the chicken, celery, scallions, and eggs, season with pepper, and toss till well blended. Add the soup mixture to the chicken mixture, stir till well blended, and scrape into the prepared casserole. Sprinkle the almonds evenly over the top and bake till golden brown, 30 to 35 minutes.

MAKES 6 SERVINGS

C A S S E R O L E   C H A T

Unbaked casseroles that contain condensed canned soup freeze well. For those that contain sour cream or yogurt, it's best to add the cream or yogurt after the casserole has been thawed.

Crazy for Casseroles

Savannah Chicken, Brown Rice, and Pimento Perloo

2¹/₂ cups water

1 teaspoon salt

1 cup raw brown rice

¹/₄ cup (¹/₂ stick) butter

1 medium-size onion, chopped

1 celery rib, chopped

¹/₂ pound fresh mushrooms, chopped

¹/₄ cup all-purpose flour

1 cup chicken broth

1 cup half-and-half

3 cups cubed cooked chicken

¹/₂ cup slivered almonds

2 ounces pimentos, drained and chopped

1 tablespoon dry sherry

Salt and black pepper to taste

Perloo (or pilaw, or piloo, or pilaf), a rice dish indigenous to the Carolina and Georgia coastal Low Country, is made with everything from tiny river shrimp to mixed seafood to various types of poultry and meats, and never is it more spectacular than when baked in a casserole with full-flavored brown rice substituted for the more traditional long-grain white. This recipe is ideal for leftover chicken (or turkey), but you could just as easily substitute 3 cups coarsely chopped boiled shrimp.

1. In a large saucepan, bring the water and salt to a brisk boil, add the rice, and stir. Cover, reduce the heat to a simmer, and cook till all the water has been absorbed and the rice is tender, 40 to 45 minutes. Fluff the rice with a fork and keep warm.

2. Preheat the oven to 350°F. Grease a 2-quart casserole and set aside.

3. In a large heavy skillet, melt the butter over moderate heat, then add the onion, celery, and mushrooms and stir for 5 minutes. Sprinkle the flour over the top and stir 3 minutes longer. Add the broth and half-and-half and stir steadily till the mixture thickens, about 10 minutes.

4. Scrape the mixture into the prepared casserole, add the rice, chicken, almonds, pimentos, and sherry, season with salt and pepper, stir till well blended, and bake, covered, till bubbly, about 30 minutes.

MAKES 6 SERVINGS

Chicken Divan with Almonds

Chicken Divan, created and served with great flourish in the Divan Parisienne Restaurant at New York's Chatham Hotel in the early twentieth century, remains one of America's most classic and delicious casseroles, a dish as appropriate to an elegant buffet as on the family supper table. In my own lifetime, the casserole was a specialty at the renowned Locke-Ober restaurant in Boston, and it was there I learned to enhance the dish by adding a few slivered almonds.

One 2-pound head broccoli, stems removed

$1/4$ cup ($1/2$ stick) butter

$1/4$ cup all-purpose flour

1 cup chicken broth

1 cup milk

Salt and black pepper to taste

$1/8$ teaspoon ground nutmeg

$1/2$ cup freshly grated Parmesan cheese

3 tablespoons dry sherry

12 slices cooked chicken or turkey

1 cup slivered almonds

$1/2$ cup heavy cream

1. Break the broccoli into florets and place them in a large saucepan with enough water to cover. Bring to a boil, reduce the heat to moderate, cook till just tender, about 10 minutes, and drain.

2. Preheat the oven to 350°F. Butter a shallow 2-quart casserole and set aside.

3. In a medium-size saucepan, melt the butter over moderate heat, then add the flour and stir for 1 minute. Gradually add the broth and milk and stir till thickened. Season with salt and pepper, add the nutmeg, $1/4$ cup of the cheese, and the sherry, stir till the cheese melts, and remove from the heat.

4. Arrange the broccoli in the prepared casserole in a single layer, sprinkle the remaining $1/4$ cup cheese over the top, arrange the chicken slices evenly over the broccoli, and sprinkle the almonds over the top.

5. In a medium-size mixing bowl, beat the heavy cream with an electric mixer till soft peaks form, fold into the cheese sauce, pour evenly over the chicken and almonds, and bake till bubbly and golden brown, about 35 minutes.

MAKES 6 SERVINGS

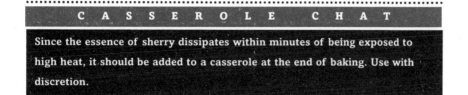

CASSEROLE CHAT

Since the essence of sherry dissipates within minutes of being exposed to high heat, it should be added to a casserole at the end of baking. Use with discretion.

Garden State Chicken and Sausage Bake

Some of the best food in this country is prepared by Italian-Americans in New Jersey, one of whom, a housewife in New Brunswick, served me this sturdy casserole more than once when I was teaching at Rutgers. With it, Gabriella would always put on the table a vinegary salad of leaf lettuce and red onions, a loaf of home-baked Italian bread, and a huge carafe of red wine, and I think she's the one who first taught me to tame the acidity of plum tomatoes in my casseroles with a teaspoon or so of sugar. Remember to prick the sausages all over before browning to release the excess fat.

4 cups peeled and coarsely chopped fresh plum tomatoes

1 teaspoon sugar

2 tablespoons olive oil

One 3-pound chicken, cut into serving pieces

6 hot Italian sausages (about 1 pound), cut in half crosswise and pricked with a fork

1 large onion, chopped

1 medium-size green bell pepper, seeded and chopped

$1/4$ pound fresh mushrooms, sliced

1 garlic clove, minced

1 teaspoon dried oregano, crumbled

$1/2$ cup chicken broth

$1/2$ cup dry white wine

Salt and black pepper to taste

1. In a large heavy saucepan, bring the tomatoes to a low boil and cook till reduced to about 2 cups. Stir in the sugar, and remove from the heat.

2. Preheat the oven to 350°F. Grease a 2- to 2$1/2$-quart casserole.

3. In a large heavy skillet, heat the oil over moderate heat, add the chicken and sausages, and brown on all sides, about 15 minutes. With tongs, transfer the chicken to the prepared casserole, then arrange the sausages over the chicken. Pour off all but about 2 tablespoons of the fat from the skillet, add the onion, bell pepper, mushrooms, and garlic, and stir till softened, about 5 minutes. Spoon the vegetables over the chicken and sausages. Add the tomatoes, oregano, broth, and wine, season with salt and pepper, cover, and bake till the chicken and sausages are very tender, about 1 hour.

MAKES 4 TO 6 SERVINGS

Smothered Chicken with Leeks and Mushrooms

3 tablespoons butter

2 tablespoons vegetable oil

One 3- to 3$^1/_2$-pound chicken, cut into serving pieces

2 medium-size leeks (white part and about 1 inch of the green), washed well and cut into 1-inch-thick rounds

3 tablespoons all-purpose flour

$^1/_2$ pound fresh mushrooms, sliced

$^1/_8$ teaspoon dried thyme, crumbled

Salt and black pepper to taste

1$^1/_2$ cups chicken broth

$^1/_2$ cup half-and-half

1. Preheat the oven to 350°F. Grease a 2-quart casserole and set aside.

2. In a large heavy skillet, heat the butter and oil together over moderate heat until the butter melts, then brown the chicken pieces on all sides and transfer to the prepared casserole.

3. Add the leeks to the skillet, cover, and sweat till softened, about 5 minutes. Sprinkle the flour over the top, stir for 1 minute, add the mushrooms and thyme, season with salt and pepper, and stir for 5 minutes. Add the broth and half-and-half and cook, stirring, till the mixture begins to thicken. Pour the mixture over the chicken, cover, and bake till the chicken is tender, about 1 hour.

MAKES 4 SERVINGS

Baked chicken smothered with all types of vegetables has, for at least a century, been as popular in the Pacific Northwest as in the Deep South, and there's simply no greater American casserole when it's prepared with care. The best smothered chicken I ever ate was made with young leeks and mushrooms by a friend's sister in St. Joseph, Missouri, and when I told her so and asked for the recipe, she said, "Why, that's the most ordinary thing I cook" and looked at me as if I were mad. If you can't find beautiful leeks, use two sliced Spanish onions—or, if they're in season, two or three Vidalias.

C A S S E R O L E   C H A T

When baking shallow-dish casseroles or gratins, spread a large sheet of aluminum foil over the bottom of the oven to catch drips.

Tarragon Chicken, Broccoli, and Black Olive Casserole

Here is a classic American chicken casserole given a new dimension with an appropriate fresh herb, briny black olives, and the substitution of two zesty cheeses for the more traditional cheddar. Leftover turkey works just as well as the chicken, but, in addition to the convenience, and for no clear reason, frozen chopped broccoli provides a better texture than fresh. Don't try to rush this cheese sauce, which should be very smooth, with no lumps.

¹/₄ cup (¹/₂ stick) butter

1 medium-size onion, finely chopped

1 cup sour cream

1 cup milk

1 cup shredded Swiss cheese

¹/₂ cup freshly grated Parmesan cheese

2 tablespoons chopped pimentos

1 tablespoon finely chopped fresh tarragon leaves or ¹/₂ teaspoon dried

Salt and black pepper to taste

¹/₄ pound egg noodles, boiled according to package directions and drained

3 cups cubed cooked chicken

One 10-ounce package frozen chopped broccoli, thawed

1 cup brine-cured black olives, drained, pitted, and cut in half

¹/₂ cup dry bread crumbs

2 tablespoons butter, melted

1. Preheat the oven to 350°F. Grease a 2-quart casserole and set aside.

2. In a large heavy saucepan, melt the butter over moderately low heat, then add the onion and stir for 2 minutes. Add the sour cream, milk, cheeses, pimentos, and tarragon, season with salt and pepper, and stir slowly till the cheeses melt and the sauce is smooth. Remove the pan from the heat.

3. In the prepared casserole, combine the noodles, chicken, broccoli, and olives and pour the cheese sauce over the top. In a small mixing bowl, combine the bread crumbs and melted butter, spoon evenly over the top of the casserole, and bake till slightly crusty, 35 to 40 minutes.

MAKES 6 SERVINGS

Crazy for Casseroles

David's Chicken, Ham, Artichoke, and Pasta Casserole

1/4 cup olive oil

2 medium-size onions, minced

2 large celery ribs, minced

1 garlic clove, minced

1/8 teaspoon ground nutmeg

2 tablespoons all-purpose flour

1/2 cup dry white wine

2 cups milk

1 cup diced cooked ham

4 cups shredded cooked chicken

4 large artichoke hearts (cooked fresh or bottled), quartered

1/2 cup sour cream

1 pound rigatoni, cooked according to package directions and drained

1 cup freshly grated Parmesan cheese

1/2 cup soft bread crumbs

2 tablespoons butter, melted

1. Preheat the oven to 350°F. Grease a 3- to 3½-quart casserole.

2. In a large heavy pot, heat the oil over low heat, add the onions, celery, garlic, and nutmeg, and stir till softened, about 7 minutes. Sprinkle the flour over the top and stir 2 minutes longer. Add the wine, increase the heat to moderate, and cook for 3 minutes. Add the milk and stir till thickened, about 3 minutes. Add the ham, chicken, artichoke hearts, and sour cream and cook for 3 minutes. Add the pasta and cheese and toss till everything is well blended.

3. Transfer to the casserole, sprinkle the crumbs evenly over the top, drizzle the melted butter over the crumbs, and bake till bubbly, about 30 minutes.

MAKES 8 SERVINGS

This up-to-date casserole was inspired by one prepared by David Page at his delightful, soul-warming restaurant in New York's Greenwich Village simply called Home. Although I've modified the casserole somewhat to better suit the home kitchen, the basic spirit of the dish is maintained and illustrates how sophisticated today's American casseroles can be when approached with careful imagination and respect.

Crusted Chicken and Black Beans I

Thanks mainly to James Beard and the celebrated American chef Jeremiah Tower, I became virtually addicted to black beans some twenty years ago and never stop coming up with new excuses to include them in various chicken and turkey casseroles. This particular version was inspired by a dish Jeremiah once served at his restaurant, Stars, in San Francisco. Like myself, feel free to experiment with the ingredients. Of course, Jeremiah would use dried beans that have been soaked overnight, but for casseroles (unlike for authentic black bean soup), I've found that the canned ones work just as well.

3 tablespoons corn oil

One 3-pound chicken, cut into serving pieces

1 large onion, chopped

1 medium-size green bell pepper, seeded and chopped

1 jalapeño, seeded and finely chopped

1 garlic clove, minced

2 teaspoons ground cumin

Salt and black pepper to taste

1 tablespoon fresh lime juice

1 large ripe tomato, peeled and chopped (juices included)

One 15 1/4-ounce can black beans, drained

2 cups chicken broth

1/2 cup soft bread crumbs

1. Preheat the oven to 350°F. Grease a 2 1/2-quart casserole and set aside.

2. In a large heavy skillet, heat the oil over moderate heat, brown the chicken pieces on all sides, and arrange in the prepared casserole.

3. Add the onion, bell pepper, jalapeño, garlic, and cumin to the skillet, season with salt and pepper, and stir till the vegetables are softened, about 5 minutes. Add the lime juice and tomato plus its juices, stir for 5 minutes, and scrape evenly over the chicken. Layer the beans over the top, add the broth, sprinkle the bread crumbs evenly over the top, cover, and bake for 30 minutes.

4. Uncover and bake till the chicken is very tender and the beans are crusty, about 30 minutes.

MAKES 6 SERVINGS

Crusted Chicken and Black Beans II

One 3-pound cooked chicken (boiled or roasted)

1 medium-size ripe tomato, peeled and chopped (juices included)

One 15 1/4-ounce can black beans, drained

1 1/2 cups bottled salsa

6 ounces Monterey Jack cheese, shredded

1 tablespoon chopped fresh cilantro leaves

1/2 teaspoon ground cumin

Salt and black pepper to taste

Four 8-inch flour tortillas, cut into quarters

2 tablespoons corn oil

1. Preheat the oven to 350°F. Grease a 2 1/2-quart casserole and set aside.

2. Remove and discard the skin and bones from the chicken, shred the meat, and place in a large mixing bowl. Add the tomato, beans, salsa, about three-quarters of the cheese, the cilantro, and cumin, season with salt and pepper, stir till well blended, and scrape into the prepared casserole. Arrange the tortilla quarters overlapping each other over the top, sprinkle with the oil, cover, and bake for 30 minutes.

3. Uncover, sprinkle the remaining cheese evenly over the top, and bake till the top is golden and crusty, 10 to 15 minutes.

MAKES 6 SERVINGS

I came up with this recipe one day when I was boiling a big old hen for chicken soup and had plenty of meat left over, but if you don't care to fool with that, the casserole can easily be made with a nicely roasted chicken picked up in a deli or super-market. This preparation is alto-gether different from my other chicken and black bean casse-role, not only in that the chicken is shredded and the texture somewhat drier, but also the top is much crustier—almost crunchy—from the tortillas. The casserole has a very Tex-Mex flavor, but remember to go easy on the cilantro and cumin, since too much of either can over-whelm the dish.

Chicken, Squash, and Blood Orange Casserole

I was eating luscious, ruby-fleshed, honey-sweet blood oranges in Spain and Italy decades ago, but only now is this juicy, inimitable fruit native to Middle Eastern countries and the Mediterranean starting to show up in our markets in any quantity. Combine the oranges with relatively bland poultry and vegetables, garlic, brown sugar, one or two herbs, and wine in a casserole such as this and you have a distinctive dish bursting with all sorts of intriguing flavors. Regular oranges, of course, could be used, but once you've tasted a blood orange, you're spoiled for life. Just make sure they're not too soft, and if your greengrocer doesn't carry them, tell him to get on the ball.

2 tablespoons vegetable oil

4 medium-size chicken legs (about 2^1/$_2$ pounds), thighs and drumsticks separated

1 medium-size butternut squash (about 1^1/$_2$ pounds), peeled, seeded, and cut into 1^1/$_2$-inch chunks

2 garlic cloves, minced

^{1}/$_2$ teaspoon dried rosemary, crumbled

Salt and black pepper to taste

2 blood oranges, peeled, white pith removed, sectioned, and juices retained

1 cup dry white wine

3 tablespoons firmly packed light brown sugar

1. Preheat the oven to 350°F. Grease a 2^1/$_2$-quart casserole and set aside.

2. In a large heavy skillet, heat the oil over moderate heat, brown the chicken pieces on all sides, and arrange in the prepared casserole.

3. Add the squash, garlic, and rosemary to the skillet, season with salt and pepper, stir about 5 minutes, then layer over the chicken. Arrange the orange sections over the top, add the wine, sprinkle the top evenly with the brown sugar, cover, and bake till the chicken is tender, about 1 hour.

MAKES 4 TO 6 SERVINGS

Nevada Basque Chicken

1 cup all-purpose flour

Salt and black pepper to taste

One 3- to 3^1/$_2$-pound chicken, cut into serving pieces

^{1}/$_4$ cup olive oil

1 medium-size onion, diced

1 medium-size green bell pepper, seeded and diced

4 medium-size ripe tomatoes, diced

^{1}/$_4$ pound smoked ham, diced

^{1}/$_2$ cup dry white wine

1. Preheat the oven to 350°F. Grease a 2- to 2^1/$_2$-quart casserole and set aside.

2. On a plate, combine the flour and salt and pepper and dredge the chicken pieces in the mixture, tapping off any excess. In a large heavy skillet, heat the oil over moderate heat, brown the chicken pieces on all sides, and arrange in the prepared casserole.

3. Add the onion, bell pepper, tomatoes, and ham to the skillet and cook, stirring, till the vegetables soften, about 10 minutes. Add the wine and continue to cook about 5 minutes. Scrape the mixture over the chicken, cover, and bake till the chicken is very tender, about 1 hour.

MAKES 4 TO 6 SERVINGS

Basque shepherds from the French and Spanish Pyrenees originally emigrated to Idaho and Nevada in the early twentieth century since they found the high pastures ideal for sheep grazing. If my one visit to the relatively barren region is any indication, not much has changed gastronomically in the past hundred years, meaning that the level of cooking sophistication is pretty much limited to lusty stews, simple casseroles, roasted meats, and good country bread found in small Basque hotels and boarding houses—along with plenty of sturdy red wine on the table. At Louis' Basque Corner in Reno, I did taste my first pygmy rabbit, but what I remember most was an utterly unpretentious chicken and ham casserole that couldn't have been more comforting and transported me back to a little Spanish restaurant I once knew in San Sebastián.

Chicken Succotash Pot

Over the years, I've prepared succotash in every guise imaginable, but perhaps the most unorthodox variation is this casserole inspired by watching a friend's mother in Kentucky bake leftover turkey drumsticks with corn, limas, and what remained of the dry packaged stuffing she'd used to make dressing for a huge roasted turkey.

In a pot of traditional chicken succotash, I'd normally shred the fowl and try to use fresh corn and limas, but when I want to stretch a chicken to feed six guests, I've found this casserole to be a perfect solution. If you want to add a bit of zest, shake a few drops of Tabasco in the stuffing-and-vegetable mixture.

3 strips lean bacon, diced

One 3-pound chicken, cut into serving pieces

6 cups packaged herb-seasoned poultry stuffing

2 medium-size onions, finely chopped

1 cup fresh or thawed frozen corn kernels

1 cup fresh or thawed frozen baby lima beans

Salt and black pepper to taste

$1/4$ cup ($1/2$ stick) butter, melted

$1^1/2$ cups chicken broth

1. Preheat the oven to 350°F. Grease a shallow $2^1/2$- to 3-quart casserole and set aside.

2. In a large heavy skillet, fry the bacon over moderate heat till cooked but not crisp and drain on paper towels. Brown the chicken pieces on all sides in the fat and transfer to a plate.

3. In a large mixing bowl, combine the stuffing, onions, corn, limas, and melted butter, season with salt and pepper, and toss till the mixture is well blended and moist.

4. Arrange half the chicken pieces in the prepared casserole, then layer half the stuffing mixture over the top. Repeat with the remaining chicken and stuffing mixture, pour over the broth, arrange the bacon pieces evenly on top, cover, and bake till the chicken is tender and top slightly browned.

MAKES 6 SERVINGS

CASSEROLE CHAT

When cutting kernels from fresh ears of corn, first cut the cobs in half to prevent flying kernels.

Chicken and Kohlrabi Soufflé

2 small kohlrabi bulbs, peeled and diced

2 medium-size red potatoes, peeled and diced

3 tablespoons butter

1 medium-size boneless, skinless whole chicken breast,
cut into 1-inch pieces

2 scallions (white part only), minced

1 tablespoon minced fresh parsley leaves

$1/2$ teaspoon dried summer savory, crumbled

$1/2$ teaspoon Worcestershire sauce

Salt and black pepper to taste

6 large eggs, beaten

2 tablespoons all-purpose flour

$1/2$ cup freshly grated Parmesan cheese

1. In a medium-size saucepan, combine the kohlrabi and potatoes and add enough water to cover. Bring to a boil, reduce the heat to low, cover, and cook till the vegetables are almost tender, about 10 minutes. Drain.

2. Preheat the oven to 350°F. Butter a $1^1/2$- to 2-quart casserole.

3. In a medium-size heavy skillet, melt the butter over moderate heat, then add the chicken, scallions, parsley, and summer savory and stir till the chicken is no longer pink, about 7 minutes. Transfer the mixture to a large mixing bowl, add the kohlrabi, potatoes, and Worcestershire, season with salt and pepper, and stir till well blended.

4. In a mixing bowl, whisk together the eggs and flour, add to the chicken mixture, stir till well blended, then scrape the mixture into the prepared casserole. Sprinkle the cheese evenly over the top and bake till golden and puffy, about 30 minutes.

MAKES 6 SERVINGS

Of all the "new" vegetables to appear frequently in supermarkets during the past few years, none is still more neglected than the rather delicate, nutty-flavored member of the cabbage family called kohlrabi. Although exotic purple kohlrabi can be found occasionally, most of the bulbs look like pale green turnips and are about three inches in diameter with crisp green leaves. Cleaned of all leaves and stems, washed, peeled, and thinly sliced, raw kohlrabi is delicious in salads, but combine it with other ingredients in a soufflé casserole such as this and you have a dish that's truly special.

Sherried Chicken Livers, Spinach, and Rice

It was a dirty stunt, I admit, since I'd heard a friend proclaim on numerous occasions how she hated any form of liver. But I had to produce a last-minute meal when four of us returned to the house after being told we'd have to wait an hour for a table in a restaurant. I knew I had about half a pound of beautiful chicken livers in the fridge intended for a pâté, and, quite frankly, I was determined to prove that anybody can learn to appreciate mild liver if it's prepared (i.e., camouflaged) carefully. When time came to serve, I simply announced that I'd thrown together a meat, spinach, and rice casserole, then watched as Ann cleaned her plate. One major trick, of course, was the sherry.

2 tablespoons butter

1/2 pound chicken livers, trimmed of fat and membranes and cut into quarters

1 1/4 cups raw long-grain rice, cooked according to package directions

One 10-ounce package frozen chopped spinach, thawed and squeezed dry

1 cup chicken broth

2 tablespoons dry sherry

Salt and black pepper to taste

1/2 cup shredded sharp cheddar cheese

1/2 cup finely chopped pecans

1. Preheat the oven to 350°F. Butter a 1 1/2-quart casserole and set aside.

2. In a small skillet, melt the butter over moderate heat, then add the chicken livers, stir till slightly browned but still pink inside, 3 to 4 minutes, and transfer to a large mixing bowl. Add the cooked rice, spinach, broth, and sherry, season with salt and pepper, stir till well blended, and scrape into the prepared casserole.

3. In a small mixing bowl, combine the cheese and pecans, stir well, sprinkle the mixture evenly over the casserole, and bake till golden, about 25 minutes.

MAKES 4 TO 6 SERVINGS

Layered Chicken Liver and Vidalia Onion Surprise

1/4 cup (1/2 stick) butter

1/4 cup vegetable oil

3 to 4 Vidalia onions (about 3 pounds), thinly sliced

1 garlic clove, minced

4 anchovy fillets, drained and minced

1/4 cup red wine vinegar

2 teaspoons sugar

1 pound chicken livers, trimmed of fat and membranes and cut in half

1 teaspoon chopped fresh thyme leaves

Salt and black pepper to taste

1 cup chicken broth

1. In a large heavy skillet, heat 2 tablespoons each of the butter and oil together over low heat till the butter melts. Add the onions, garlic, and anchovies, stir well, cover, and cook till the onions soften, about 15 minutes.

2. In a small mixing bowl, combine the vinegar and sugar and stir till the sugar dissolves. Pour over the onions, cover, continue to cook till the onions are very soft and golden, 20 to 30 minutes, and transfer to a plate.

3. Preheat the oven to 325°F. Grease a 1 1/2-quart casserole and set aside.

4. In a medium-size skillet, heat the remaining 2 tablespoons butter and oil together over moderate heat until the butter melts, then add the livers and thyme, cook till the livers are slightly browned but still pink inside, about 5 minutes, and transfer to a plate.

5. Layer half the livers in the prepared casserole, layer half the onions over the livers, and season with salt and pepper. Layer the remaining livers and onions, pour the broth over the top, and bake till the top is golden brown, 20 to 25 minutes.

MAKES 4 SERVINGS

The secret to this delectable casserole is the anchovies, which virtually disappear while the onions are slowly sweated almost to the point of caramelization. Even though the Vidalias are sweeter than regular onions, the sugar is still needed to give them the right texture. And don't worry: the casserole will not be too sweet.

Turkey Tetrazzini

This Tetrazzini (see the other on page 106), made with egg yolks, half-and-half, and no chicken broth, is much richer than my standard chicken and ham version and is always a big hit on formal buffets. If you want a little more textural contrast, you might also add ¹/₂ cup or more of slivered toasted almonds to the spaghetti mixture before transferring it to the casserole.

¹/₄ cup olive oil

1 small onion, finely chopped

1 small green bell pepper, seeded and finely chopped

¹/₂ pound fresh mushrooms, sliced

2 tablespoons all-purpose flour

Salt and black pepper to taste

2¹/₂ cups half-and-half

3 cups diced cooked turkey

3 tablespoons dry sherry

2 large egg yolks, beaten

8 ounces thin spaghetti, cooked according to package directions and drained

¹/₂ cup freshly grated Parmesan cheese

Sweet paprika to taste

1. Preheat the oven to 350°F. Butter a 2¹/₂-quart casserole and set aside.

2. In a large heavy skillet, heat the oil over moderate heat, add the onion, bell pepper, and mushrooms and stir till the vegetables soften, about 5 minutes. Sprinkle the flour over the top, season with salt and pepper, and stir for about 1 minute. Add the half-and-half and stir till the mixture thickens, about 5 minutes. Add the turkey and sherry, stir for about 1 minute, transfer the mixture to a large mixing bowl, and let stand a few minutes.

3. Add the egg yolks to the bowl and stir till well blended. Add the spaghetti, toss till well blended, transfer to the prepared casserole, and smooth the top with a spoon. Sprinkle the cheese and paprika evenly over the top and bake till nicely browned, 20 to 30 minutes.

MAKES 6 TO 8 SERVINGS

Crazy for Casseroles

Emma's Turkey Drumstick and Cabbage Surprise

1 small head cabbage, cored and cut into chunks

1 large onion, chopped

2 carrots, scraped and chopped

$1/2$ pound fresh mushrooms, sliced

1 teaspoon dried tarragon, crumbled

Pinch of red pepper flakes

Salt and black pepper to taste

2 cups chicken broth

4 medium-size turkey drumsticks

3 garlic cloves, thinly sliced

2 tablespoons vegetable oil

1. In a large pot, combine the cabbage, onion, carrots, mushrooms, tarragon, and red pepper flakes, season with salt and black pepper, and toss. Add the broth, bring to a boil, reduce the heat to low, cover, and simmer for 30 minutes.

2. Preheat the oven to 350°F. Grease a 2-quart casserole and set aside.

3. Carefully pull the skin of each turkey drumstick back to the end of the leg, make 3 or 4 slits in each drumstick, stuff each slit with a garlic slice, and carefully pull the skin back up. In a large heavy skillet, heat the oil over moderate heat, brown the drumsticks on all sides, and transfer to a plate.

4. To assemble the casserole, arrange two of the drumsticks on the bottom of the prepared casserole and spoon half the boiled vegetables evenly over the top. Repeat with the remaining two drumsticks and vegetables, pour the cooking broth from the pot over the top, cover, and bake till the drumsticks are very tender, $1^1/2$ to $1^3/4$ hours.

MAKES 4 SERVINGS

Emma was the housekeeper for a family I knew well while living in Missouri, and I don't think I ever met a more natural cook who was as adept at putting together an elegant venison terrine as making Brunswick stew. I hounded Emma for lots of recipes, but none of her dishes impressed me more than this earthy casserole she once made in enough quantity to feed a dozen guests. And what was the big "surprise"? I asked her. "Why, honey, it's the garlic I stuff in each turkey leg, that's what. Bet you couldn't even tell it was there, but that's the big secret." When I find medium-size turkey drumsticks on sale, I always buy and freeze a few, never forgetting dear Emma's conviction that big legs tend to be tough and stringy.

Green Mountain Turkey and Smoked Ham Pot

Turkey, smoked ham, aged cheddar cheese, and apple brandy—what combination could better represent the wonderful provender we associate with the state of Vermont, where I once spent an entire glorious summer. Due, of course, to draconian interstate regulations enacted years ago, it's a myth that most "Vermont turkeys" touted in out-of-state markets and restaurants are the superlative birds that were once shipped throughout the country. Virtually all of the few thousand plump, succulent, authentic gobblers still produced there are being consumed strictly on home territory. If you can find genuine Vermont smoked ham and a superior Vermont cheddar (like Cabot) for this casserole, so much the better. If you have plenty of whole ham left over and want still another special treat, bake and serve it with a luscious raisin sauce the way Vermonters have been doing since colonial days.

1/4 cup (1/2 stick) butter

1 medium-size onion, minced

1 large celery rib, minced

1/4 cup all-purpose flour

2 cups milk

One 10 3/4-ounce can Campbell's condensed cream of celery soup

2 cups cubed cooked turkey

1 cup cubed smoked ham

2 tablespoons minced pimentos

2 tablespoons apple brandy or cider

Salt and black pepper to taste

1/2 cup shredded Vermont cheddar cheese

1. Preheat the oven to 350°F. Butter a 2-quart casserole and set aside.

2. In a large heavy saucepan, melt the butter over moderate heat, then add the onion and celery and stir for 1 minute. Sprinkle the flour over the top and stir 2 minutes longer. Add the milk and stir constantly till slightly thickened. Add the soup, turkey, ham, pimentos, and brandy, season with salt and pepper, and stir till well blended. Scrape the mixture into the prepared casserole, sprinkle the cheese evenly over the top, and bake till bubbly and golden brown, about 30 minutes.

MAKES 6 SERVINGS

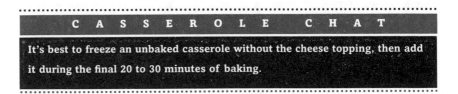

CASSEROLE CHAT

It's best to freeze an unbaked casserole without the cheese topping, then add it during the final 20 to 30 minutes of baking.

Crazy for Casseroles

After-Holiday Turkey and Rice Supper

2 tablespoons butter

$^1/_2$ pound fresh mushrooms, sliced

2 cups diced cooked turkey

Salt and black pepper to taste

1 cup raw long-grain rice, cooked according to package directions

12 pimento-stuffed green olives, sliced

$1^1/_2$ cups Cream Sauce (page 6)

$^1/_2$ cup soft bread crumbs

2 tablespoons butter, melted

$^1/_2$ cup almonds, toasted (page 340) and chopped

1. Preheat the oven to 350°F. Butter a 2-quart casserole and set aside.

2. In a small skillet, melt the butter over moderate heat, then add the mushrooms, stir for 5 minutes, and transfer to a medium-size mixing bowl. Add the turkey, season with salt and pepper, toss, and set aside.

3. In another medium-size mixing bowl, combine the cooked rice and pimentos, toss well, then spoon half the mixture into the prepared casserole. Add half the turkey mixture, cover with the remaining rice mixture, top with the remaining turkey mixture, and pour the cream sauce evenly over the top.

4. In a small mixing bowl, combine the bread crumbs, melted butter, and almonds, toss till well blended, sprinkle the mixture evenly over top of the casserole, and bake till golden brown, about 30 minutes.

MAKES 6 SERVINGS

I'm forever searching for novel ways to utilize leftover Thanksgiving and Christmas turkey, and there remains no better source than my vast library of quaint but often highly inspired regional cookbooks printed by churches and charity leagues. Some of these hail back to the 1940s and '50s, others are more modern, but whatever the vintage, I can always be assured of finding plenty of good, practical casserole recipes like this one from an Arkansas housewife who seemed to make an art of extending leftovers.

Turkey Dressing Bake

Going back decades to the days when home cooks at large church social functions, country clubs, and even sports events came up with all sorts of novel ways to utilize leftovers impressively, this casserole is unusual in that the dressing is baked just till custardy, cut into squares, and served with a clever pimento sauce. Obviously, it's an ideal holiday casserole for either the dinner or buffet table, but, unless you want an altogether different (and disappointing) texture, don't try to use leftover stuffing—as I once did with embarrassing results. And here's still another time when there simply is no successful substitute for canned soup.

1¼ cups packaged herb-seasoned poultry stuffing

1 small onion, finely chopped

1 celery rib, finely chopped

¼ teaspoon poultry seasoning

2 cups diced cooked turkey

¼ cup (½ stick) butter

¼ cup all-purpose flour

¼ teaspoon salt

¼ teaspoon black pepper

2 cups chicken broth

3 large eggs

Half of a 10¾-ounce can Campbell's condensed cream of mushroom soup

¼ cup milk

½ cup sour cream

¼ cup chopped pimentos

1. In a medium-size mixing bowl, combine the bread stuffing, onion, celery, and poultry seasoning, then sprinkle over the bottom of a buttered 2-quart casserole. Distribute the turkey evenly over the top.

2. Preheat the oven to 325°F.

3. In a medium-size heavy saucepan, melt the butter over moderate heat, then add the flour, salt, and pepper and stir for 1 minute. Add the broth, stir till thickened, and remove from the heat.

4. In a small mixing bowl, beat the eggs, add a small amount of the hot broth, stirring constantly, then add the mixture to the broth, stirring constantly till well blended and smooth. Pour the sauce over the turkey and dressing and bake till custardy, about 45 minutes.

5. Meanwhile, in a medium-size saucepan, combine the soup, milk, sour cream, and pimentos and stir over moderate heat till well blended and hot.

6. To serve, cut the turkey dressing into squares and top each portion with the pimento sauce.

MAKES 6 SERVINGS

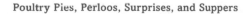

Turkey, Broccoli, and Noodle Buffet Casserole

After all the festive hoopla of Thanksgiving or Christmas dinner is over, you've invited a few friends over for a low-key buffet supper, and the last thing you need is more major shopping and cooking. There's no better solution than this simple casserole utilizing leftover turkey (or chicken) and a few staples that should always be in the cabinet or fridge. What does add distinctive flavor to the dish are the smoked almonds.

$^1/_4$ cup ($^1/_8$ stick) butter

$^1/_4$ cup all-purpose flour

$^1/_2$ teaspoon Dijon mustard

Salt and black pepper to taste

$3^1/_2$ cups milk

$^1/_2$ pound sharp cheddar cheese, shredded

8 ounces medium-wide egg noodles, cooked according to package directions and drained

4 cups diced cooked turkey

One 10-ounce package frozen broccoli florets, cooked according to package directions and drained

$^1/_2$ cup coarsely chopped smoked almonds

1. Preheat the oven to 350°F. Butter a 2-quart casserole and set aside.

2. In a medium-size, heavy saucepan, melt the butter over moderate heat, then add the flour, mustard, and salt and pepper to taste and stir for 2 minutes. Gradually add the milk, stir constantly till thickened, and remove from the heat. Add the cheese, stir till it melts, and set the sauce aside.

3. Arrange the cooked noodles in the prepared casserole, layer the turkey over the top, then layer the broccoli over the turkey. Pour the sauce evenly over all, sprinkle the almonds over the top, and bake till bubbly, about 30 minutes.

MAKES 6 TO 8 SERVINGS

Duck and Green Olive Supper

One 4- to 4$^1/_2$-pound duckling

Salt and black pepper to taste

$^1/_4$ pound sliced lean bacon, diced

2 small onions, sliced

$^1/_4$ teaspoon dried thyme, crumbled

$^1/_4$ teaspoon dried marjoram, crumbled

1 bay leaf, finely crushed

1$^1/_2$ tablespoon all-purpose flour

1$^1/_2$ cups beef broth or bouillon

$^1/_2$ cup dry red wine

12 large pitted green olives

1. Preheat the oven to 325°F. Grease a 2-quart casserole and set aside.

2. Season the duckling inside and out with salt and pepper, prick the skin well, place on a rack in a large roasting pan, and roast for 45 minutes.

3. Meanwhile, in a large, deep skillet, fry the bacon till almost crisp, remove it with a slotted spoon, and scatter in the casserole. Pour off all but about 2 tablespoons of the fat. Add the onions, thyme, marjoram, and bay leaf, season with salt and pepper, stir well, and cook for 5 minutes over moderate heat, stirring. Sprinkle over the flour, stir, and cook 3 minutes longer, stirring. Gradually add the broth and wine and bring to a boil. Reduce the heat to moderate, cook till the liquid is slightly reduced, about 10 minutes, and remove from the heat.

4. Disjoint the duckling into serving pieces and arrange the pieces over the bacon in the casserole. Scatter the olives evenly over and around the duckling, pour the contents of the skillet over the top, cover, and bake till the duck is tender and the sauce nicely thickened, 20 to 30 minutes.

MAKES 4 SERVINGS

Duck and green olives are one of the great culinary marriages, and never do I love the combination more than in this slightly smoky, herby casserole that is really best if allowed to sit a few hours after baking, then reheated. And if you really like olives as much as I do, don't be shy about adding a few more. Most ducklings today (fresh or frozen) average between 4 and 4$^1/_2$ pounds, but if you can find a hefty 5- to 5$^1/_2$-pounder, you'll have more than enough meat for four persons.

Duck, Tangerine, and Mushroom Supreme

I love duck, the only problem being what to do with the leftovers when I've roasted two 4-pound ducklings necessary to feed four people and appetites are timid. The most logical answer, of course, is a delectable salad or casserole, and one of the most successful of the latter is this layered combination of duck, tangerines, onion, and mushrooms enriched with tangy red currant jelly and a bit of lemon peel. Use this recipe also for any leftover roasted goose.

3 tangerines, peeled, white pith removed, sectioned, and seeded

1 cup orange juice

$1/2$ cup red currant jelly, melted

$1/4$ cup ($1/2$ stick) butter

1 small onion, minced

$1/2$ pound fresh mushrooms, thinly sliced

$2^1/2$ to 3 cups diced cooked duck

$1/8$ teaspoon dried basil, crumbled

$1/8$ teaspoon ground nutmeg

Pinch of ground ginger

2 tablespoons finely chopped fresh parsley leaves

Salt and black pepper to taste

$1/2$ cup soft bread crumbs

1 teaspoon grated lemon peel

1. Place the tangerine sections in a shallow baking dish. In a small mixing bowl, combine the orange juice and melted jelly, stir till well blended, pour over the tangerines, and let marinate for 30 minutes.

2. Meanwhile, melt 2 tablespoons of the butter in a small skillet over moderate heat, then add the onion and mushrooms, stir till softened, about 5 minutes, and remove from the heat.

3. Preheat the oven to 350°F. Butter a $1^1/2$-quart casserole and set aside.

4. In a medium-size mixing bowl, combine the duck, basil, nutmeg, ginger, and parsley, season with salt and pepper, toss well, and transfer half the mixture to the prepared casserole. Arrange the tangerines over the duck, cover with the onion and mushrooms, spoon the remaining duck mixture over the top, and spoon half of the marinade over the duck.

5. In a small mixing bowl, combine the bread crumbs and lemon peel and sprinkle evenly over the top of the casserole. Cut the remaining 2 tablespoons butter into small pieces, dot the top of the casserole with them, and bake till lightly browned, 25 to 30 minutes.

MAKES 4 TO 6 SERVINGS

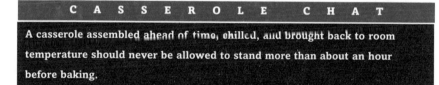

C A S S E R O L E   C H A T

A casserole assembled ahead of time, chilled, and brought back to room temperature should never be allowed to stand more than about an hour before baking.

Long Island Duck and Black Bean Casserole

The first white Peking ducks were brought to Connecticut and Long Island on clipper ships in the late nineteenth century, and today half the ducklings sold in the U.S. are produced on Long Island. Since I have a home at the eastern end of the Island, I have no problem procuring fresh ducks anytime I want them, but it's only been in recent years with the arrival of immigrants from South and Central America that I've been exposed to any number of new ways of preparing one of my favorite birds. Long Island ducklings do tend to be fatty, so, whether you're using fresh or frozen birds, do remove at least part of the fat before browning the pieces. When preparing this particular casserole, I also might add a little dry mustard and finely chopped fresh rosemary (but not too much) to the dredging mixture.

Two 4-pound ducks

$1/4$ cup all-purpose flour

Salt and black pepper to taste

$1/8$ teaspoon cayenne pepper

2 tablespoons butter

2 ounces salt pork, rind discarded and diced

2 medium-size onions, finely chopped

2 garlic cloves, minced

Two 15-ounce cans black beans

1. Cut the ducks into serving pieces and remove and discard as much fat as possible. Preheat the oven to 350°F. Grease a 3-quart casserole and set aside.

2. On a plate, combine the flour, salt and black pepper, and cayenne and dredge the duck pieces in the mixture, tapping off any excess.

3. In a large heavy skillet, heat the butter and salt pork over moderate heat till the pork renders most of its fat, then add the onions and garlic and stir till softened, about 5 minutes. Transfer the pork cracklings and onions to the prepared casserole.

4. In batches, brown the duck pieces on all sides in the rendered fat, then arrange them in the casserole. Add the beans plus their liquid, season with salt and pepper, cover, and bake till the duck and beans are very tender, about 2 hours.

MAKES 6 SERVINGS

3 tablespoons vegetable oil

One 4- to 5-pound duckling, excess fat removed and cut into serving pieces

2 celery ribs (leaves included), chopped

$1/2$ teaspoon dried thyme, crumbled

1 bay leaf

$1/2$ teaspoon black peppercorns

Salt to taste

1 cup chicken broth

$1/2$ cup apple cider

3 cups peeled and diced rutabaga

12 small white onions, peeled

$1/2$ teaspoon sugar

1. Preheat the oven to 350°F. Grease a 3- to 3½-quart casserole and set aside.

2. In a large heavy skillet, heat the oil over moderate heat, brown the duckling pieces on all sides, transfer to the prepared casserole, and pour off all but about 1 tablespoon of the fat from the skillet. Add the celery, thyme, bay leaf, peppercorns, salt, broth, and cider to the casserole, cover, and bake for 1 hour.

3. Meanwhile, combine the rutabaga and onions in the skillet, sprinkle the sugar over the top, brown lightly over moderate heat, and remove from the heat.

4. After the duckling has baked for 1 hour, layer the rutabaga and onion over the top, baste with a little of the juice in the casserole, cover, and continue to bake till the duck and rutabaga are tender, about 30 minutes.

MAKES 6 SERVINGS

Pearl Byrd Foster, who hailed from Virginia but eventually ran one of New York City's most famous restaurants in the 1960s and '70s, was the one who originally taught me many glorious ways of cooking with rutabagas. "They're hard as nails, and you almost need a hacksaw to peel them," she would rant, "but no vegetable makes better stews and casseroles." Although earthy 2- to 3-pound rutabagas are now usually available year round, the best (like their first cousin, the yellow turnip) are harvested in the fall and add tremendous depth to any duck or goose dish. To preserve their freshness as much as possible, rutabagas are almost always dipped in melted paraffin, but even so, I like to neutralize their slight bitterness by adding a little sugar. If you can't find good rutabagas, firm yellow turnips can be substituted.

Holiday Goose, Sausage, and Chestnut Royale

This is a truly regal casserole worthy of the most festive holiday occasion. Although chestnuts have not been harvested in America for close to a century because of a blight that infected the trees in 1904, almost 20 million pounds of succulent European varieties are imported each year. Frozen chestnuts, stocked widely in supermarkets but not shelled and peeled, are of identical quality to fresh, much less perishable, and can be stored almost indefinitely without risk of rotting or drying up. To prepare them for cooking, cut a deep X on the flat side of the nuts with a sharp paring knife, toss them into boiling water for about 10 minutes, then remove both the shells and inner skins. If, on the other hand, you have a low degree of patience, some specialty food shops now stock shelled, peeled, and expensive frozen European chestnuts.

One 8- to 9-pound goose

4 strips lean bacon, diced

3 medium-size onions, sliced

3 medium-size carrots, scraped and cut into thin rounds

2 garlic cloves, minced

1 cup dry red wine

2 cups chicken broth

1 cup tomato sauce

$1/2$ teaspoon dried thyme, crumbled

$1/8$ teaspoon ground fennel seeds

1 bay leaf

Salt and black pepper to taste

30 chestnuts, shelled and peeled (see headnote)

6 sweet Italian sausages

1. Trim as much fat as possible from the goose and discard. Cut the goose into 8 to 10 serving pieces and pat dry with paper towels.

2. In a 3- to 3½-quart cast-iron or enameled iron casserole, render the bacon over moderate heat, then add the goose pieces and brown on all sides. Add the onions, carrots, and garlic and stir till softened, about 5 minutes. Add the wine, increase the heat to high, and boil till the wine is almost a glaze. Add the broth, tomato sauce, thyme, fennel, and bay leaf, season with salt and pepper, stir, reduce the heat to low, cover, and simmer for 1 hour.

3. Meanwhile, place the chestnuts in a saucepan with enough water to cover, bring to a low boil, cook for 30 minutes, drain, and set aside.

4. Arrange the sausages in a medium-size skillet and prick all over with a fork. Add enough water to come halfway up the sides, bring to a low

boil, cook for 10 minutes, and drain. Cut the sausages into small rounds and set aside.

5. Preheat the oven to 350°F.

6. Skim any fat from the liquid in the casserole, layer the chestnuts, then the sausages over the goose and vegetables, cover, and bake till the goose is very tender, about 1 hour, basting the chestnuts and sausages from time to time and adding a little more broth if necessary.

MAKES 6 TO 8 SERVINGS

Creole Squab, Mushroom, and Lima Bean Bake

In New Orleans and the Louisiana bayou country, some cooks use squabs almost the way others use ordinary chicken, and the flavor difference is pronounced in any number of dishes. Squabs, which are young pigeons, weigh about a pound, have darkish, full-flavored meat, and, like Rock Cornish hens, are utterly succulent when braised or slowly baked. Squabs are now available fresh or frozen and completely dressed in finer markets all over the country.

3 tablespoons butter

2 tablespoons vegetable oil

4 dressed squabs (³/₄ to 1 pound each)

1 large onion, finely chopped

2 celery ribs, finely chopped

2 carrots, scraped and finely chopped

3 tablespoons all-purpose flour

2 cups chicken broth

¹/₂ cup dry red wine

¹/₂ pound fresh mushrooms, sliced

1 cup fresh or frozen lima beans

¹/₂ teaspoon cayenne pepper

Salt and black pepper to taste

1. Preheat the oven to 350°F. Grease a 2¹/₂- to 3-quart casserole and set aside.

2. In a large heavy skillet, heat the butter and oil together over moderate heat till the butter melts, then brown the squabs on all sides and transfer to a plate. Add the onion, celery, and carrots to the skillet and stir till softened, about 7 minutes. Sprinkle the flour over the top and stir 1 minute longer. Increase the heat to high and gradually add the broth and wine, stirring constantly till the sauce thickens slightly. Add the mushrooms, limas, and cayenne, season with salt and black pepper, stir, and remove from the heat.

3. Arrange the squabs breast side up in the prepared casserole, pour on any juices that might have accumulated around them, pour the vegetable sauce evenly over the top, cover, and bake till the squabs are tender, about 45 minutes.

MAKES 4 SERVINGS

Crazy for Casseroles

Colonial Pheasant and Leek Casserole

Two 2-pound pheasants, dressed and each cut into 6 serving pieces

1 cup all-purpose flour

$^1/_4$ cup ($^1/_2$ stick) butter

2 medium-size leeks (white part only), washed well and cut crosswise into 2-inch lengths

2 carrots, scraped and cut into 2-inch lengths

1 garlic clove, minced

$^1/_2$ pound fresh mushrooms, quartered

$^1/_2$ teaspoon dried rosemary, crumbled

Salt and black pepper to taste

1 cup chicken broth

$^1/_2$ cup dry red wine

2 tablespoons gin

$^1/_2$ cup heavy cream

1. Preheat the oven to 325°F. Butter a 3-quart casserole and set aside.

2. Dredge the pheasant pieces in the flour, tapping off any excess. In a large heavy skillet, melt the butter over moderate heat, then brown the pheasant pieces on all sides and arrange in the prepared casserole. Add the leeks, carrots, garlic, mushrooms, and rosemary to the skillet, season with salt and pepper, and stir till softened, about 8 minutes. Add the broth, wine, gin, and heavy cream, stir till slightly reduced, about 5 minutes, pour over the pheasant, cover, and bake till the pheasant is very tender, about 1$^1/_4$ hours.

MAKES 6 SERVINGS

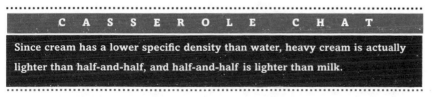

C A S S E R O L E   C H A T

Since cream has a lower specific density than water, heavy cream is actually lighter than half-and-half, and half-and-half is lighter than milk.

Who knows when the ring-necked pheasant was introduced in the U.S.? Some say that a consul in Shanghai brought the first specimens to Oregon in the late nineteenth century, but, then, how does that explain that George Washington and Thomas Jefferson had the birds on their Virginia estates almost a century earlier? No matter; today pheasants are found in at least 30 states, which makes it baffling that you don't find the fowl in more restaurants and home kitchens given their distinctive savor. Since the lean meat of pheasant can be dry unless carefully basted while roasting, I love to bake it slowly in a casserole with all sorts of vegetables. While fresh 2- to 4-pound pheasants are sometimes available in butcher shops, the frozen ones are much more plentiful and completely acceptable. If, however, you can't find pheasants, this can be made with six large chicken legs (about 4$^1/_2$ pounds) with the skin removed. I like to believe that Mr. Jefferson's cook must have prepared pheasant like this on a regular basis.

Minnesota Quail with Wild Rice and Raisins

Much as I love quail, the lean, white-meated birds can be dry and sometimes tough unless they're braised or baked in sufficient liquid to keep them moist, as in this unusual casserole that an old friend from southern Minnesota likes to prepare. Raised mainly today on game farms in the Upper Midwest, New Jersey, and the South, quail are by far our most plentiful game birds, which forever makes me wonder why they're not served in more restaurants. Weighing about eight to ten ounces, the small birds can be found fresh in better markets, but, frankly, I can tell very little difference between the fresh and frozen.

1 cup raw wild rice, rinsed in a sieve

2 cups water

$^1/_2$ cup orange juice

$^1/_2$ cup seedless golden raisins

$^1/_2$ cup all-purpose flour

1 teaspoon dried tarragon, crumbled

$^1/_2$ teaspoon sweet paprika

Salt and black pepper to taste

6 quails (about 10 ounces each), dressed

3 tablespoons butter

2 tablespoons vegetable oil

1 medium-size leek (white part only), split lengthwise, washed well, patted dry, and finely chopped

1 cup half-and-half

1. In a medium-size saucepan, combine the rice and water, bring to a boil, reduce the heat to low, cover, and simmer till the rice has absorbed all the liquid, about 45 minutes. Set aside.

2. In a small saucepan, combine the orange juice and raisins, bring to a simmer, cook for 5 minutes, remove from the heat, and set aside.

3. Preheat the oven to 350°F. Butter a 2- to $2^1/_2$-quart casserole and set aside.

4. In a paper or plastic bag, combine the flour, tarragon, paprika, and salt and pepper, add the quails, and shake, tapping off any excess flour and reserving the flour. In a large heavy skillet, heat the butter and oil together over moderate heat till the butter melts, then brown the quails quickly on all sides and transfer to a plate. Add the leek to the skillet, stir for 5 minutes, and transfer to the plate. Add the reserved flour to the

drippings in the skillet and stir for 1 minute. Add the half-and-half, bring almost to a boil, and stir for 1 minute. Add the orange-raisin mixture, stir till well blended, and remove the sauce from the heat.

5. Layer the rice in the bottom of the prepared casserole, scatter the leek evenly over the rice, and spoon half the sauce over the top. Arrange the quails snugly breast side up over the top, spoon the remaining sauce over the quails, cover, and bake till bubbly and the quails are tender, 30 to 35 minutes.

MAKES 4 TO 6 SERVINGS

Fish and Shellfish Shroups, Royales, and Supremes

Michigan Baked Fish Casserole

Michigan has a rich immigrant heritage of Cornish, Irish, Finns, Czechs, Dutch, Germans, and Ukranians, all of whom made full use of the Great Lakes' bounty of whitefish, perch, trout, and salmon. Michiganians still pride themselves on simple home cooking and nothing is prized more than an honest fish casserole served with a fresh mushroom salad and a good yeast bread—followed, of course, by a tart dessert made with the area's delectable cherries. And if you really want to cook like the locals, you'll add a thin layer of cooked cranberry, navy, or red kidney beans to the casserole.

6 tablespoons ($^3/_4$ stick) butter

6 slices Canadian bacon

1 medium-size onion, chopped

$^1/_2$ pound fresh mushrooms, chopped

$^1/_4$ cup dry bread crumbs

$1^1/_2$ to 2 pounds fresh small fish fillets
(such as whitefish, perch, bass, or trout)

6 tablespoons all-purpose flour

1 cup milk

1 cup shredded sharp cheddar cheese

$^1/_2$ teaspoon dried oregano, crumbled

Salt and black pepper to taste

2 medium-size ripe tomatoes, sliced

1. Preheat the oven to 325°F. Butter a 2-quart casserole and set aside.

2. In a medium-size skillet, heat 2 tablespoons of the butter over moderate heat, then brown the Canadian bacon briefly on each side and transfer to a plate. Melt another 2 tablespoons of butter in the skillet, then add the onion, mushrooms, and bread crumbs, stir for about 5 minutes, and scrape the mixture evenly over the bottom of the prepared casserole. Arrange the fish fillets over the top, then arrange the bacon slices over the fish.

3. In a small heavy saucepan, melt the remaining 2 tablespoons butter over moderate heat, then add the flour and whisk for 1 minute. Gradually whisk in the milk till the mixture is smooth, then add the cheese and oregano, season with salt and pepper, and stir till the cheese melts. Pour the sauce evenly over the casserole, arrange the tomatoes over the top, cover, and bake till bubbly, about 30 minutes.

MAKES 6 SERVINGS

Pierre's Scalloped Fish with Apples

1 pound fresh fish fillets (such as sea bass, red snapper, or grouper), cut into small pieces

2 Granny Smith apples, left unpeeled, cored, and cut into slices

1 cup milk

1 large egg, beaten

2 tablespoons butter, melted

1 teaspoon Dijon mustard

2 teaspoons fresh lemon juice

1 teaspoon firmly packed dark brown sugar

Salt and black pepper to taste

1½ cups dry bread crumbs

1 tablespoon butter, cut into small pieces

1. Preheat the oven to 350°F. Butter a 1-quart casserole and set aside.

2. In a large mixing bowl, combine the fish, apples, milk, and egg and mix well.

3. In a small mixing bowl, combine the melted butter, mustard, lemon juice, and brown sugar, season with salt and pepper, mix till well blended, add to the fish mixture, and stir again till well blended, taking care not to break up the fish too much.

4. Sprinkle ½ cup of the bread crumbs evenly over the bottom of the prepared casserole, spread the fish mixture evenly over that, and sprinkle the remaining 1 cup crumbs over the top. Dot with the butter and bake till lightly browned, about 30 minutes.

MAKES 4 SERVINGS

Pierre Franey was one of the most creative and versatile chefs I've ever had the privilege of knowing, and I'll never forget the day at his home in Springs on Long Island when, confronted with extra sea bass fillets after a photo shoot for a cookbook, he whipped up this unusual casserole for a couple of close friends who'd dropped by. Never would I have thought of combining fish, apples, and brown sugar, but it turned out to be one of the most memorable casseroles I'd ever tasted.

Sarasota Red Snapper and Goat Cheese Casserole

The casserole my Greek-American friend in Sarasota, Florida, served one night was made with only tender, local snapper throats and the very finest feta cheese cured in barrels at a neighborhood deli. You don't have to have these rare ingredients, however, to produce an equally delicious casserole using ordinary red snapper fillets and virtually any full-flavored, semidry goat cheese. Do note that to prevent the fish from overcooking, the casserole is baked at a relatively high temperature for no more than 20 minutes.

3 tablespoons olive oil (preferably Greek)

1 medium-size onion, chopped

1 garlic clove, minced

$1/2$ cup dry white wine

3 cups canned crushed tomatoes

$1/4$ cup capers, drained

1 teaspoon dried oregano, crumbled

$1/4$ teaspoon red pepper flakes

Salt and black pepper to taste

2 pounds red snapper fillets, each cut into halves or thirds

$1/2$ pound goat cheese, crumbled

2 tablespoons ouzo, Pernod, or other licorice-flavored liqueur

1. Preheat the oven to 400°F. Grease well a 2-quart casserole and set aside.

2. In a large saucepan, heat the olive oil over moderate heat, add the onion and garlic, and stir for 2 minutes. Add the wine, tomatoes, capers, oregano, red pepper flakes, season with salt and black pepper, bring to a boil, reduce the heat to low, and let simmer for 10 minutes. Remove the sauce from the heat.

3. Layer half the snapper pieces skin side down in the prepared casserole, season with salt and pepper, spoon half the tomato sauce over the pieces, and sprinkle half the cheese over the top. Repeat with the remaining snapper, sauce, and cheese, drizzle the ouzo over the top, and bake till golden, about 20 minutes.

MAKES 6 SERVINGS

Flounder and Spinach Bake

One 10-ounce package frozen chopped spinach, cooked according to package directions, drained well, and squeezed dry

1 pound fresh small flounder fillets

Salt and black pepper to taste

One 10 3/4-ounce can Campbell's condensed cream of shrimp soup

2 tablespoons dry sherry mixed with 1 tablespoon all-purpose flour

1/4 cup freshly grated Parmesan cheese

2 tablespoons butter, cut into bits

1. Preheat the oven to 350°F.

2. Butter a shallow 1½-quart casserole and layer the spinach across the bottom. Arrange the flounder fillets evenly over the spinach and season with salt and pepper.

3. In a medium-size mixing bowl, combine the condensed soup and sherry mixture, stir till well blended and smooth, and pour over the fish. Sprinkle the cheese evenly over the top, dot with the butter bits, and bake till golden, about 25 minutes.

MAKES 4 SERVINGS

The only fish I love more than flounder is its first cousin, fluke (rarely available outside the waters of Long Island and southern New England), so when a retired chef I was visiting in Vero Beach, Florida, served this easy, sapid casserole one night after a half-day of deep-sea fishing, I couldn't get the recipe fast enough. Needless to say, the casserole can be made with any non-oily, white-fleshed fish.

CASSEROLE CHAT

Lean fish is an ideal candidate for casseroles that contain sufficient liquid since it doesn't dry out, as it tends to do with other methods of cooking. Also, fatty fish such as bluefish and mackerel can give a casserole an oily texture.

Boston Salt Cod, Potato, and Onion Casserole

New England fishermen were salting cod as a means of preserving the fish as far back as the eighteenth century, and with westward expansion in the nineteenth century, it was the Scandinavians who introduced salt cod to the Upper Midwest. Why the fish is not more popular today baffles me, for when rehydrated in several changes of water, salt cod cooked in casseroles is not only tastefully mild but moist and almost silken in texture. Cooking salt cod with potatoes and onions is a classic Boston method, and there's simply no better seafood casserole.

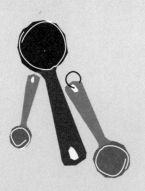

1/2 pound salt cod

3 tablespoons butter

1 small onion, minced

1 garlic clove, minced

3/4 cup all-purpose flour

1 cup chicken broth

1 cup half-and-half

Black pepper to taste

1 tablespoon olive oil

2 large Idaho potatoes

1/2 cup freshly grated Parmesan cheese

1. Place the cod in a large glass bowl, add enough cold water to cover, and soak at least 12 hours, changing the water twice. Drain and pat dry.

2. In a small heavy saucepan, melt the butter over moderate heat, then add the onion and garlic and stir for 1 minute. Add about 2 tablespoons of the flour and stir for 1 minute. Add the broth and whisk till the mixture is smooth. Add the half-and-half, season with pepper, continue to whisk till the sauce thickens, about 3 minutes, and remove from the heat.

3. Preheat the oven to 350°F. Grease a 1- to 1 1/2-quart casserole.

4. Cut the cod into 1/4-inch strips and dredge in the remaining flour, tapping off excess. In a large skillet, heat the oil over moderate heat, add the cod, cook 1 minute on each side, and drain on paper towels.

5. Peel the potatoes, cut into thin discs, and arrange half the discs over the bottom of the casserole. Layer half the cod over the potatoes and pour half the sauce over the top. Repeat with the remaining potatoes, cod, and sauce, sprinkle the cheese over the top, and bake for 1 hour. Uncover and bake till nicely browned, about 25 minutes.

MAKES 4 SERVINGS

184

Crazy for Casseroles

Herbed Salmon and Corn Scallop

1¹/₂ pounds fresh salmon fillets, skinned and cut into cubes

Salt and black pepper to taste

2 juniper berries, finely crushed

¹/₄ teaspoon dried chervil, crumbled

Juice and grated rind of 1 lemon

1¹/₄ cups plain yogurt

One 10-ounce package frozen corn kernels, thawed

1 cup shredded Swiss cheese

1¹/₂ cups dry bread crumbs

3 tablespoons butter, melted

1. Preheat the oven to 375°F.

2. Butter a shallow 2-quart casserole and arrange the fish over the bottom. Season with salt and pepper, sprinkle over the juniper berries, chervil, and lemon juice, cover with a sheet of aluminum foil, and bake for 15 minutes.

3. Add the lemon rind, yogurt, corn, and cheese and stir gently till well blended. Sprinkle the bread crumbs evenly over the top, drizzle the butter over the crumbs, and bake till golden brown, about 25 minutes.

MAKES 4 TO 6 SERVINGS

Slightly smoky, aromatic juniper berries, which are available whole and dried in better markets, grow on shrub-like trees throughout much of Europe and enhance not only many ham and wild game dishes (not to mention various gins) but virtually any salmon prepara-tion. Combine the berries with a little licorice-flavored chervil, as in this unusual scallop, and casserole cookery takes on a whole new sophistication. If you can't find the chervil, ground dried fennel produces just as good results.

CASSEROLE CHAT

To transport a hot meat, poultry, or fish casserole to another location, pack it in a well-insulated container or a large roasting pan lined with towels. Even better, transport the casserole chilled, then reheat when ready to serve.

Tuna, Pea, and Brown Rice Casserole

This is but one of dozens of tuna casseroles that were virtual staples on American tables during the 1940s and '50s, the only ingredient missing being crumbled potato chips as a topping—which I personally loathe. Today, as yesterday, the casserole is simple, economical, and, yes, tasty enough to serve even the snootiest friends when a quick meal is in order. Regular long-grain white rice can be substituted, but the brown variety has considerably more flavor.

1 cup brown rice, cooked according to package directions

One 10³/₄-ounce can Campbell's condensed golden mushroom soup

One 6-ounce can chunk light tuna packed in oil, drained

1 cup frozen peas, cooked according to package directions and drained

Black pepper to taste

2 tablespoons dry bread crumbs

¹/₄ cup shredded sharp cheddar cheese

1. Preheat the oven to 350°F. Generously butter a 1¹/₂-quart casserole with at least 1 tablespoon of butter and set aside.

2. In a large mixing bowl, combine the rice and condensed soup and mix till well blended. Flake the tuna and add it to the rice-soup mixture along with the peas, season with pepper, and stir till well blended.

3. Sprinkle the bread crumbs evenly over the bottom of the prepared casserole, scrape the tuna-and-rice mixture into the casserole, sprinkle the cheese evenly over the top, and bake till bubbly, 25 to 30 minutes.

MAKES 4 TO 6 SERVINGS

M.F.K. Fisher's Baked Tuna with Mushroom Sauce

Two 6-ounce cans chunk light tuna packed in oil, drained and flaked

1 large onion, thinly sliced

1 medium-size green bell pepper, seeded and cut into thin strips

2 teaspoons minced fresh parsley leaves

One 10$^3/_4$-ounce can Campbell's condensed cream of mushroom soup

$^1/_2$ cup water

$^1/_2$ cup shredded sharp cheddar cheese

1. Preheat the oven to 400°F.

2. Butter a 1-quart casserole and make layers of tuna, onion, and bell pepper, sprinkling the parsley over the top layer.

3. Dilute the condensed soup with the water, stir well, and pour evenly over the top of the casserole. Sprinkle the cheese evenly over the top and bake till golden, about 20 minutes.

MAKES 4 SERVINGS

Today, M.F.K. Fisher is recognized as one of the pivotal figures in American gastronomy, and if Mary Frances didn't find a thing wrong with using canned soup in this tuna casserole she served me once at lunch at her ranch in Sonoma, California, neither should we. Of course, she called the mushroom soup a "sauce," which only added to her old-fashioned and distinctive charm.

Tex-Mex Tuna Casserole

What my friend Mary Greenwood in Houston found "Tex-Mex" about the black olives and macaroni in her tuna casserole remains a mystery, but I had to admit that the olives did add a special savor that was nothing less than delectable. When I make this casserole, I do add a few shakes of Tabasco to the soup-and-milk mixture and, if I think about it in time, I drizzle about 2 tablespoons of melted butter over the crushed tortilla chips for a more supple texture.

One 10³/₄-ounce can Campbell's condensed cream of broccoli soup

1 cup milk

One 4-ounce jar chopped pimentos, drained

¹/₄ cup sliced pitted black olives, drained

Two 6-ounce cans chunk light tuna packed in oil, drained and flaked

³/₄ cup shredded Monterey Jack cheese with jalapeño

2¹/₂ cups corkscrew macaroni, cooked according to package directions and drained

¹/₃ cup crushed tortilla chips

1. Preheat the oven to 350°F. Grease a 2-quart casserole and set aside.

2. In a large mixing bowl, combine the condensed soup and milk and stir till well blended. Add the pimentos, olives, tuna, cheese, and macaroni and stir till well blended.

3. Scrape the mixture into the prepared casserole and bake till bubbly, about 20 minutes. Sprinkle the tortilla chips evenly over the top and bake 10 minutes longer.

MAKES 6 SERVINGS

Tuna-Stuffed Bell Pepper Bake

4 large green bell peppers

1 cup raw long-grain rice, cooked according to package directions

One 6-ounce can chunk light tuna packed in oil, drained

1 small onion, finely chopped

One 10-ounce package frozen corn kernels, thawed

1/2 cup finely chopped fresh mushrooms

Salt and black pepper to taste

Paprika to taste

1 ripe tomato, peeled, seeded, and finely chopped

1/2 cup shredded sharp cheddar cheese

3 cups hot water

1. Preheat the oven to 350°F.

2. Cut a wide circle around the stems of the peppers, lift off the lids, and discard. Scoop out and discard the seeds and membranes, trim the bottoms of the peppers so they will stand upright, and arrange in a 2-quart casserole.

3. In a large mixing bowl, combine the rice, tuna, onion, corn, and mushrooms, season with salt, pepper, and paprika, and mix till well blended. Stuff equal amounts of the mixture into the peppers, spoon equal amounts of the chopped tomato over the mixture, and sprinkle equal amounts of cheese over the tops.

4. Pour the hot water around the peppers and bake till the tops are golden, 30 to 35 minutes. Carefully lift the peppers out of the casserole with a slotted spoon, place on a large plate, and serve piping hot.

MAKES 4 SERVINGS

This is probably my favorite hot preparation of canned tuna and the ideal dish to serve a hungry family or friends on a cold night. The dish can also be made with any leftover cooked and flaked fish, such as broiled flounder, bluefish, and haddock. I like to serve the stuffed peppers with freshly baked cornbread and various pickles.

California Tuna, Potato, and Olive Casserole

Only now are most American chefs learning what southern Europeans have known for centuries: that the best way to prepare fresh tuna is to bake it. Of course, grilled tuna steaks (always cooked rare and usually tough) are the current rage in restaurants and on outdoor decks all over the country, few cooks realizing that only the prized belly cut of tuna has sufficient fat to guarantee moistness and tenderness when quickly seared. I refuse to eat those bleeding slabs with the texture of cardboard, and so will you once you taste this succulent casserole that the great California chef Jeremiah Tower taught me to make when he was in the kitchen of Stars in San Francisco.

1½ pounds fresh tuna steak (preferably the belly cut), cut into ¼-inch-thick slices

3 medium-size red potatoes, peeled and cut into thin slices

2 medium-size onions, thinly sliced

12 large black pitted olives

¼ cup capers, drained and rinsed

3 ripe tomatoes, peeled and chopped (juices included)

¼ cup chopped fresh parsley leaves

Salt and black pepper to taste

½ cup dry bread crumbs

½ cup olive oil

1. Preheat the oven to 350°F.

2. Grease a 2-quart casserole and arrange half the tuna slices over the bottom. Layer half the potatoes over the tuna, layer half the onions over the potatoes, and sprinkle half the olives and capers each evenly over the top. Spoon half the tomatoes over that, sprinkle half the parsley over the tomatoes, and season with salt and pepper. Repeat the layering with the remaining tuna, potatoes, onions, olives, capers, tomatoes, parsley, and salt and pepper.

3. Sprinkle the bread crumbs evenly over the top, drizzle the crumbs evenly with the oil, and bake till just golden, about 25 minutes.

MAKES 6 SERVINGS

Shrimp Savvy

Whether chopped or ground to make casserole dips, incorporated in various brunch bakes, quiches, and pies, or featured in elaborate jambalayas, pilaus, and pasta dishes, shrimp has always been a cardinal ingredient in American casseroles. I would no more include canned shrimp in my casserole recipes than I'd include canned crabmeat, and I often attribute much of the disrepute of casserole cookery during the last few decades to the careless use of such inferior ingredients back in the 1940s and '50s in far too many kitchens. Of course, even the term "fresh shrimp" is an oxymoron, since virtually all shrimp sold in markets today has been previously frozen. Fortunately, shrimp, unlike most crabmeat and other seafood, suffers minimum damage from freezing, reason enough why when I find shrimp on sale, I don't hesitate to buy plenty and refreeze what I don't use in cartons of water (never just by themselves). Never fail to sniff any shrimp you plan to purchase and if there's the least trace of spoilage or iodine, walk away.

Needless to say, nothing is more unappetizing (or gritty) than shrimp that hasn't been deveined, so be sure to make this extra effort even when the shrimp are to be chopped or combined with other ingredients. The only other sin that many people commit is overcooking shrimp to the point where they're tough and dry as cardboard. If there's adequate liquid in a casserole, shrimp can withstand fairly lengthy simmering without losing their integrity, but in classic dishes like Chicago Shrimp de Jonghe (page 23) or a shrimp and spinach casserole (pages 24 and 199) that contain minimum liquid, as much attention as practical should be paid to not overcooking the shrimp.

Although most shrimp used in this book are cooked in the casserole itself, for recipes that call simply for boiled or partially boiled shrimp, the basic method bears repeating:

Place the raw shrimp in a saucepan with enough water to cover (a half squeezed lemon can also be added), bring slowly to a boil, remove from the heat, and let stand 2 to 4 minutes, depending on the size of the shrimp. Drain in a colander and, when cool enough to handle, peel and devein the shrimp.

Monterey Shrimp, Asparagus, and Artichoke Royale

While the majority of shrimp in the U.S. are fished in the Atlantic Ocean and Gulf of Mexico, the Pacific varieties found from Monterey down to Santa Barbara, called coonstripe, side-stripe, and spot, are some of the sweetest and most delectable anywhere. Given the region's abundance of fresh, meaty asparagus and globe artichokes, there's little wonder that casseroles such as this one show up regularly not only in homestyle coastal restaurants but in many homes.

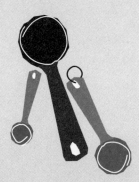

6 tablespoons (³/₄ stick) butter

¹/₄ pound fresh mushrooms

1 pound fresh asparagus, bottoms trimmed, steamed till just tender, drained, and quartered

One 14-ounce can artichoke hearts, drained and quartered

1 pound fresh shrimp, cooked in boiling water till just cooked through, drained, peeled, and deveined

³/₄ cup all-purpose flour

³/₄ cup milk

³/₄ cup half-and-half

¹/₄ cup dry sherry

1 tablespoon Worcestershire sauce

Salt and black pepper to taste

Cayenne pepper to taste

¹/₄ cup freshly grated Parmesan cheese

Paprika to taste

1. Preheat the oven to 375°F. Butter a 2-quart casserole and set aside.

2. In a skillet, melt 2 tablespoons of the butter over moderate heat, add the mushrooms, stir till softened, about 8 minutes, and set aside.

3. Layer the asparagus in the bottom of the prepared casserole, then the artichokes over the asparagus, and the mushrooms over the artichokes, then layer the shrimp over the mushrooms.

4. Melt the remaining 4 tablespoons butter in a saucepan over moderate heat, add the flour, and whisk for 1 minute. Add the milk and half-and-half and whisk till thickened. Add the sherry and Worcestershire, season with salt and peppers, and continue to whisk till thickened. Pour over the casserole, sprinkle with the cheese and paprika, and bake 20 to 25 minutes.

MAKES 6 SERVINGS

Crazy for Casseroles

Herbed Shrimp, Pasta, and Cheese Casserole

2 large eggs

1 cup evaporated milk

1 cup plain yogurt

$^1/_2$ pound feta cheese, crumbled

$^1/_2$ cup shredded Swiss cheese

$^1/_3$ cup chopped fresh parsley leaves

$^1/_3$ cup chopped fresh basil leaves

1 teaspoon dried oregano, crumbled

4 garlic cloves, minced

$^1/_2$ pound angel hair pasta, cooked according to package directions and drained

$1^1/_2$ pounds fresh medium-size shrimp, boiled in water till just cooked through, drained, peeled, and deveined

One 16-ounce jar medium-hot green salsa

$^1/_3$ pound mozzarella cheese, shredded

1. Preheat the oven to 350°F. Grease a shallow 3-quart casserole and set aside.

2. In a large mixing bowl, blend together the eggs, evaporated milk, and yogurt, then add the feta and Swiss cheeses, parsley, basil, oregano, and garlic and stir till well blended.

3. Spread half the pasta over the bottom of the prepared casserole, layer half the shrimp over the pasta, and spoon the salsa evenly over the top. Spread the remaining pasta over the salsa, and pour the egg mixture over the top. Layer on the remaining shrimp, sprinkle the mozzarella cheese evenly over the shrimp and bake till golden, about 30 minutes. Let stand 10 minutes before serving.

MAKES AT LEAST 8 SERVINGS

This rich, elaborate, but easy-to-prepare shrimp casserole was created by one of three sisters in Charlotte, North Carolina, who entertains almost as much as my own mother. The casserole is always served as a main buffet dish with no more than a large tossed green salad, rolls, and plenty of iced tea. Do feel free to experiment with any number of different cheeses, including crumbled goat and genuine Parmigiano-Reggiano.

Creole Curried Shrimp and Squash Casserole

In New Orleans, this popular curried casserole would normally be made with the area's big Gulf shrimp and the green, mild-flavored, pear-shaped vegetable of the squash family known as mirlitons (also called chayotes when available in Latin grocery stores outside the region). Yellow crookneck squash is a totally acceptable substitute for the more exotic vegetable, and I've also used eggplant and zucchini. What really gives the casserole its distinction, however, is the subtle addition of brown sugar—light or dark.

3 tablespoons butter

3 tablespoons all-purpose flour

Salt and black pepper to taste

1 1/4 cups chicken broth

1/2 cup heavy cream

1 teaspoon curry powder

1 tablespoon light brown sugar

1 tablespoon fresh lemon juice

1/2 pound fresh small shrimp, peeled and deveined

2 tablespoons olive oil

1 medium-size onion, chopped

1 small green bell pepper, seeded and chopped

4 medium-size yellow squash, cut into 1/4-inch-thick rounds

1/2 cup dry bread crumbs

1/2 cup freshly grated Parmesan cheese

2 tablespoons butter, melted

1. Preheat the oven to 350°F. Butter a 1 1/2- to 2-quart casserole and set aside.

2. In a large saucepan, melt the butter over moderate heat, add the flour, season with salt and pepper, and whisk till the mixture bubbles. Add the broth and whisk till well blended and smooth. Add the cream, curry powder, brown sugar, and lemon juice and stir till well blended. Add the shrimp, stir, and set aside.

3. In a small skillet, heat the oil over moderate heat, add the onion and green pepper, stir for about 5 minutes to soften, and set aside.

4. Layer half the squash over the bottom of the prepared casserole, layer half the onion and green pepper evenly over the squash, and spoon half

Crazy for Casseroles

the shrimp mixture over the top. Repeat with the remaining squash, onion and green pepper, and shrimp mixture, cover the casserole, and bake for 20 minutes.

5. Meanwhile, in a small mixing bowl, toss the bread crumbs and cheese with the melted butter. Spread evenly over the top of the casserole and continue to bake, uncovered, till golden brown, about 20 minutes.

MAKES 4 TO 6 SERVINGS

Low Country Shrimp and Two-Rice Casserole

During the days of the great rice plantations in coastal South Carolina and Georgia, casseroles made with tiny, sweet river shrimp and long-grain rice were common to every household. This updated version includes a combination of long-grain and wild rice and is also very good made with just brown rice. If your shrimp are large, cut them in half for this dish.

3/4 cup (1 1/2 sticks) butter

1 medium-size onion, sliced

1/2 pound fresh mushrooms, sliced

1/2 green bell pepper, seeded and diced

2 cups mixed cooked long-grain and wild rice

1 to 1 1/2 pounds fresh shrimp, peeled and deveined

1 tablespoon Worcestershire sauce

Tabasco sauce to taste

Salt and black pepper to taste

1/2 cup all-purpose flour

1 1/2 cups chicken broth

1/2 cup dry white wine

1. Preheat the oven to 350°F. Butter a 2-quart casserole and set aside.

2. In a large heavy skillet, melt 4 tablespoons of the butter over moderate heat, add the onion, mushrooms, and bell pepper, and stir till softened, about 8 minutes. Add the rice, toss till well blended, then spread the mixture across bottom of the prepared casserole.

3. In a medium-size mixing bowl, combine the shrimp and Worcestershire, season with Tabasco and salt and pepper, toss well, and arrange evenly over the rice and vegetables.

4. In a medium-size heavy saucepan, melt the remaining 1/2 cup (1 stick) butter over moderate heat, add the flour, and whisk for 1 minute. Add the broth and wine, whisk till well blended and slightly thickened, pour the sauce evenly over the casserole, and bake till bubbly, about 25 minutes.

MAKES 6 SERVINGS

Crazy for Casseroles

Sally's Shrimp Stroganoff

One 10¾-ounce can Campbell's condensed cream of mushroom soup

One 8-ounce container sour cream

1 teaspoon dillweed, crumbled

Salt and black pepper to taste

4 scallions (white part and some of the green), chopped

¼ cup sliced pimento-stuffed green olives

4 ounces sharp cheddar cheese, shredded

1 pound fresh small shrimp, peeled and deveined

1 tablespoon prepared horseradish

One 8-ounce package egg noodles, cooked according to package directions and drained

1. Preheat the oven to 350°F. Grease a shallow 2½-quart casserole and set aside.

2. In a large mixing bowl, combine the condensed soup, sour cream, and dill, season with salt and pepper, and mix well. Add the scallions, olives, half of the cheese, the shrimp, and horseradish and mix well. Add the noodles and stir till well blended.

3. Scrape the mixture into the prepared casserole, cover, and bake for 30 minutes. Uncover, sprinkle the remaining cheese evenly over the top, and bake till golden, about 20 minutes.

MAKES 6 TO 8 SERVINGS

Sally was the sister of a friend I had while living in Missouri, a delightful, slightly crazy gal who didn't think twice about using canned soups in her many casseroles and could whip one up just as easily for twenty guests as for the four in her family. When I commented how impressed I was with her seafood version of classic beef stroganoff, a puzzled look came over her face. "I never knew it was made with anything except shrimp." In any case, this makes a nice buffet dish.

Shrimp Royal

This rather elaborate casserole is tagged "Royal" instead of "Royale" for the simple reason that my sister's married name is Royal and she created the dish while living in coastal Wilmington, North Carolina. At first I balked at her using bread crumbs to crust a rice dish, then marveled at the subtle textural contrast between the soft rice and crispy golden topping. The rice should remain quite moist in this casserole, so don't overcook.

2 tablespoons butter

2 medium-size onions, finely chopped

1/2 pound fresh mushrooms, sliced

2 pounds fresh medium-size shrimp, peeled and deveined

2 medium-size ripe tomatoes, peeled and diced

1/8 teaspoon paprika

Salt and black pepper to taste

1/3 cup semisweet sherry

1 teaspoon Worcestershire sauce

1/2 cup half-and-half

2 tablespoons all-purpose flour

4 cups cooked long-grain rice

1/2 cup dry bread crumbs

2 tablespoons butter, melted

1. Preheat the oven to 350°F. Butter a 2 1/2- to 3-quart casserole.

2. In a large, deep, heavy skillet, melt the butter over moderate heat, add the onions, mushrooms, and shrimp, and stir till the shrimp are just pink, about 5 minutes. Add the tomatoes and paprika, season with salt and pepper, reduce the heat to low, cover, and cook for 5 minutes. Stir in the sherry and Worcestershire.

3. In a small mixing bowl, combine the half-and-half and flour, stir till a light paste forms, add to the shrimp mixture, and bring to a boil, stirring constantly. Reduce the heat to low and cook 1 minute longer. Add the rice, toss well, and scrape the mixture into the prepared casserole.

4. In a small mixing bowl, toss the bread crumbs and melted butter together, spoon the crumbs evenly over the top, and bake till golden, 20 to 25 minutes.

MAKES 6 TO 8 SERVINGS

Chicago Shrimp, Spinach, and Feta Cheese Casserole

3 tablespoons butter

One 10-ounce package frozen chopped spinach, cooked according to package directions, drained well, and squeezed dry

2 tablespoons chopped fresh chives

1 garlic clove, minced

Salt and black pepper to taste

3 tablespoons dry white wine

$^1/_4$ pound fresh mushrooms, sliced

1 medium-size ripe tomato, peeled and diced

$^1/_2$ pound fresh medium-size shrimp, peeled and deveined

$^1/_4$ cup vinaigrette dressing of your choice

$^1/_4$ pound feta cheese (preferably Greek), crumbled

1. Preheat the oven to 350°F. Grease a 1- to 1$^1/_2$-quart casserole and set aside.

2. In a large heavy skillet, melt the butter over moderate heat, add the spinach, chives, and garlic, season with salt and pepper, and toss for about 2 minutes. Add the wine, stir 2 minutes longer, then scrape the mixture into the prepared casserole.

3. Layer the mushrooms over the spinach, distribute the diced tomato over the mushrooms, and arrange the shrimp over the top. Pour the vinaigrette evenly over everything, sprinkle the cheese all around, and bake till slightly browned, 20 to 25 minutes.

MAKES 4 SERVINGS

Since my paternal grandfather was Greek, it was only natural that much of the food I was exposed to as a child had a Greek-American slant. Then, many years later, I had occasion to frequent some of the small, unpretentious restaurants in Chicago's Greektown, one of which prided itself on this delectable shrimp and spinach casserole oozing with tangy feta cheese and served in copious portions with chopped iceberg lettuce salad on the side. My rendition comes close to reproducing the original I remember.

Hootie's Hot Seafood Shroup

My sister, Hootie, first served this simple but tasty casserole years ago when she was living in Wilmington, North Carolina, and while she still can't tell me exactly what a "shroup" is (I judge "shrimp" plus "soup"), the dish is now a standard item on the buffet of any number of family members and friends. To allow the major flavors to meld, she insists the casserole should be allowed to sit overnight in the refrigerator, and since the soup is salty, there's no need to add salt.

5 slices white bread

$1/2$ pound fresh medium-size shrimp, peeled and deveined

$1/2$ pound fresh lump crabmeat, picked over for shells and cartilage

$1/4$ cup mayonnaise

1 small onion, diced

$1/2$ small green bell pepper, seeded and diced

1 celery rib, diced

Black pepper to taste

$1^{1}/2$ cups milk

2 large eggs

One $10^{3}/4$-ounce can Campbell's condensed cream of mushroom soup

$1/2$ cup grated sharp cheddar cheese

Paprika to taste

1. Cut about half of the bread into dice, spread over the bottom of a 2-quart casserole, and scatter the shrimp and crabmeat over the top.

2. In a small mixing bowl, combine the mayonnaise, onion, bell pepper, and celery, season with pepper, mix till well blended, and spread the mixture evenly over the seafood.

3. Trim and discard the crusts from the remaining bread slices, cut the bread into small dice, and spread over the mayonnaise mixture.

4. In a medium-size mixing bowl, beat together the milk and eggs, pour evenly over the bread, cover with plastic wrap, and refrigerate overnight.

5. Preheat the oven to 350°F.

6. Spoon the soup over the casserole and bake for 30 minutes. Sprinkle the cheese and paprika evenly over the top and bake till golden, about 20 minutes.

MAKES 6 SERVINGS

Crazy for Casseroles

Chilled Seafood, Mango, and Rice Casserole

1 cup raw brown rice, cooked according to package directions

1 pound fresh medium-size cooked shrimp, boiled in water till just cooked through, drained, peeled, and deveined

$^3/_4$ pound fresh lump crabmeat, picked over for shells and cartilage

3 ripe mangoes, peeled, pitted, and coarsely chopped

$^1/_4$ cup chopped fresh chives

2 teaspoons celery seeds

Salt and black pepper to taste

2 cups mayonnaise

$^3/_4$ cup sour cream

2 teaspoons Dijon mustard

1 tablespoon prepared horseradish

1 tablespoon fresh lemon juice

Chopped fresh parsley for garnish

1. Spread the rice evenly over the bottom of a 2- to 2$^1/_2$-quart casserole, layer the shrimp over the rice, then layer the crabmeat over the shrimp.

2. In a large mixing bowl, combine the mangoes, chives, and celery seeds, season with salt and pepper, and toss till well blended. Add the mayonnaise, sour cream, mustard, horseradish, and lemon juice, stir till well blended, and spread evenly over the top of the casserole. Cover with plastic wrap and refrigerate at least 2 hours before serving.

3. To serve, garnish the edges with parsley.

MAKES 6 SERVINGS

Who says that all casseroles must be hot, especially in this age when culinary rules are broken every day, often to good advantage? The truth is that this dish did indeed originate as a traditional hot rice and seafood casserole. Then, since I happen to love the combination of shrimp and mango (or papaya) in salads, one steamy summer day when I was expecting friends for lunch, I began experimenting with these two and other fresh ingredients, and one thing led to another, and what I ended up with was not a salad but this concoction prepared and served in one of my prettiest casseroles. Suffice it to say that the chilled dish was a huge hit and that I've made it many times since—often with regular long-grain white rice when I don't have the more flavorful brown rice on hand.

Crab Norfolk

Created in 1924 by a certain W. O. Snowden at the Snowden & Mason restaurant in Norfolk, Virginia, this utterly simple casserole has become a classic all over the country. The original dish was baked and served in specially designed small, oval aluminum pans, but today either individual ramekins or a single casserole is used. Traditionally, crab Norfolk is served with fluffy white rice, and I also love it with minted green peas.

1 pound fresh lump crabmeat, picked over for shells and cartilage

2 tablespoons cider vinegar

$^1/_4$ cup ($^1/_2$ stick) butter, melted

$^1/_2$ teaspoon Worcestershire sauce

$^1/_4$ teaspoon Tabasco sauce

Salt and freshly ground black pepper to taste

1. Preheat the oven to 350°F.

2. In a large mixing bowl, combine all the ingredients and toss lightly till well blended, taking care not to break up the crabmeat.

3. Scrape the mixture into a 1-quart casserole and bake just till bubbly, about 20 minutes.

MAKES 4 SERVINGS

Crazy for Casseroles

Classy Crabmeat

Nothing is more delectable in baked casseroles than fresh, sweet crabmeat, and since the succulent meat from eastern blue and Gulf crabs is usually available in finer markets throughout the South and Midwest, I find no excuse in ever resorting to the bland, often mushy, canned or frozen products. The choicest and most expensive meat (called "lump") from these crabs comes from the back and should be used in casseroles that truly highlight the crabmeat (such as Crab Imperial); claw meat, which contains more shell and cartilage but is considerably less costly, is appropriate in mixed seafood dishes. Equally noble and sweet is the pinkish white Dungeness crabmeat found fresh all along the West Coast, as well as the scarlet leg meat of Alaska king crabs, which is available only frozen but is nonetheless delicious. No matter which fresh crabmeat you use, remember to pick it over carefully for shell and cartilage, while making every effort not to break up the delicate meat any more than necessary. Generally, fresh crabmeat is very perishable, so I never buy more than the amount needed for a given casserole.

Ben Benson's Lump Crabmeat and Wild Mushroom Ramekins

It's no secret to New Yorkers and tourists alike that Ben Benson's in Manhattan is one of the country's greatest steak houses. What many don't realize, however, is that the restaurant also serves some of the most original and delectable seafood dishes anywhere, these exceptional ramekins being just one example. The ramekins do make nice individual servings, but you can also use a buttered 1½-quart casserole instead.

1 cup milk

1 cup heavy cream

1 cup half-and-half

1¼ cups finely chopped shallots or scallions (white part only)

¼ cup (½ stick) butter, cut into pieces

1 cup all-purpose flour

Salt and black pepper to taste

3 tablespoons olive oil

1 garlic clove, minced

1 pound fresh wild mushrooms (ceps, shiitakes, or morels), chopped

1 pound fresh lump crabmeat, picked over for shells and cartilage

½ to ¾ cup dry bread crumbs, to your taste

¼ cup chopped fresh chives

1. Preheat the oven to 400°F. Butter four 2- to 2½-cup ramekins and set aside.

2. In a large heavy saucepan, combine the milk, heavy cream, and half-and-half and bring to a low boil. Add 1 cup of the shallots, the butter, and flour, season with salt and pepper, and stir over low heat till the sauce is smooth, about 7 minutes. Keep the sauce warm.

3. In a large heavy skillet, heat the oil over moderate heat, add the remaining ¼ cup shallots and the garlic, and stir for 1 minute. Add the mushrooms, season with salt and pepper, stir till they're soft and tender, about 10 minutes, and remove from the heat.

4. Divide the mushrooms equally among the prepared ramekins, top each with about 2 tablespoons of the sauce, and layer equal amounts of the crabmeat over the top.

5. In a small mixing bowl, combine the bread crumbs and chives, stir well, and spoon equal amounts over each ramekin. Drizzle equal amounts of the remaining sauce over the tops and bake till just heated through and slightly golden on top, about 10 minutes.

MAKES 4 SERVINGS

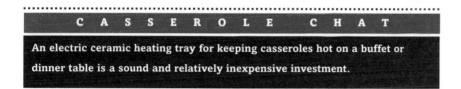

C A S S E R O L E   C H A T

An electric ceramic heating tray for keeping casseroles hot on a buffet or dinner table is a sound and relatively inexpensive investment.

Crabmeat Soufflé Supreme

The name Helen Corbitt is, sadly, almost unknown today, but throughout the 1950s and '60s, she was not only the director of restaurants for Neiman-Marcus department stores but the author of numerous highly respectable cookbooks. I once heard Helen referred to as "the casserole lady," a plausible tag if this sublime casserole soufflé is any indication of her talents. Do note that for a fluffy, delicate soufflé, this must be baked in a water bath, and don't be surprised if the casserole fails to feed six unless you include a number of side dishes.

1/4 cup (1/2 stick) butter

1/4 cup all-purpose flour

1 1/4 cups milk

1 teaspoon salt

Freshly ground black pepper

1 tablespoon Madeira wine

1 tablespoon fresh lemon juice

4 large eggs, separated

1/2 pound fresh lump crabmeat, picked over for shells and cartilage

1 cup finely slivered cooked ham

1 cup finely slivered cooked chicken breast

1 cup freshly grated Parmesan cheese

1. Preheat the oven to 350°F. Butter lightly a 2-quart casserole and set aside.

2. In a large, heavy saucepan, melt the butter over moderate heat, add the flour, and whisk for 1 minute. Add the milk and whisk till thickened. Add the salt and pepper, Madeira, lemon juice, and egg yolks, whisking constantly and rapidly, and remove from the heat. Add the crabmeat, ham, and chicken, stir till well blended, and let cool.

3. In a large mixing bowl, beat the egg whites with an electric mixer till stiff peaks form. Fold the whites into the cooled crabmeat mixture, scrape into the prepared casserole, and sprinkle the cheese evenly over the top. Place the casserole in a large roasting pan with enough hot water to come halfway up the sides of the casserole and bake till the top is golden, about 45 minutes.

MAKES 6 SERVINGS

Crazy for Casseroles

Crabmeat and Artichoke Bridge Casserole

2 tablespoons butter

$^{1}/_{2}$ pound fresh mushrooms, diced

12 canned or bottled artichoke hearts, quartered

1 pound fresh claw or lump crabmeat, picked over for shells and cartilage

$1^{1}/_{2}$ cups Cream Sauce (page 6)

$^{1}/_{4}$ cup dry sherry

1 tablespoon Worcestershire sauce

Salt and black pepper to taste

$^{1}/_{4}$ cup freshly grated Parmesan cheese

Paprika to taste

1. Preheat the oven to 350°F. Butter a 1- to 1$^{1}/_{2}$-quart casserole and set aside.

2. In a small skillet, melt the butter over moderate heat, add the mushrooms, stir till softened and most of the liquid evaporates, about 8 minutes, and remove from the heat.

3. Layer the artichokes over the bottom of the prepared casserole, layer the mushrooms over the artichokes, then layer the crabmeat over the mushrooms.

4. In a medium-size mixing bowl, combine the cream sauce, sherry, and Worcestershire, season with salt and pepper, stir till well blended, and pour evenly over the casserole. Sprinkle the cheese and paprika over the top and bake till golden, about 20 minutes.

MAKES 4 TO 6 SERVINGS

Heaven only knows when meat from the blue crab and artichoke hearts were first baked together in a casserole all along the Eastern seaboard. Near Castroville in northern California, the self-proclaimed artichoke capital of the world, I once even had one made with luxurious Dungeness crab. In any case, the classic casserole has evolved throughout the country almost as a staple at bridge parties, and while I became bored playing bridge years ago, I've certainly never been bored with this casserole as the ideal solution for a simple luncheon get-together of close friends. (Tip: With the artichokes diced instead of quartered, it's also a great dish for cocktail parties—served with melba toast.) Just be sure to use only fresh crabmeat.

Savannah Deviled Crab Crusted with Pecans

Unbeknownst to aficionados of blue crabs from Chesapeake Bay, Pacific Dungeness and king crab, Louisiana buster crabs, and Florida stone crabs, the deepwater rock crabs fished along the Georgia coast, yield some of the sweetest and most delectable crabmeat on earth. Combine it with meaty Georgia pecans, as in this tangy casserole, and you'll understand why the local dishes of Savannah remain some of the most delectable (and neglected) in the entire South. Be warned that old, rancid pecans will destroy the casserole, which is another reason why all fresh pecans should be stored in the freezer (up to six months) till ready to use.

1 pound fresh lump crabmeat, picked over for shells and cartilage

1 large celery rib, finely chopped

1 medium-size green bell pepper, seeded and finely chopped

4 scallions (white part and some of the green), finely chopped

$1/4$ cup finely chopped fresh parsley leaves

$1/2$ teaspoon dry mustard

Salt and black pepper to taste

Tabasco sauce to taste

$1/4$ cup heavy cream

$1/2$ cup (1 stick) butter, melted

$1^1/2$ cups crushed soda crackers

$1/2$ cup finely chopped pecans

1. Preheat the oven to 350°F. Butter a $1^1/2$-quart casserole and set aside.

2. In a large mixing bowl, combine the crabmeat, celery, bell pepper, scallions, parsley, and mustard, season with salt and pepper, and stir gently till well blended. Season with Tabasco, add the heavy cream, half the melted butter, and the crackers and stir gently till well blended.

3. Scrape the mixture into the prepared casserole, sprinkle the pecans evenly over the top, drizzle the remaining butter over the pecans, and bake till golden brown, about 30 minutes.

MAKES 4 SERVINGS

The Pines Crabmeat Imperial

1 pound fresh lump crabmeat, picked over for shells and cartilage

1 cup homemade or Hellmann's mayonnaise

1 tablespoon fresh lemon juice

1 teaspoon Worcestershire sauce

Salt and freshly ground black pepper to taste

Fine dry bread crumbs

$1/4$ cup ($1/2$ stick) butter, melted

Lemon wedges, seeded

Preheat the oven to 375°F.

"Put the crabmeat in a large bowl and add the mayonnaise, lemon juice, Worcestershire, and salt and pepper. Mix everything gently with your hands, lifting the crabmeat up and down in the air the way a child lifts soapsuds to play with them (this motion separates the mixture in such a way that the crabmeat has the airy quality of a soufflé). Divide equal handfuls of the mixture among four ovenproof seafood shells and sprinkle the top of each with a few bread crumbs. Now drizzle some of the butter over the tops and place the shells on a heavy baking sheet. Bake them up 15 to 20 minutes, till just lightly browned and crusty on top but not at all burned. Serve with lemon wedges."

MAKES 4 SERVINGS

Although possibly the best crab imperial anywhere today is the luscious version served at the venerable Haussner's restaurant in Baltimore, Maryland, for me the quintessential casserole remains the one I relished as a college student some forty years ago at a family restaurant called The Pines in Chapel Hill, North Carolina. After I raved and raved over the dish, my mother finally asked the owner for the recipe, rendered here exactly the way it was typed on a sheet of paper. Since then, I've often tampered slightly with the recipe, sometimes adding a tablespoon of chopped pimentos, other times a quarter teaspoon of dry mustard, and almost always sprinkling a little paprika over the top. The trick is to add subtle new dimension to the casserole without in any way overwhelming the delicate crabmeat.

Old-Fashioned Yankee Oyster Pie

No matter that this classic casserole is still called a pie in coastal Connecticut, Rhode Island, and Massachusetts. Of course, the supply of oysters in New England today is a mere fraction of what it was a century ago (due to overfishing and pollution), but that doesn't mean there aren't still all sorts of casseroles made with prized bluepoints, Lynnhavens, Cotuits, and Wellfleets. If you want to add a little extra dimension to the pie without destroying the integrity of the oysters, you can mix a few shaved almonds with the bread crumbs sprinkled over the top. Just be sure not to overcook the oysters.

10 ounces oyster crackers, crushed

3 pints shucked fresh oysters, liquor reserved

$^1/_2$ cup (1 stick) butter, melted

2 cups half-and-half

2 teaspoons Worcestershire sauce

Salt and black pepper to taste

Dash of Tabasco sauce

1. Preheat the oven to 350°F.

2. Butter a 2-quart casserole and arrange half the crushed crackers over the bottom. Layer half the oysters over the crackers and drizzle about one-quarter of the butter over the top. Repeat with another layer of crackers, oysters, and butter, reserving $^1/_2$ cup of the crackers and $^1/_4$ cup of the butter for the top.

3. In a small mixing bowl, combine the half-and-half, $^1/_2$ cup of the reserved oyster liquor, and the Worcestershire, season with salt and pepper and Tabasco, mix till well blended, and pour over the casserole. Sprinkle the remaining cracker crumbs evenly over the top, drizzle the remaining $^1/_4$ cup butter over the crumbs, and bake just till bubbly, 20 to 25 minutes.

MAKES 6 TO 8 SERVINGS

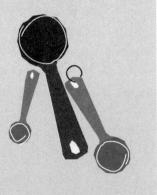

West Coast Oyster and Spinach Casserole

$^1/_4$ cup ($^1/_2$ stick) butter

1 small onion, minced

2 tablespoons all-purpose flour

1 pint shucked fresh oysters, liquor reserved

1 cup milk

Salt and black pepper to taste

$^1/_4$ teaspoon ground nutmeg

One 10-ounce package frozen chopped spinach, cooked according to package directions and drained well

$^1/_2$ cup dry bread crumbs

1. Preheat the oven to 350°F. Butter a 1$^1/_2$-quart casserole and set aside.

2. In a large heavy saucepan, melt 2 tablespoons of the butter over moderate heat, add the onion, and stir for 1 minute. Sprinkle the flour over the top and stir 1 minute longer. Add the oyster liquor and milk and stir constantly till bubbly. Season with salt and pepper, add the nutmeg, gently fold in the oysters, and simmer just till the edges of the oysters begin to curl. Remove from the heat.

3. Arrange the spinach over the bottom of the prepared casserole and spoon the oyster mixture over the spinach. Sprinkle the bread crumbs evenly over the top, dot with the remaining 2 tablespoons butter cut into small pieces, and bake for 15 minutes. Turn off the oven and let the casserole stand in the oven 15 minutes longer to set before serving.

MAKES 4 SERVINGS

All along the East Coast of the U.S. I've eaten every oyster casserole imaginable, but when a lady I know down at Morro Bay, California, made this preparation with purplish black Pacific oysters and truly fresh California leaf spinach, the occasion was a revelation. Most Pacific oysters (especially the prized Olympias) are, alas, rarely available outside the region and, quite frankly, the "fresh" spinach I usually find in East Coast markets looks like it's seen better days. As a result, I use the finest Eastern fresh oysters available (preferably Chincoteagues) and frozen spinach for this casserole, and I haven't had a complaint yet.

Oyster Macaroni and Cheese

Generally, I, like my mother, make macaroni and cheese with no more than a simple custard, but when my veterinarian's wife told me about this unorthodox, main-course creation prepared with fresh oysters in a tangy cheese sauce, I had to get the recipe and try it out on close friends. Suffice it to say that the casserole is sublime, the briny flavor of the oysters and their liquor adding amazing new depth to the classic concept. Do watch the casserole carefully to make sure the interior doesn't get too dry. Depending on your oven, it might be ready after baking only about 20 minutes.

$^1/_2$ pound elbow macaroni

Salt to taste

2 tablespoons butter

1 small onion, minced

1 tablespoon all-purpose flour

$^1/_4$ teaspoon dry mustard

Black pepper to taste

Cayenne pepper to taste

2 cups milk

$^1/_2$ pound sharp cheddar cheese, shredded

12 shucked fresh oysters, $^1/_2$ cup liquor reserved

$^1/_2$ cup dry bread crumbs

2 tablespoons butter, melted

1. Place the macaroni in a large pot of salted boiling water, cook for 8 minutes, uncovered, drain in a colander, and set aside.

2. Preheat the oven to 350°F. Butter a 2-quart casserole and set aside.

3. In a small heavy saucepan, melt the butter over moderate heat, add the onion, and stir for 2 minutes. Add the flour and mustard, season with salt and both peppers, and stir 1 minute longer. Gradually add the milk and all but about 2 ounces of the cheese, reduce the heat to low, and stir slowly till the cheese melts and the sauce is smooth. Remove the pan from the heat.

4. Layer about one-half the drained macaroni in the prepared casserole, stir in half of the sauce, and arrange half of the oysters over the top. Repeat with the remaining macaroni and oysters, spoon the remaining sauce over the top, pour on the oyster liquor, and sprinkle with the remaining cheese.

5. In a small mixing bowl, combine the bread crumbs and melted butter, spoon evenly over the top, and bake till the casserole is bubbly and crusted, 25 to 30 minutes.

MAKES 6 TO 8 SERVINGS

Deviled Oysters and Pecans

This recipe, adapted from a Southern church pamphlet from the 1950s, has to be one of the most delicious oyster casseroles I've ever encountered and just goes to prove that many home cooks back then knew exactly what they were doing. It's simple, subtle, and ideal for a stylish luncheon or small dinner buffet.

1/2 cup (1 stick) butter

1 small onion, chopped

1 small green bell pepper, seeded and chopped

1 garlic clove, minced

1/2 pound fresh mushrooms, chopped

1 teaspoon dry mustard

Salt and black pepper to taste

1 cup dry bread crumbs

1 quart shucked fresh oysters, liquor reserved

1/4 cup heavy cream

1 teaspoon Worcestershire sauce

1 cup chopped pecans

1. Preheat the oven to 350°F. Butter a 2-quart casserole and set aside.

2. In a large heavy skillet, melt the butter over moderate heat, add the onion, bell pepper, garlic, and mushrooms and stir for 5 minutes. Add the mustard, season with salt and pepper, and stir 2 minutes longer. Add the bread crumbs, stir till well blended, and remove from the heat.

3. In a small mixing bowl, combine the oyster liquor, heavy cream, and Worcestershire, stir till well blended, and set aside.

4. Spoon half the crumb mixture over the bottom of the prepared casserole, layer the oysters over the top, and sprinkle the pecans evenly over the oysters. Spoon the remaining crumb mixture over the pecans, pour the cream mixture over the top, and bake till golden, about 30 minutes.

MAKES 6 SERVINGS

Crazy for Casseroles

Curried Oyster and Wild Rice Bake

¹/₄ cup (¹/₂ stick) butter, melted

1 cup raw wild rice, cooked according to package directions and kept hot

1 quart shucked fresh oysters, drained

Salt and black pepper to taste

Tabasco sauce to taste

Half of a 10³/₄-ounce can Campbell's condensed cream of chicken soup

³/₄ cup half-and-half

2 teaspoons mild curry powder

¹/₄ teaspoon dried thyme, crumbled

1. Preheat the oven to 325°F. Butter a 1¹/₂- to 2-quart casserole and set aside.

2. Add the butter to the hot rice, stir till well blended, then layer half the rice over the bottom of the prepared casserole. Arrange the oysters over the rice, season with salt and pepper and Tabasco, and layer the remaining rice over the oysters.

3. In a medium-size saucepan, combine the condensed soup and half-and-half over moderate heat, add the curry powder and thyme, and stir till the curry has dissolved completely. Pour the mixture evenly over the top of the casserole and bake till bubbly, about 25 minutes.

MAKES 4 TO 6 SERVINGS

Oysters baked with wild rice is a popular casserole from New England to the Upper Midwest and the combination lends itself beautifully to a little mild curry powder—but not too much. If you're not crazy about the flavor of thyme, leave it out.

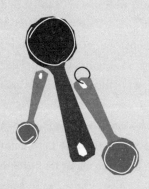

Jay's Scalloped Clams

Long Island, New York, where I have a home, is known for its vast variety of both hard- and soft-shell clams (littlenecks, cherrystones, razors, skimmers, and the like), and no activity is more relished by locals than clamming in the area's many bays, inlets, and sounds. Generally, I prefer my clams simply steamed in clam broth with maybe a little onion, but when my colleague Jay Jacobs, an obsessed clammer and accomplished cook, came up with this remarkable casserole one day for lunch, a new dish was quickly added to my repertory. Although there's nothing like fresh clams for flavor and tenderness, those who simply don't have access to fresh quahogs or steamers will have to settle for canned minced clams, which are not bad. Do be warned that clams tend to toughen when cooked, so be careful not to overcook. This casserole makes both a delightful first course and, served with a salad and bread, a nice luncheon dish.

2 cups minced fresh clams

1 small onion, finely chopped

3 tablespoons finely chopped fresh parsley leaves

$^1/_2$ cup (1 stick) butter, melted

1 teaspoon Worcestershire sauce

1 tablespoon dry sherry

Salt and black pepper to taste

$1^1/_2$ cups coarsely crushed soda crackers

$^3/_4$ cup half-and-half

$^1/_2$ cup fresh bread crumbs

2 tablespoons butter, cut into bits

1. Preheat the oven to 350°F. Butter a $1^1/_2$-quart casserole and set aside.

2. In a large mixing bowl, combine the clams, onion, parsley, melted butter, Worcestershire, and sherry, season with salt and pepper, and stir till well blended. Add the crushed crackers and stir till well blended. Add the half-and-half and stir gently but thoroughly.

3. Scrape the mixture into the prepared casserole. Scatter the bread crumbs evenly over the top, dot with the butter bits, and bake just till bubbly, about 20 minutes.

MAKES 4 SERVINGS

Scallop Casserole

$^1/_2$ pound small fresh mushrooms (or larger ones cut in half)

1 pound fresh sea scallops, drained

Salt and black pepper to taste

2 tablespoons butter

2 tablespoons all-purpose flour

$^1/_2$ cup sweet white wine

Half of a 12-ounce can evaporated milk

Pinch of ground nutmeg

1. Preheat the oven to 350°F.

2. Butter a $1^1/_2$-quart casserole, arrange the mushrooms over the bottom, layer the scallops evenly over the mushrooms, and season with salt and pepper.

3. In a small saucepan, melt the butter over moderate heat, add the flour, and stir for 1 minute. Gradually add the wine and stir till the sauce thickens. Gradually stir in the evaporated milk, add the nutmeg, season with salt and pepper, pour the sauce evenly over the top of the casserole, and bake till bubbly, about 25 minutes.

MAKES 4 TO 6 SERVINGS

Generally, I prefer my scallops simply dusted in fine dry bread crumbs and sautéed quickly in a little butter and lemon juice, but this is one casserole preparation that never fails to impress everyone at my table. I have found that bay scallops are just too delicate for any casserole, so be sure to use sea scallops. This casserole can be served either as a first course or a luncheon dish for four.

Lobster Thermidor

Who knows for sure the origins of this classic lobster casserole that's always had such snob appeal in upscale American restaurants, country clubs, and even the White House? Was it first made in France for Napoleon during the month of "Thermidor" to celebrate the First Republic's new calendar? Was it created later on in the nineteenth century at Maire's restaurant in Paris for the premiere of Victorian Sardou's play *Thermidor*? Whatever, the dish had certainly crossed the Atlantic in a number of guises by 1896 when a recipe appeared in Fannie Farmer's famous *Boston Cooking School Cookbook*, and it's been part of the American repertoire ever since. The irony is that the rich casserole is so easy to prepare, especially if you use leftover boiled or steamed lobster.

6 tablespoons (³/₄ stick) butter

¹/₂ pound fresh mushrooms, sliced

3 tablespoons all-purpose flour

2 cups half-and-half

¹/₄ cup dry sherry

4 cups chunks cooked lobster meat

Salt and black pepper to taste

¹/₂ cup freshly grated Parmesan cheese

1. Preheat the oven to 400°F. Butter a shallow 2¹/₂- to 3-quart casserole and set aside.

2. In a medium-size skillet, melt 3 tablespoons of the butter over moderate heat, add the mushrooms, stir till softened and most of the liquid evaporates, about 5 minutes, and remove from the heat.

3. In a large heavy saucepan, melt the remaining 3 tablespoons butter over moderate heat, add the flour, and whisk till smooth. Gradually add the half-and-half, whisking till the sauce is thickened and smooth. Add the sherry and cook 1 minute longer. Remove from the heat, add the lobster, season with salt and pepper, and stir till well blended.

4. Scrape the mixture into the prepared casserole, sprinkle the cheese evenly over the top, and bake till lightly browned, about 20 minutes.

MAKES 8 SERVINGS

Spicy Leftover Lobster Casserole

1½ cups fresh bread crumbs

¼ cup (½ stick) butter, melted

2 cups diced cooked lobster meat

2 celery ribs, finely chopped

3 large hard-boiled eggs, coarsely chopped

2 cups Cream Sauce (page 6)

¼ teaspoon Tabasco sauce

Salt and black pepper to taste

1. Preheat the oven to 350°F. Butter a shallow 2-quart casserole and set aside.

2. In a medium-size mixing bowl, combine the bread crumbs and butter, stir till well blended, then layer half the mixture over the bottom of the prepared casserole.

3. In a large mixing bowl, combine the lobster, celery, chopped eggs, cream sauce, and Tabasco, season with salt and pepper, mix till well blended, and spoon the mixture evenly over the bread crumbs. Layer the remaining bread crumbs evenly over the lobster mixture and bake till lightly browned, about 30 minutes.

MAKES 6 SERVINGS

When I steam lobsters in the summer for an elaborate shore dinner, I always throw an extra critter in the pot with the idea of having enough meat later on to make a nice lobster salad, a chunky bisque, or a sumptuous casserole such as this one. I might also add a little sherry, Madeira, or rum to the lobster mixture, and if I want to really go overboard, I might mix plenty of freshly grated Parmesan cheese with the bread crumbs.

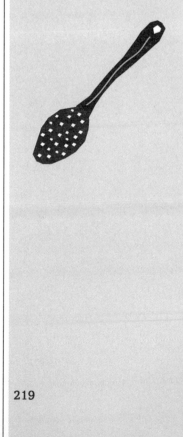

Pasta and Rice Puddings, Bakes, and Casseroles

Johnnie Marzetti

Some try to pinpoint a certain 1920s Marzetti's restaurant in Columbus, Ohio, as the original venue of this famous American casserole; others say simply the dish was created somewhere in the Midwest and given an Italianate name to make it sound more "sophisticated." In any case, there are as many versions (and spellings) of Midwestern Johnnie Marzetti as there are of Southern pilau, and the ingredients can vary wildly. Different pastas are used, ground veal or pork or sausage are often substituted for the beef, and some cooks insist that an iron skillet is preferable to a traditional casserole dish. Feel free to experiment; everybody else does.

$^{1}/_{4}$ cup olive oil

$1^{1}/_{2}$ pounds ground beef round

2 medium-size onions, chopped

$^{1}/_{2}$ green bell pepper, seeded and chopped

$^{1}/_{2}$ pound fresh mushrooms, sliced

2 garlic cloves, minced

Salt and black pepper to taste

One 28-ounce can crushed tomatoes

1 teaspoon dried oregano, crumbled

One 12-ounce package medium-wide egg noodles

$^{1}/_{2}$ pound sharp cheddar cheese, shredded

3 ounces mozzarella cheese, shredded

$^{1}/_{4}$ cup dry bread crumbs

2 tablespoons butter, melted

1. In a large heavy skillet, heat the oil over moderate heat, add the beef, breaking it up with a fork, and stir for about 3 minutes. Add the onions, bell pepper, mushrooms, and garlic, season with salt and pepper, stir well, and continue to cook till the beef and vegetables are slightly browned, about 8 minutes. Add the tomatoes and oregano and stir till well blended. Bring to a simmer, cook about 15 minutes, and remove from the heat.

2. Preheat the oven to 350°F. Grease a 2-quart casserole and set aside.

3. In a large pot of boiling salted water, cook the noodles according to package directions till just tender and drain.

4. Spoon about half the meat sauce over the bottom of the prepared casserole, spread the noodles evenly over the sauce, and sprinkle half the cheddar over the top. Spoon the remaining sauce over the noodles, then sprinkle the remaining cheddar plus the mozzarella over the top.

5. In a small mixing bowl, combine the bread crumbs and melted butter, toss well, scatter the crumbs over the casserole, and bake till lightly browned, about 30 minutes.

MAKES 6 SERVINGS

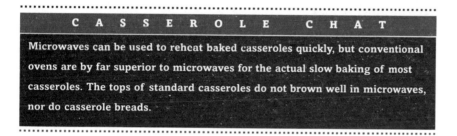

CASSEROLE CHAT

Microwaves can be used to reheat baked casseroles quickly, but conventional ovens are by far superior to microwaves for the actual slow baking of most casseroles. The tops of standard casseroles do not brown well in microwaves, nor do casserole breads.

Blue Plate Noodle, Beef, and Cheese Casserole

In many respects, this is the granddaddy of all American noodle casseroles, the type that I remember eating in S & W cafeterias of the South back in the 1950s and '60s and that I'm sure is still being served on college campuses throughout the country. Of course, these blue plate specials can be steam-table abominations, but if one like this is prepared carefully with good ingredients, it is comfort food at its best and fully respectable for a very casual winter evening served with no more than sesame bread sticks and a nice salad.

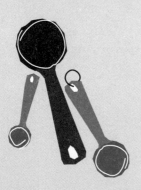

1/2 pound egg noodles, cooked according to package directions and drained

6 scallions (white part and some of the green), chopped

2 pounds ground beef round

1 garlic clove, minced

One 15-ounce can crushed tomatoes

One 15-ounce can tomato sauce

1 teaspoon sugar

Salt and black pepper to taste

Tabasco sauce to taste

3/4 pound sharp cheddar cheese, shredded

One 8-ounce package cream cheese

One 8-ounce container sour cream

1. In a large mixing bowl, toss the noodles and scallions together.

2. Preheat the oven to 350°F. Grease a 2 1/2-quart casserole and set aside.

3. In a large skillet, combine the beef and garlic, breaking up the meat, and cook over moderate heat until it's no longer pink. Drain off the fat, add the tomatoes, tomato sauce, and sugar, season with salt, pepper, and Tabasco, stir for 10 minutes, and remove from heat.

4. In a large mixing bowl, combine all but about 1 cup of the cheddar, the cream cheese, and sour cream and mix till well blended.

5. Spoon one-third of the meat sauce over the bottom of the prepared casserole, layer half the noodles and half the cheese mixture over the top, then repeat the procedure once more. Spoon the remaining sauce over the top, sprinkle the reserved 1 cup cheddar evenly over the sauce, and bake till bubbly and golden brown, about 30 minutes.

MAKES 6 TO 8 SERVINGS

Crazy for Casseroles

Baked Penne with Ham, Peas, and Jack Cheese

1 pound penne pasta

3 tablespoons olive oil

1 small onion, finely chopped

1 large ripe tomato, peeled, seeded, and finely chopped

3 tablespoons all-purpose flour

4 cups milk

Salt and black pepper to taste

2 cups shredded Monterey Jack cheese

One 10-ounce package frozen peas, thawed

$1/2$ pound cooked ham, diced

1. In a large pot of boiling salted water, cook the pasta according to the package directions till just tender, drain, and transfer to a large mixing bowl.

2. Preheat the oven to 350°F. Grease a 3-quart casserole and set aside.

3. In a large heavy saucepan, heat the oil over moderate heat, add the onion and tomato, and stir for 2 minutes. Sprinkle the flour over the top and continue to stir for about 1 minute. Gradually add the milk, whisking rapidly till the sauce is smooth. Season with salt and pepper, add 1 cup of the cheese, and stir till it melts and the sauce is smooth.

4. Add the cheese sauce, peas, and ham to the pasta and toss till well blended. Scrape the mixture into the prepared casserole, sprinkle the remaining 1 cup cheese evenly over the top, and bake till bubbly and golden brown, about 30 minutes.

MAKES 6 TO 8 SERVINGS

Talk about a no-nonsense pasta casserole that's as appropriate for a stylish buffet as for a hearty family meal. Penne has a wonderful toothy texture, but any small tubular pasta works just as well. And so basic is this casserole that all sorts of small vegetables, diced meats, and cheeses can be used.

Saginaw Chamoisette Casserole

A dear friend of mine, Marion German, inherited this recipe from her mother in Saginaw, Michigan, where, at the Bethlehem Lutheran Church, the casserole has been featured at church dinners for at least the past 80 years. Nobody has any idea about the derivation of "chamoisette," but so popular is the casserole throughout the community that it's also prepared for guild luncheons, family reunions, and any number of other social get-togethers. For variety, some ladies often substitute diced cooked chicken or turkey for the beef, and while the whole wheat noodles do give the dish much of its distinction, macaroni or any small pasta shells can also be used.

CHAMOISETTE SAUCE:

2 pounds medium-size ripe tomatoes, peeled and cut into quarters (juices included)

$1/2$ cup chopped onion

$1/2$ cup chopped celery

$1/2$ cup seeded and chopped green bell pepper

$1/2$ teaspoon dried basil, crumbled

1 teaspoon fresh lemon juice

CASSEROLE:

$1/2$ pound whole wheat noodles

1 tablespoon vegetable oil

1 pound ground beef sirloin

1 garlic clove, minced

2 teaspoons soy sauce

Salt and black pepper to taste

$1/2$ cup dry bread crumbs

$2/3$ cup freshly grated Parmesan cheese

2 tablespoons butter, cut into pieces

1 cup finely chopped fresh parsley leaves

1. To make the sauce, combine all the ingredients in a large heavy saucepan and slowly bring to a boil over moderate heat. Reduce the heat to low and simmer for 15 minutes, stirring but not mashing the tomatoes. Remove from the heat.

2. In a large pot of boiling salted water, cook the noodles according to package directions till just tender, drain, and set aside.

3. Preheat the oven to 375°F. Grease a 2-quart casserole and set aside.

4. In a large heavy skillet, heat the oil over moderate heat, add the ground beef and garlic, and stir to break up the meat. Add the soy sauce,

season with salt and pepper, continue to stir till the meat browns, then transfer the mixture to a large mixing bowl. Add the noodles and sauce and fold till well blended.

5. Scrape the mixture into the prepared casserole, sprinkle the bread crumbs, then the cheese evenly over the top, dot with the butter, and bake till golden brown, about 30 minutes. To serve, sprinkle a border of chopped parsley around the edges.

MAKES 4 TO 6 SERVINGS

Seafood Lasagne

If memory serves, the first seafood lasagne I ever tasted was prepared with a simple shrimp sauce at a small south-side Italian-American restaurant in Chicago. There's certainly nothing wrong with noodles baked in a smooth seafood cream sauce, but for a really spectacular main dish, I personally like to layer ingredients separately for an almost custardy casserole. Here I highlight shrimp and crabmeat, but I might also use any white fish that has been poached and flaked.

$^1/_2$ pound fresh shrimp, peeled, deveined, boiled in water to cover till just cooked, drained, and chopped

$^1/_2$ pound fresh lump crabmeat, picked over for shells and cartilage

6 lasagne noodles

3 tablespoons butter

1 medium-size onion, finely chopped

$^1/_2$ pound fresh mushrooms, thinly sliced

1 tablespoon fresh lemon juice

Salt and black pepper to taste

3 large eggs, beaten

2 cups half-and-half

$^1/_4$ cup freshly grated Parmesan cheese

$^3/_4$ cup shredded mozzarella cheese

1. Preheat the oven to 350°F. Butter a 2-quart casserole and set aside.

2. In a large mixing bowl, combine the shrimp and crabmeat, toss well, and set aside.

3. In a large pot of boiling salted water, cook the noodles according to package directions till just tender and drain.

4. In a large skillet, melt the butter over moderate heat, add the onion and mushrooms, and stir till softened, about 5 minutes. Add the sautéed onion and mushrooms and lemon juice to the mixed seafood, season with salt and pepper, and toss again.

5. In another large mixing bowl, combine the eggs, half-and-half, and Parmesan and stir till well blended. Add about two-thirds of the egg mixture to the seafood mixture and stir till well blended.

6. Spread about one-third of the seafood mixture over the bottom of the prepared casserole. Cover with 2 of the noodles, then spread another third of the mixture over the noodles, cover with 2 more noodles, and spread the remaining mixture over the top. Cover with the remaining 2 noodles, pour the remaining egg mixture over the noodles, and sprinkle the mozzarella evenly over the top. Bake till bubbly and golden, about 45 minutes, and let stand 10 minutes before serving.

MAKES 6 SERVINGS

Orzo, Shrimp, and Pea Casserole

Orzo refers to barley in Italian, which makes it all the more ironic that this small, oval pasta with such creamy texture is primarily a staple in Greek cuisine. Living in a family that was partly Greek, I was virtually raised on lamb baked with orzo, chicken and orzo simmered in yogurt, and any number of orzo and vegetable casseroles, but it was not till I visited some Greek-American friends in Sarasota, Florida, that I was exposed to this amazing creation featuring orzo and local shrimp and peas. If you like herby casseroles, feel free to add a little oregano, thyme, or summer savory.

6 strips lean bacon

3 scallions (white part only), finely chopped

1 garlic clove, minced

3 cups chicken broth

1 1/2 cups orzo pasta

1 cup freshly grated Parmesan cheese

Salt and black pepper to taste

1 pound fresh small shrimp, peeled and deveined

1 1/2 cups fresh or frozen and thawed peas

1 cup sour cream

1. In a medium-size skillet, fry the bacon over moderate heat till almost crisp and drain on paper towels. Pour off all but about 1 tablespoon of the fat, add the scallions and garlic, stir till softened, and set aside. Crumble the bacon.

2. Preheat the oven to 350°F. Butter a 2-quart casserole and set aside.

3. In a large heavy saucepan, bring the broth to a boil, add the orzo, reduce the heat to low, cover, and cook till all the liquid is absorbed, about 15 minutes.

4. Transfer the orzo to the prepared casserole, add the bacon, scallions and garlic, and 1/2 cup of the cheese, season with salt and pepper, and stir well. Add the shrimp and peas and stir gently just to mix the shrimp and peas into the orzo. Spread the sour cream evenly over the top, sprinkle with the remaining 1/2 cup cheese, and bake till bubbly and golden, about 25 minutes.

MAKES 6 SERVINGS

Fusilli, Crabmeat, and Almond Bake

³/₄ pound fusilli pasta

6 tablespoons (³/₄ stick) butter

3 tablespoons all-purpose flour

3 cups milk

¹/₂ cup heavy cream

¹/₈ teaspoon cayenne pepper

Salt and black pepper to taste

1 large egg yolk, beaten

¹/₄ cup sherry

1 pound fresh lump crabmeat, picked over for shells and cartilage

¹/₂ cup sliced almonds

¹/₂ cup freshly grated Parmesan cheese

1. In a large pot of boiling salted water, cook the pasta till just tender, drain, and transfer to a large mixing bowl. Add 2 tablespoons of the butter and toss till it melts and coats the pasta.

2. Preheat the oven to 350°F. Butter a 2- to 2¹/₂-quart casserole.

3. In a large heavy saucepan, melt the remaining 4 tablespoons butter over moderate heat, add the flour, and whisk for about 1 minute. Gradually add the milk, whisking rapidly till the sauce is smooth. Add the heavy cream and cayenne, season with salt and pepper, return to a simmer, and whisk for about 5 minutes. Remove the pan from the heat and very rapidly whisk in the egg yolk. Add the sherry and stir well.

4. Add about ¹/₂ cup of the sauce to the pasta, toss well, and layer it over the bottom of the prepared casserole. In a medium-size mixing bowl, toss together the crabmeat and almonds, then layer the mixture evenly over the pasta. Spoon the remaining sauce over the top, sprinkle evenly with the cheese, and bake till golden brown, about 30 minutes.

MAKES 6 SERVINGS

Department store "tea rooms" have sadly disappeared in most Eastern cities, but in many large Southern and Midwestern centers, some stores still pride themselves on their quaint restaurants where busy shoppers can break for a casual lunch and enjoy a composed salad, fancy sandwich and soup, or a small hot pasta casserole such as this one featuring crabmeat and almonds. The casserole is perfect for bridge lunches any time of year, and I've served it more than once to friends on my deck in early spring when the weather is just warm enough to eat outdoors.

Vegetarian Noodle Casserole

I'm certainly no vegetarian, but when a pasta casserole like this one bursting with all sorts of fresh seasonal vegetables was served at a luncheon at the Stanford Court hotel in San Francisco to accompany a big platter of steamed crabs, I wasted no time chatting with the chef. The casserole can indeed stand on its own when the thermometer soars and appetites are dull, and I've substituted everything from blanched sugar snap peas to cherry tomatoes to young sliced cucumbers. You might also experiment with different types of firm cheeses.

6 ounces egg noodles

3 tablespoons butter

1 medium-size onion, chopped

1 celery rib, chopped

1 small red bell pepper, seeded and chopped

$1/2$ cup coarsely chopped broccoli florets

$1/2$ cup coarsely chopped yellow squash

$3/4$ cup milk

1 cup shredded sharp cheddar cheese

Salt and black pepper to taste

$1/4$ cup dry bread crumbs

2 tablespoons butter, melted

1. In a large pot of boiling salted water, cook the noodles according to package directions till just tender, drain, and transfer to a large mixing bowl.

2. Preheat the oven to 350°F. Butter a 2-quart casserole and set aside.

3. In a large heavy skillet, melt the butter over moderate heat, add the onion, celery, bell pepper, broccoli, and squash and cook, stirring, till the vegetables soften, about 8 minutes. Reduce the heat to low, add the milk and cheese, season with salt and pepper, and stir till the cheese melts. Pour the mixture over the noodles and toss till well blended.

4. Scrape the mixture into the prepared casserole, cover, and bake for 15 minutes.

5. In a small mixing bowl, combine the bread crumbs and melted butter, toss well, spoon evenly over top of the casserole, and continue to bake, uncovered, till slightly crusty on top, 15 to 20 minutes.

MAKES 6 SERVINGS

Crazy for Casseroles

Spiced Noodle and Apple Pudding

$^1/_2$ pound wide egg noodles

2 medium-size apples, peeled, cored, and finely chopped

1 cup seedless golden raisins

$^1/_2$ cup sour cream

2 large eggs, beaten

$^1/_4$ cup ($^1/_2$ stick) butter, melted

$^1/_2$ cup sugar

$^1/_2$ teaspoon ground cinnamon

$^1/_4$ teaspoon ground cloves

Salt and black pepper to taste

1. Preheat the oven to 350°F. Butter a 2-quart casserole and set aside.

2. In a large pot of boiling salted water, cook the noodles according to package directions till just tender, drain, and transfer to a large mixing bowl. Add all the remaining ingredients to the noodles and toss till well blended.

3. Scrape the mixture into the prepared casserole and bake till the top is crisp and nicely browned, about 45 minutes.

MAKES 6 SERVINGS

Although noodle pudding has been a dessert staple in Jewish cuisine for generations, in the German-American communities of the Upper Midwest the spicy casserole is more often served as a side dish to all sorts of ham, pork, and wild game preparations. What's perhaps most interesting about the pudding is that it's good hot, lukewarm, or even cold.

Sweet Maa's Macaroni and Cheese Casserole

No, macaroni and cheese was not created by the Kraft food company in the 1930s; the dish can actually be traced in America back to the time of Thomas Jefferson. (The origins of "macaroni cheese"— or "macrow"—in England are even earlier.) The casserole evolved slowly from simple layered macaroni baked with cheddar or Swiss cheese on top to a much more elaborate production involving cheese sauces and custards and every seasoning from mustard to Worcestershire sauce to grated onion. The version here, made with a custard, was my great grandmother's, and since Sweet Maa was a nineteenth-century Southern lady, I like to think that it represents maybe the second stage in the development of macaroni and cheese as one of America's great casseroles. The cardinal rules of making macaroni and cheese are that plenty of cheese must be used and that the casserole should never be allowed to overcook and dry out.

1 pound (2 cups) elbow macaroni

$^1/_2$ pound sharp cheddar cheese, thinly sliced

2 large eggs, beaten

$^1/_2$ cup milk, plus more as needed

3 tablespoons butter, melted

Salt and black pepper to taste

1. In a large pot of boiling salted water, cook the macaroni according to package directions till just tender and drain.

2. Preheat the oven to 350°F.

3. Butter a 2-quart casserole, then layer half the macaroni over the bottom, followed by a layer of half the cheese slices, then a layer of the remaining macaroni.

4. In a small mixing bowl, combine the eggs, $^1/_2$ cup of milk, and the melted butter, season with salt and pepper, stir till well blended, and pour over the casserole. Top with the remaining cheese slices and add just enough milk to cover all the macaroni but not the top layer of cheese. Bake till the custard is slightly firm and the top lightly browned, 25 to 30 minutes. Serve piping hot.

MAKES 4 TO 6 SERVINGS

CASSEROLE CHAT

In boiling dried pasta "according to package directions" to be used in casseroles, cook the minimum time—generally about 8 minutes. Always use 1 gallon of salted water for each pound of pasta.

Crazy for Casseroles

Three-Cheese Macaroni Casserole

1 pound elbow macaroni

$^1\!/_4$ cup ($^1\!/_2$ stick) butter

3 tablespoons all-purpose flour

4 cups whole milk

$^1\!/_2$ teaspoon dry mustard

2 cups shredded extra-sharp cheddar cheese

1 cup shredded fresh mozzarella cheese

1 cup freshly grated Parmesan cheese

1 teaspoon sweet paprika

Salt and black pepper to taste

1 cup dry white bread crumbs

2 tablespoons butter, melted

1. In a large pot of boiling salted water, cook the macaroni till just tender, drain, and transfer to a large mixing bowl.

2. Preheat the oven to 350°F. Butter a 2$^1\!/_2$- to 3-quart casserole.

3. In a large heavy saucepan, melt the butter over moderate heat, add the flour, and whisk till well blended and smooth, about 1 minute. Gradually whisk in the milk, then add the mustard and whisk till the sauce thickens slightly, about 5 minutes. Reduce the heat to low, add the cheddar, mozzarella, $^1\!/_2$ cup of the Parmesan, and the paprika, season with salt and pepper, and stir till the cheeses melt and the sauce is smooth. Add the sauce to the macaroni, stir till the noodles are well coated, scrape into the casserole, and sprinkle the remaining $^1\!/_2$ cup Parmesan over the top.

4. In a small mixing bowl, combine the bread crumbs and melted butter, sprinkle evenly over the top, and bake till bubbly and slightly browned, about 30 minutes. Serve piping hot.

MAKES 6 TO 8 SERVINGS

This is a very modern version of macaroni and cheese in that a sauce replaces the traditional custard, three different cheeses plus dry mustard provide more sophisticated texture and flavor, and the casserole is given a crusty finish with the bread crumb topping. Remember that the dish is only as good as the quality of its cheeses, meaning that it's futile to even prepare it unless you're willing to buy the finest aged American, Canadian, or even English cheddar available, fresh semi-firm mozzarella, and genuine Parmigiano-Reggiano. There's nothing to equal macaroni and cheese piping hot right from the oven, but it can be reheated successfully if moistened with a little extra milk and covered tightly with aluminum foil. This casserole can also be prepared and served in a 12-inch cast-iron skillet.

Baked Manicotti

Before manicotti fell victim to the vogue of northern Italian cooking that swept through Italian-American kitchens about 20 years ago, there wasn't a *ristorante* or trattoria in the U.S. that didn't pride itself on the rich, sumptuous casserole. In my experience, manicotti was always strictly a restaurant dish, which is unfortunate since it's not that difficult to prepare and so impressive to serve at home. The crepes can be filled with ground meats, but here I've used the more traditional ricotta cheese filling.

CREPES:

1 cup milk

2 large eggs, beaten

$1/2$ teaspoon salt

1 cup all-purpose flour, plus more if needed

Olive oil

FILLING:

1 pound ricotta cheese

$1/4$ cup freshly grated Parmesan cheese

2 tablespoons minced fresh parsley leaves

Salt and black pepper to taste

Pinch of ground nutmeg

1 large egg, beaten

SAUCE AND TOPPING:

3 cups Tomato Sauce (page 7)

$1/4$ cup freshly grated Parmesan cheese

1. To prepare the crepes, combine the milk, eggs, and salt in a medium-size mixing bowl and stir till well blended. Gradually add the flour and stir till the batter is smooth, adding a little more flour if necessary. For each crepe, drop about 1 tablespoon of batter onto a lightly oiled small skillet over moderate heat, spread into a 4-inch circle, brown lightly on one side, about 2 minutes, flip over, brown the other side, and transfer the crepe to a plate. Repeat the procedure till all the batter is used up, piling the crepes on top of each other.

2. Preheat the oven to 350°F. Grease a $2^{1/2}$- to 3-quart casserole and set aside.

3. To prepare the filling, combine all the ingredients in a large mixing bowl and stir till well blended.

Crazy for Casseroles

4. Spoon about 2 tablespoons of filling in the center of each crepe, fold the edges toward the center, press the edges together, and arrange the crepes seam side down in the prepared casserole. When all the crepes have been layered, pour the sauce over the top, sprinkle with the Parmesan, and bake till bubbly, about 30 minutes.

MAKES 6 SERVINGS

Stuffed Cannelloni Casserole

I am never without cartons of homemade spaghetti sauce (with and without meat) in the freezer, which come in handy not only when I want to serve quick bowls of thin pasta but when I need a good sauce for a casserole such as this using pasta shells stuffed with spinach and cheese. You could fill the shells with ground beef or veal sautéed with onions, garlic, and herbs, in which case only a well-seasoned tomato sauce should be used, along with shredded mozzarella or grated Parmesan for the top. In either case, if you're caught short on spaghetti sauce and don't have time to make some, you can substitute about 2 cups of seasoned canned crushed tomatoes or, if you really insist, a bottled sauce.

24 large cannelloni shells

One 10-ounce package frozen chopped spinach, thawed and squeezed dry

1 cup shredded mozzarella cheese

1 cup freshly grated Parmesan cheese

1 cup ricotta cheese

2 large eggs, beaten

1 teaspoon dried oregano, crumbled

1 teaspoon dried basil, crumbled

Salt and black pepper to taste

2 cups spaghetti sauce of your choice

1. In a large pot of boiling salted water, cook the shells according to the package directions till just tender and drain.

2. In a large mixing bowl, combine the spinach, $1/2$ cup of the mozzarella, the Parmesan, ricotta, eggs, oregano, and basil, season with salt and pepper, and mix till well blended.

3. Preheat the oven to 350°F.

4. Butter a 2-quart casserole and spoon half the spaghetti sauce over the bottom. Fill each pasta shell with 2 tablespoons of the spinach-and-cheese mixture and arrange the shells over the sauce. Spoon the remaining sauce over the shells, sprinkle the remaining $1/2$ cup mozzarella evenly over the top, and bake till bubbly and lightly browned, about 30 minutes.

MAKES 6 SERVINGS

Farfalle and Wild Mushroom Supreme

1 pound farfalle pasta

$^1\!/_2$ cup (1 stick) butter

1 small onion, finely chopped

1 pound fresh wild mushrooms (chanterelles, ceps, or shiitakes), stems removed or trimmed and cut into pieces

$^1\!/_2$ cup dry white wine

$1^1\!/_2$ cups half-and-half

Salt and black pepper to taste

2 tablespoons all-purpose flour

$^1\!/_4$ cup milk

2 large eggs

$^1\!/_2$ cup grated pecorino cheese

1. In a large pot of boiling salted water, cook the farfalle till just tender, drain, and transfer to a bowl. Add $^1\!/_4$ cup of the butter and toss to coat.

2. Preheat the oven to 350°F. Butter a 3-quart casserole and set aside.

3. In a large heavy saucepan, melt 2 tablespoons of the butter over moderate heat, add the onion, and stir till softened. Add the mushrooms and stir till most of the liquid evaporates, about 5 minutes. Add the wine, cover, and simmer for 5 minutes. Add the half-and-half, season with salt and pepper, and simmer 5 minutes longer.

4. In a small mixing bowl, combine the remaining 2 tablespoons butter and the flour, mix till it becomes a paste, and gradually add it to the sauce, whisking rapidly till smooth. In another small mixing bowl, whisk together the milk and eggs, add to the sauce, and stir till well blended. Pour the sauce over the pasta and toss till well blended. Scrape the mixture into the prepared casserole, sprinkle the cheese evenly over the top, and bake till golden, 25 to 30 minutes.

MAKES 8 TO 10 SERVINGS

Since the market availability of exotic pastas and fresh wild mushrooms is today amazing compared with just ten years ago, this luscious casserole, the pride of an Italian-American friend in Manhattan, couldn't be more modern. Farfalle, which is a flat sheet of macaroni pinched into the form of a butterfly, is a delightful pasta, but you could also use fusilli or orecchiette for a similar effect. Here I prefer to finish the casserole with a really zesty pecorino cheese, which, by the way, is considerably less expensive than Parmigiano-Reggiano and ideal for many pasta casseroles.

Tortellini, Mushroom, Olive, and Blue Cheese Casserole

So standard are cheddar, Swiss, Parmesan, and mozzarella cheeses in pasta casseroles that most cooks forget that certain small pastas like tortellini and cappelletti are never so sensuous as when dressed with a tangy, rich, silky blue cheese sauce. Of course, Stilton, Gorgonzola, Roquefort, or any of the other noble European blues could be used, but since I'll put Iowa's Maytag Blue up against any of the expensive imports, that's the one I recommend. For an even more intense flavor sensation, I might well substitute about a quarter cup of rinsed capers for the diced olives. Notice that this casserole needs no salt with the blue cheese.

Two 9-ounce packages cheese tortellini

$^1/_4$ cup ($^1/_2$ stick) butter

1 small onion, finely chopped

1 garlic clove, minced

$^1/_4$ pound fresh mushrooms, finely chopped

3 tablespoons all-purpose flour

2 cups milk

1 cup half-and-half

$^1/_2$ cup dry white wine

Black pepper to taste

1$^1/_2$ cups crumbled blue cheese

1 cup diced California black olives

$^1/_2$ cup freshly grated Parmesan cheese

1. In a large pot of boiling salted water, cook the tortellini till just tender, drain, and transfer to a large mixing bowl.

2. Preheat the oven to 350°F. Butter a 2$^1/_2$-quart casserole and set aside.

3. In a large heavy saucepan, melt the butter over moderate heat, add the onion, garlic, and mushrooms, and stir till the vegetables soften and most of the mushroom liquid evaporates, about 5 minutes. Sprinkle the flour on top and stir 1 minute longer. Gradually add the milk, whisking rapidly, then add the half-and-half and whisk till the sauce thickens. Add the wine, season with pepper, reduce the heat slightly, and whisk till the sauce is smooth, about 5 minutes. Remove the pan from the heat, add the blue cheese, and stir till the cheese melts and the sauce is smooth.

4. Add the sauce and olives to the pasta, toss till well blended, and scrape into the prepared casserole. Sprinkle the Parmesan evenly over the top and bake till bubbly and golden brown, about 30 minutes.

MAKES 6 TO 8 SERVINGS

Mrs. Wilkes's Savannah Red Rice

4 strips lean bacon

2 medium-size onions, chopped

2 medium-size green bell peppers, seeded and chopped

2 cups cooked long-grain white rice

One 16-ounce can stewed tomatoes

1 cup tomato sauce

Salt and black pepper to taste

Tabasco sauce to taste

2 tablespoons freshly grated Parmesan cheese

1. Preheat the oven to 325°F. Grease a 2-quart casserole and set aside.

2. In a large skillet, fry the bacon over moderate heat till almost crisp, then drain on paper towels, reserving the grease in the skillet. Crumble the bacon.

3. Add the onions and bell pepper to the skillet and cook, stirring, till slightly browned, about 10 minutes. Add the rice, tomatoes, and tomato sauce, season with salt and pepper and Tabasco, and stir 5 minutes longer.

4. Scrape the mixture into the prepared casserole, sprinkle the top evenly with the cheese, and bake till the rice is slightly dry, about 30 minutes.

MAKES 6 SERVINGS

Mrs. Wilkes's Boarding House in Savannah, Georgia, was a legend even when I was visiting the restaurant as a college student, and people from all over still line up outside at lunchtime today to eat exemplary fried chicken, okra and tomatoes, black-eyed peas, cornbread, pecan pie, and numerous other Southern specialties at large communal tables. This is my adaptation of Mrs. Wilkes's red rice, and if you want to turn the dish into a main course for four, as I often do, simply experiment by adding to the rice and tomatoes small peeled and deveined shrimp or sliced link sausages that have been lightly browned.

A Rice Primer

Curiously enough, the original French "casserole" denoted a simple rice preparation, and one of the first legitimate American-style casseroles (in Fannie Farmer's *Boston Cooking-School Cook Book* of 1896) was little more than a mixture of steamed long-grain rice and mutton. Today, rice is still a major component of dozens of classic casseroles (especially in the South), and special attention should be paid to the cooking of the varieties involved.

By far the most popular rice used in casseroles is long-grain white (or Carolina) rice. For 3 cups cooked rice, bring 2 1/4 cups of water or broth plus 1 teaspoon salt to a boil in a 3-quart saucepan. Add 1 cup of long-grain rice, reduce the heat to low, cover, and cook till all the liquid is absorbed, about 20 minutes. Fluff the rice with a fork.

Brown rice is simply unpolished long-grain white rice still containing the germ and outer layer of bran, which gives the grain its brownish hue. Many consider its flavor to be superior to that of ordinary white rice. For 3 cups cooked rice, bring 2 1/4 cups of water or broth plus 1 teaspoon salt to a boil in a 3-quart saucepan. Add 1 cup of brown rice, reduce the heat to low, cover, and cook till all the liquid is absorbed, 45 to 50 minutes. Fluff the rice with a fork.

Nut-flavored wild rice (also called "Indian rice") is actually not a rice at all but a luxurious aquatic grass grown in the Upper Midwestern states. It is very expensive but delicious in certain casseroles. For 2 1/2 cups cooked rice, first rinse 1 cup raw rice well in a strainer under cold running water. Bring 2 cups of water plus 1/2 teaspoon salt to a boil in a 3-quart saucepan. Add the rinsed wild rice, reduce the heat to low, cover, and cook till tender, 40 to 45 minutes. Fluff with a fork, let simmer about 5 minutes longer, and drain well.

Green Rice Casserole

2^1/$_2$ cups cooked long-grain white rice

1^1/$_2$ cups shredded sharp cheddar cheese

1 cup ricotta cheese

1 cup sour cream

1 garlic clove, minced

Salt and black pepper to taste

One 10-ounce package frozen chopped spinach, thawed

1 medium-size green bell pepper, seeded and coarsely chopped

4 scallions (white part and some of the green), chopped

1. Preheat the oven to 350°F. Butter a 2-quart casserole and set aside.

2. In a large mixing bowl, combine the rice, about three-quarters of the cheddar, the ricotta, sour cream, and garlic, season with salt and pepper, and mix till well blended. Add the spinach, bell pepper, and scallions and mix till well blended.

3. Scrape the mixture into the prepared casserole. Sprinkle the remaining cheddar evenly over the top and bake till golden, about 30 minutes.

MAKES 6 SERVINGS

I've traced green rice casseroles in the U.S. back to the 1930s and they still appear in regional cookbooks to this day. Originally, they seem to have been made only with minced parsley or watercress, but gradually cooks began also using green peas, broccoli, spinach, green bell peppers, chives, and, in the South, various bitter greens. I got the clever idea of adding ricotta cheese from my good friend and colleague Jean Anderson. This makes an easy and attractive buffet dish.

Singapore Rice Casserole

This is the sort of quaintly named rice casserole found in any number of regional church cookbooks dating back to the 1940s and '50s, and I often wonder if the cost of exotic ingredients like saffron was as exorbitant then as now. This particular one comes from northern Illinois, and it is suggested that it be served with any curry dish or meatballs.

2 cups chicken broth

¹/₄ cup (¹/₂ stick) butter

1 small onion, chopped

1 cup raw long-grain white rice

1 teaspoon salt

¹/₄ teaspoon saffron threads

¹/₂ cup seedless dark raisins

1. Preheat the oven to 350°F. Butter a 1-quart casserole and set aside.

2. In a small saucepan, bring the chicken broth to a boil and keep hot.

3. In a medium-size heavy saucepan, melt 2 tablespoons of the butter over moderate heat, add the onion and stir till slightly browned, about 5 minutes. Add the rice, salt, and saffron and stir well. Add the hot broth and stir for 1 minute.

4. Transfer the mixture into the prepared casserole and bake for 20 minutes. Add the remaining 2 tablespoons butter in pieces plus the raisins, stir well, and continue to bake till all the broth is absorbed but the rice is still moist, 5 to 10 minutes.

MAKES 4 SERVINGS

Curried Rice, Leek, and Pine Nut Bake

1 cup raw long-grain white rice

$1/4$ cup pine nuts

3 tablespoons butter

3 leeks (white part only), washed well, patted dry, and diced

1 teaspoon curry powder

2 cups chicken broth

Salt and black pepper to taste

1. Preheat the oven to 350°F. Butter a $1^{1}/_{2}$-quart casserole and set aside.

2. In a shallow baking pan, spread out the rice and nuts, place in the oven, toast, stirring a few times, till golden, 8 to 10 minutes, and set aside.

3. In a large skillet, melt the butter over moderate heat, add the leeks, and stir till softened, about 5 minutes. Transfer to a large heavy saucepan, add the toasted rice and nuts, curry powder, and broth, season with salt and pepper, and bring to a boil.

4. Transfer the contents of the pan to the prepared casserole and bake till the rice has absorbed all the liquid and is tender, about 30 minutes.

MAKES 4 TO 6 SERVINGS

What gives this casserole its sublime character is the initial toasting of the rice and nuts before they're baked with the leeks. I've also substituted either diced sautéed carrots or mushrooms for the leeks, as well as added about a half cup of seedless golden raisins to whatever vegetable I use. In any case, the casserole is wonderful with roasted poultry or virtually any game dish.

Nutty Two-Rice and Raisin Casserole

Frankly, I could sit down and eat this earthy, nutty casserole all by itself with nothing more than a plate of arugula and a good bottle of red wine. The casserole was inspired by a similar rice dish once prepared by Lidia Bastianich at her restaurant, Felidia, in New York and served with delectable venison. I've substituted pecans for toasted pine nuts, orange juice for sweet white wine, and added a few raisins, all of which seem to give the casserole a more American identity. Serve it with any game or pork dish or with roasted poultry. Do notice that the casserole should be baked just till the rices are soft—not dried out.

5½ cups water

1 cup raw wild rice

1 cup raw brown rice

¼ cup (½ stick) butter

1 medium-size onion, finely chopped

1 cup seedless golden raisins

1 cup crumbled pecans

½ cup chopped fresh parsley leaves

½ cup orange juice

Salt and black pepper to taste

½ cup freshly grated Parmesan cheese

1. In a medium-size heavy saucepan, bring 3 cups of the water to a boil, add the wild rice, and stir. Reduce the heat to low, cover, and cook till just tender, 30 to 35 minutes. Drain and transfer to a large mixing bowl.

2. At the same time, bring the remaining 2½ cups water to a boil in another medium-size heavy saucepan, add the brown rice, and stir. Reduce the heat to low, cover, and cook till the water is all absorbed and the rice is just tender, about 25 minutes. Add the brown rice to the wild rice, add 2 tablespoons of the butter, and toss well.

3. Preheat the oven to 350°F. Butter a 2-quart casserole and set aside.

4. In a small skillet, melt the remaining 2 tablespoons butter over moderate heat, add the onion, and stir till golden, about 5 minutes. Add the onion to the two rices, along with the raisins, pecans, parsley, and orange juice, season with salt and pepper, and toss till well blended.

5. Scrape the mixture into the prepared casserole. Sprinkle the cheese over the top, cover, and bake till the rices are soft, 20 to 25 minutes.

MAKES 6 SERVINGS

Crazy for Casseroles

Casseroles for a Crowd

Three-Soup Chicken and Almond Casserole Scarborough

When a friend in Charlotte, North Carolina, Ann Scarborough, first told me about this casserole she liked to serve on buffets for small crowds, I must confess I snickered over the *three* different canned soups used as a base. Then Ann invited me to one of her shindigs, and when I tasted the casserole, served with wild rice and a tart green salad, my pomposity was considerably deflated. Yes, the casserole is indeed baked a full 1¹/₂ hours at a relatively low temperature. Don't ask me why the chicken doesn't toughen. It simply doesn't, and the flavor is amazing.

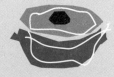

12 boneless, skinless chicken breast halves (about 5 pounds)

Salt and black pepper to taste

1¹/₄ cups (7 ounces) slivered almonds

One 10³/₄-ounce can Campbell's condensed cream of mushroom soup

One 10³/₄-ounce can Campbell's condensed cream of celery soup

One 10³/₄-ounce can Campbell's condensed cream of chicken soup

³/₄ cup dry white wine

¹/₂ pound fresh mushrooms, sliced

1 tablespoon fresh chopped basil leaves

1 cup freshly grated Parmesan cheese

1. Preheat the oven to 325°F.

2. Grease a 3-quart casserole and arrange the chicken breasts over the bottom, overlapping them if necessary. Season with salt and pepper, then sprinkle about two-thirds of the almonds evenly over the top.

3. In a large mixing bowl, combine the three soups, wine, mushrooms, and basil, stir till well blended, and pour over the chicken. Sprinkle the cheese and remaining almonds evenly over the top, cover, and bake for 1 hour. Uncover and continue to bake till golden brown, about 30 minutes.

MAKES 8 TO 10 SERVINGS

Canned Convenience

My dear friend and colleague, the food writer Jean Anderson, has called the twentieth century "The Age of Campbell's. And Heinz. And Lipton." And never is her assessment more valid than when applied to the development of American casseroles. Ever since Campbell's published *Helps for the Hostess* in 1916 and illustrated for the first time how canned soups could be used both as ingredients and as easy substitutes for fancy sauces, casserole cookery has never been quite the same. Food snobs no doubt balk at the very idea of cooking anything with canned soups, but, as I've discovered from long and often embarrassing experience, the truth is that there are some regional American casseroles (like Flounder and Spinach Bake on page 183, Poppy Seed Chicken on page 136, and Broccoli Casserole Supreme on page 303) that simply don't work without the soups. Actually, I've used very few canned soups in this book, but when a recipe does call for one (and I use only Campbell's), that means you're only asking for trouble if you try to substitute another liquid or create some snazzy sauce. Some may consider it to be a dubious honor, but part of the unique distinction of American casseroles is the clever and delicious role that canned soups have played in the development of so many classics.

Craig's Chicken Spaghetti

When Craig Claiborne was my neighbor in East Hampton on Long Island, it was almost a ritual once a year for him to invite at least a dozen close friends over to his famous house for his pride and joy: chicken spaghetti. I think Craig spent half the day preparing the elaborate casserole that his mother had originally taught him how to make in Mississippi, but every time I tasted it, I knew it was time and effort well spent. I've made the casserole only once, served family style to ten guests with only a huge red-tipped lettuce, watercress, and Belgian endive salad, sesame bread sticks, and carafes of red wine. It was something of an ordeal to prepare, but when the feast was over, literally everyone at the table asked for the recipe. Succinctly, the dish is a masterpiece of casserole art.

One 3¹/₂ pound chicken with giblets

Salt to taste

3 cups canned peeled Italian plum tomatoes, coarsely chopped (juices included)

7 tablespoons butter

3 tablespoons all-purpose flour

¹/₂ cup heavy cream

¹/₈ teaspoon ground nutmeg

Black pepper to taste

¹/₂ pound fresh mushrooms, quartered

2 cups finely chopped onions

1¹/₂ cups finely chopped celery

1¹/₂ cups seeded and chopped green bell pepper

1 tablespoon minced garlic

¹/₄ pound ground beef round

¹/₄ pound ground pork

1 bay leaf

¹/₂ teaspoon red pepper flakes

1 pound spaghetti

¹/₂ pound sharp cheddar cheese, shredded

Freshly grated Parmesan cheese

1. Place the chicken and giblets in a kettle with enough water to cover and add salt. Bring to a boil, reduce the heat to low, cover, and simmer till tender, about 45 minutes. Remove the chicken and, when cool enough to handle, shred the meat and set aside. Return the skin and bones to the pot, cook the broth down over moderate heat till reduced to 5 cups, about 30 minutes, strain into a bowl, and set aside. Discard the skin and bones.

2. Meanwhile, place the tomatoes in a medium-size saucepan, cook down over moderate heat to half the original volume, stirring often.

Crazy for Casseroles

3. Melt 3 tablespoons of the butter in another medium-size saucepan over moderate heat, add the flour, and whisk till well blended and smooth. Add 1 cup of the broth plus the cream, whisking rapidly, and when smooth, add the nutmeg, and season with salt and pepper. Reduce the heat to low and continue to cook for about 10 minutes, stirring often. Set the white sauce aside.

4. In a large skillet, heat the remaining 4 tablespoons of butter over moderate heat, add the mushrooms, and stir till golden. Add the onions, celery, and bell pepper and stir till the vegetables are crisp-tender, about 5 minutes. Add the garlic, beef, and pork and cook, stirring and breaking the meat apart with a large, heavy spoon, till the meats lose their pink color. Add the bay leaf, pepper flakes, reduced tomatoes, and white sauce and stir till well blended.

5. In a large pot of boiling salted water, cook the spaghetti till just tender, drain and rinse under cold running water.

6. Preheat the oven to 350°F.

7. Butter a flameproof 5- to 6-quart casserole, then spoon enough of the meat sauce over the bottom to cover it lightly and add about one-third of the spaghetti. Add one-third of the shredded chicken, another layer of meat sauce, and a layer of one-third of the cheddar. Continue making layers, ending up with a layer of spaghetti topped with a thin layer of meat sauce and cheddar. Pour in about 2 cups of the broth to almost cover the top layer of spaghetti, place the casserole on top of the stove, and bring it just to the boil. Cover with a lid or aluminum foil, place in the oven, and bake for 15 minutes. Uncover and bake till lightly browned on top, about 15 minutes longer. Serve immediately with Parmesan cheese on the side.

MAKES 12 OR MORE SERVINGS

Lizzie's Low Country Chicken Bog

When I was a student in France, I remember how a fellow Fulbright, Bobby King from Conway, South Carolina, used to talk about the glorious Low Country dishes produced by his family's black cook, Lizzie. Many years later, when we renewed our old friendship, he happened to mention how he'd learned to reconstruct some of Lizzie's recipes (she never wrote anything down), the most exceptional of which was the chicken bog she'd prepare when Bobby's parents wanted to entertain a large number of guests. Bobby remembers eating this casserole in the forties and fifties, but no doubt its origins can be traced back hundreds of years. Notice that the casserole is not layered, the only seasoning is salt and pepper, the sausages are not browned first, and the broth is not skimmed of fat so that the rice will be glossy and full-flavored. A genuine bog must be slightly soggy (unlike a pilau) and you should watch the rice carefully after about 15 minutes of baking.

Two 3-pound fryer chickens, cut into serving pieces

4 celery ribs, cut into 2-inch pieces

3 medium-size onions, chopped

2 carrots, scraped and cut into thin rounds

4 cups raw long-grain white rice

$^1/_2$ cup (1 stick) butter, cut into pieces

10 breakfast sausage links

Salt and black pepper to taste

1. In a large heavy pot, combine the chicken, celery, onions, and carrots with enough water to cover. Bring to a boil, reduce the heat to low, cover, and simmer till the chicken is tender, 35 to 40 minutes. With a slotted spoon, transfer the chicken to a platter and, when cool enough to handle, remove and discard the skin and bones, shred the meat, and set aside. Transfer the vegetables to a plate and reserve the broth.

2. Preheat the oven to 375°F.

3. In a cast-iron or enameled iron 5-quart casserole, combine the rice and butter with 8 cups of the reserved broth, bring to a boil, reduce the heat to low, cover, and cook for 15 minutes. Add the chicken, vegetables, and sausage, season with salt and pepper, stir, and bake, covered, till most of the water is absorbed and the rice is tender but still very moist, 15 to 20 minutes. Stir well before serving piping hot.

MAKES 10 TO 12 SERVINGS

CASSEROLE CHAT

Since new non-enameled cast-iron casseroles have a porous surface that can rust and produce off-flavors, they should be seasoned by rubbing oil over the entire surface, placing in a preheated 300°F oven for 30 minutes, then cooling.

Chicken and Sausage Casserole

6 to 7 ripe tomatoes, peeled, seeded, and chopped (juices included)

1 teaspoon sugar

2 tablespoons olive oil

Two 2½- to 3-pound chickens, cut into serving pieces

10 to 12 sweet or hot Italian sausages (about 2 pounds), pricked with a fork

2 large onions, chopped

2 large green bell peppers, seeded and chopped

½ pound fresh mushrooms, sliced

2 garlic cloves, minced

2 teaspoons dried oregano, crumbled

Salt and black pepper to taste

1 cup chicken broth

1 cup dry white wine

1. Place the tomatoes and their juices and the sugar in a large saucepan, cook them down over moderate heat till reduced to about 4 cups, and remove from the heat.

2. Preheat the oven to 350°F.

3. In a heavy, flameproof 4- to 5-quart casserole, heat the oil over moderate heat, add the chicken in batches, brown on all sides, and transfer to a plate. Add the sausages, in batches if necessary, brown on all sides, transfer to a plate, and pour off all the fat in the casserole.

4. Return the chicken and sausages to the casserole in layers, sprinkle the onions, bell peppers, mushrooms, and garlic over the top, then sprinkle with the oregano and season with salt and pepper. Add the tomatoes, broth, and wine, stir slightly, cover, and bake till the chicken, sausages, and vegetables are very tender, 40 to 50 minutes.

MAKES 10 SERVINGS

Italian-Americans have created, without question, some of the best casseroles in our entire repertory, and when I was teaching in New Jersey, I had the good fortune to be exposed to a number of these naturally gifted home cooks adept at turning out all sorts of layered dishes. I don't think Italians are capable of preparing what others call an intimate meal, their social philosophy of the more the merrier being almost ingrained in their fun-loving culture. If memory serves, for example, the housewife in East Brunswick who served this particular specialty one Saturday evening invited at least a dozen friends and placed a separate casserole on each of two groaning dinner tables. And that's the way it should be.

Plantation Chicken and Shrimp Pilau

Casserole cookery seems almost indigenous to the coastal Carolina and Georgia Low Country, and nothing exemplifies the art more than the area's numerous rice pilaus that include everything from chicken to seafood to wild game. How *pullao* from India evolved in this region as pilau, purlow, perloo, and heaven knows what other names remains as much a mystery as the Spanish origins of Louisiana's jambalaya. But when guests are invited into the stately homes of Charleston and Savannah for a festive meal (or to much less formal outdoor get-togethers at beach houses on one of the off-shore islands), it's almost certain that one of the dishes will be a sumptuous pilau such as this one that combines chicken and seafood. Do remember that, unlike a Low Country bog, the rice in a pilau must be dry and fluffy.

10 strips lean bacon, cut into ¼-inch pieces

2 large onions, finely chopped

2½ cups raw long-grain white rice

4 cups chicken broth

5 medium-size ripe tomatoes, peeled, seeded, and chopped

¼ cup fresh lemon juice

1 tablespoon Worcestershire sauce

1 tablespoon salt

1 teaspoon black pepper

½ teaspoon cayenne pepper

3 cups diced cooked chicken

2 pounds fresh medium-size shrimp, peeled and deveined

One 4-ounce jar pimentos, drained and chopped

½ cup minced fresh parsley leaves

1. Preheat the oven to 350°F.

2. In a large heavy skillet, fry the bacon over moderate heat till crisp, drain on paper towels, and crumble.

3. Pour about 6 tablespoons of the bacon grease into a heavy, flameproof 4- to 4½-quart casserole, add the onions, and cook, stirring over moderate heat, till softened, about 7 minutes. Add the rice and stir till well coated with the fat. Add the broth, tomatoes, lemon juice, Worcestershire, salt, black pepper, and cayenne and bring the liquid to a boil. Cover the casserole and bake for 25 minutes.

4. Add the chicken, shrimp, bacon, and pimentos, stir till well blended, cover, and bake for another 20 minutes. Remove from the oven and let stand for 10 minutes. Sprinkle with the parsley and fluff with a fork.

MAKES 10 TO 12 SERVINGS

Holiday Turkey, Squash, and Broccoli Soufflé

3 cups peeled, seeded, and diced acorn or butternut squash

3 cups quartered broccoli florets

3 cups diced cooked turkey

1 cup freshly grated Parmesan cheese

$^3/_4$ cup dry bread crumbs

$^1/_2$ cup diced pimentos

2 tablespoons chopped fresh parsley leaves

1 teaspoon dried rosemary, crumbled

Salt and black pepper to taste

1 cup milk

$^1/_2$ cup half-and-half

3 large eggs

1. Preheat the oven to 350°F. Butter a 3-quart casserole and set aside.

2. In a large pot, combine the squash and broccoli with enough salted water to cover, bring to a boil, reduce the heat to low, cover, and simmer, till tender, about 15 minutes. Drain.

3. Transfer the vegetables to a large mixing bowl, add the turkey, cheese, bread crumbs, pimentos, parsley, and rosemary, season with salt and pepper, and toss till well blended.

4. In a medium-size mixing bowl, whisk together the milk, half-and-half, and eggs till well blended and add to the vegetables and turkey. Stir till well blended, scrape into the prepared casserole, and bake till puffy and lightly browned, about 30 minutes.

MAKES 10 SERVINGS

I must confess that my favorite Thanksgiving or Christmas meal is a day-after casual dinner buffet featuring a leftover-turkey hash loaf, stew, or casserole sufficient to feed eight or ten festivity-weary but hungry family members and friends. The whole idea is that the dish be relatively simple and the flavors uncomplicated and comforting. With this particular homey soufflé casserole, I'd serve no more than a congealed fruit salad, hot biscuits or rolls, maybe some pickles, an unpretentious white wine, and homemade cookies.

Turkey and Ham Bake Supreme

When I was teaching at the University of Missouri in Columbia, a food-obsessed faculty wife who could cook anything once served a casserole much like this one at a Sunday dinner given for everyone in my department. When I got the recipe and gave it to my mother, she doctored the dish (for the better) by adding sherry and water chestnuts, and later on it was my idea to give it even more zip with real Parmesan cheese. In many respects, it's the quintessential American casserole, still another way to use up lots of leftover turkey and ham—or, for that matter, any cooked meats—and feed lots of people. For a bit of color, you might also add a cup of green peas and a few chopped pimentos.

^{1}/$_2$ cup (1 stick) butter

2 large onions, finely chopped

^{1}/$_2$ cup all-purpose flour

1^1/$_2$ teaspoons salt

Black pepper to taste

2 cups milk

1 cup half-and-half

^{1}/$_2$ pound fresh mushrooms, sliced

5 tablespoons dry sherry

5 cups diced cooked turkey

5 cups diced cooked ham

Two 5-ounce cans water chestnuts, drained and sliced

1 cup shredded Swiss cheese

^{1}/$_4$ cup freshly grated Parmesan cheese

2^1/$_2$ cups dry bread crumbs

^{1}/$_2$ cup (1 stick) butter, melted

1. Preheat the oven to 350°F.

2. In a heavy, flameproof 3- to 3^1/$_2$-quart casserole, melt 6 tablespoons of the butter over moderate heat, add the onions, and cook, stirring, till soft but not browned, about 5 minutes. Sprinkle the flour and salt over the onions, season with pepper, and stir 2 minutes longer. Reduce the heat to low and gradually add the milk and half-and-half, stirring constantly till the mixture is thickened and smooth. Remove the casserole from the heat.

3. In a small skillet, melt the remaining 2 tablespoons butter over moderate heat, add the mushrooms, and cook, stirring, till golden, about 5 minutes. Add the mushrooms to the milk mixture, then add the sherry,

turkey, ham, and water chestnuts and stir till well blended. Sprinkle the two cheeses evenly over the top.

4. In a medium-size mixing bowl, combine the bread crumbs and melted butter, stir till well blended, spoon the mixture evenly over the cheeses, and bake till lightly browned on top, about 35 minutes. Serve piping hot.

MAKES 10 TO 12 SERVINGS

Mary's Texas Olive Tamale Pie

In Texas and throughout much of the Southwest, tamale pies are often made either with a sturdy top cornmeal crust or a softer top and bottom cornmeal "mush" crust. Both can be delicious, but never did I taste a better pie than this one with olives and no separate crust that my old friend Mary Greenwood and her beau, Sam, served in a handsome casserole one Saturday night down in Houston to a contingent of visiting Yankees. To get the right texture, just be sure when preparing the cornmeal mixture to add the meal slowly to the water, whisking constantly till very smooth.

3 tablespoons bacon grease

1 medium-size onion, chopped

1 medium-size green bell pepper, seeded and chopped

2 garlic cloves, minced

1 1/2 pounds ground beef round

1 1/2 tablespoons chili powder

1/2 teaspoon dried oregano, crumbled

1/2 teaspoon ground cumin

One 28-ounce can crushed tomatoes

1/2 cup beef broth

One 12-ounce can corn kernels, drained

30 pitted black olives, cut in half

Salt and black pepper to taste

3 cups water

2 cups yellow cornmeal

2 tablespoons butter

1 1/2 cups grated Monterey Jack cheese

1. In a large, deep, heavy skillet, heat the bacon grease over moderate heat, add the onion, bell pepper, and garlic, and stir for 5 minutes. Add the beef, chili powder, oregano, and cumin and stir till the meat is no longer pink. Add the tomatoes and broth, bring to a simmer, and cook for 30 minutes. Add the corn and olives, season with salt and pepper, stir well, and continue to cook for 15 minutes.

2. Preheat the oven to 350°F. Grease a 3-quart casserole and set aside.

Crazy for Casseroles

3. Pour the water into a large heavy saucepan, salt it to taste, bring to a boil, and gradually add the cornmeal, whisking rapidly till smooth, about 1 minute. Add the butter and stir till well blended.

4. Add the cornmeal mixture to the meat sauce, stir till well blended and smooth, then scrape into the prepared casserole. Sprinkle the cheese evenly over the top and bake till golden brown, about 35 minutes.

MAKES 8 TO 10 SERVINGS

Easy Moussaka

Who says that moussaka must involve a complicated béchamel sauce to be really good? That's what I always thought till a lady in Kansas City served this version to a group of March of Dimes gourmet gala judges and told me about substituting a simple half-and-half and sour cream cheese sauce. Moussaka, served with garlicky bread and a vinegary salad, is virtually designed to feed lots of people, and so long as you don't allow the eggplant to absorb too much oil while being browned (it sucks up oil like a sponge and can become disgustingly soggy), I dare say you won't have much of this left over. For the most authentic flavor, do try to use ground lamb instead of beef if you have a willing butcher.

5 medium-size eggplants

Salt to taste

Olive oil for frying

$^1/_2$ cup dry bread crumbs

3 medium-size onions, chopped

2 garlic cloves, minced

Black pepper to taste

2$^1/_2$ pounds ground lamb shoulder or beef round

2 cups tomato sauce

$^1/_4$ cup dry red wine

3 tablespoons tomato paste

$^1/_2$ teaspoon dried oregano, crumbled

$^1/_4$ teaspoon ground cinnamon

1 bay leaf, crumbled

$^1/_4$ cup minced fresh parsley leaves

1$^1/_2$ cups half-and-half

1$^1/_2$ cups sour cream

$^1/_8$ teaspoon ground nutmeg

$^1/_2$ cup freshly grated Parmesan cheese

1. Peel the eggplants, cut lengthwise into 3-inch-thick slices, salt the slices, and let them drain in a large colander in the sink for about 1 hour. Rinse the slices and pat dry with paper towels.

2. In a large heavy skillet, heat about 2 tablespoons of the oil over moderate heat, add about 4 slices of eggplant, brown on both sides, and drain on paper towels. Repeat the procedure with additional oil and eggplant till all the slices are browned, never using more than about 2 tablespoons of oil for each batch and not overcooking the eggplant.

3. Preheat the oven to 350°F. Grease a shallow 3- to 3½-quart casserole, sprinkle the bread crumbs evenly over the bottom, and set aside.

4. In a large heavy skillet, heat about 3 tablespoons olive oil over moderate heat, add the onions and garlic, season with salt and pepper, and stir till golden, about 8 minutes. Add the meat, break up any chunks, and stir till browned, about 10 minutes. Add the tomato sauce, wine, tomato paste, oregano, cinnamon, bay leaf, and parsley, stir well, reduce the heat to low, and let the sauce simmer for 15 to 20 minutes.

5. Alternating, layer the eggplant and meat sauce in the prepared casserole till everything is used up. In a medium-size mixing bowl, combine the half-and-half, sour cream, nutmeg, and cheese, whisk till well blended, spread evenly over the casserole, and bake till puffy and lightly browned, about 1¼ hours.

MAKES 10 SERVINGS

New Mexican Meat and Chile Pepper Casserole

Variations on this zesty casserole are found throughout the American Southwest, but few utilize milk and eggs as I do to transform a rather ponderous concoction into a much lighter, soufflé-style dish. This is a great buffet casserole for eight to ten guests, but if any is left over, I think nothing of stuffing the mixture into two or three seeded bell pepper halves, sprinkling more cheese over the top, drizzling a little oil over the cheese, and baking them very slowly for a simple, intimate dinner.

3 tablespoons corn oil

1 pound ground beef round

$^3/_4$ pound ground pork

1 large onion, chopped

1 garlic clove, minced

$^1/_4$ teaspoon ground cumin

Three $4^1/_2$-ounce cans green chiles, drained and chopped

$^3/_4$ pound Monterey Jack cheese, shredded

2 cups milk

6 large eggs

$^1/_2$ cup all-purpose flour

Salt and black pepper to taste

Tabasco sauce to taste

1. Preheat the oven to 350°F. Grease a $2^1/_2$- to- 3-quart casserole and set aside.

2. In a large heavy skillet, heat the oil over moderate heat, add the beef, pork, onion, garlic, and cumin and stir till the meats lose their pink color. Drain off any fat and set the skillet aside.

3. Spoon half the chiles over the bottom of the prepared casserole and sprinkle half the cheese evenly over that. Layer the meat mixture evenly over the cheese, then top with the remaining chiles and cheese.

4. In a large mixing bowl, whisk together the milk and eggs till well blended, add the flour, season with salt and pepper and Tabasco, and whisk till well blended and smooth. Pour over the top of the casserole and bake till golden brown, about 35 minutes.

MAKES 10 SERVINGS

Ham, Mushroom, and Noodle Special

1/4 cup (1/2 stick) butter

1/4 cup all-purpose flour

4 cups milk

1/2 pound sharp cheddar cheese, shredded

1/8 teaspoon ground nutmeg

1/8 teaspoon cayenne pepper

Salt and black pepper to taste

1 1/2 cups heavy cream

1 tablespoon vegetable oil

1 medium-size onion, finely chopped

1/2 pound fresh mushrooms, finely chopped

3/4 pound cooked ham, cut into small cubes

1 pound egg noodles, cooked according to package directions and drained

1/2 cup freshly grated Parmesan cheese

1. Preheat the oven to 350°F. Butter a 3-quart casserole and set aside.

2. In a large heavy saucepan, melt 3 tablespoons of the butter over moderate heat, add the flour, and whisk till well blended and smooth. Whisking rapidly, add the milk till well blended, then add the cheddar, nutmeg, and cayenne, season with salt and black pepper, and stir till the cheese melts. Stir in the cream, bring to a boil, stirring, and remove from the heat.

3. In a large, deep skillet, heat the remaining 1 tablespoon butter and the oil together over moderate heat, add the onion and mushrooms, and stir till softened, about 5 minutes. Add the ham and stir well. Add the cheese sauce, stir to combine, then add the noodles and stir till well blended.

4. Scrape the mixture into the prepared casserole, sprinkle the Parmesan evenly over the top, and bake till golden brown, about 30 minutes.

MAKES 8 TO 10 SERVINGS

I came up with this straightforward casserole early one winter evening when, as sometimes happens, guests invited for dinner asked if they could bring friends and, quite frankly, I had no intention of going back to the market for more of the beef short ribs I'd intended to bake. I'm never, ever without leftover ham in the fridge or freezer, some type of fresh or dried mushroom, packages of various noodles, and plenty of genuine Parmesan cheese, a habit that has paid high dividends more than once and that I urge everybody to imitate. This casserole is just as good made with leftover cooked chicken or turkey, and feel free to sprinkle a few herbs into the sauce for added flavor.

Sausage Lasagne

You can use, of course, browned hot or sweet Italian sausages cut into ¹/₂-inch-thick rounds for this lasagne, but I personally prefer the flavor of good (and preferably spicy) bulk pork sausage. For years, I also used traditional ricotta cheese, then, when I once decided at the last minute to have lasagne and salad available for a group of friends expected for cocktails and didn't have time to go shopping for ricotta, I simply substituted cottage cheese I had in the fridge. Frankly, I couldn't tell much difference, and most of my guests not only stayed for supper but devoured every morsel. As to whether I'd ever resort to one of those bottled marinara sauces in place of making my own, the answer is a nasty No!

1 pound bulk pork sausage

1 garlic clove, minced

2 teaspoons dried oregano, crumbled

1 teaspoon dried basil, crumbled

1¹/₂ teaspoons salt

One 16-ounce can crushed tomatoes

Two 6-ounce cans tomato paste

10 ounces lasagne noodles

3 cups creamy-style cottage cheese

2 large eggs, beaten

¹/₄ cup chopped fresh parsley leaves

Black pepper to taste

¹/₂ cup freshly grated Parmesan cheese

1 pound mozzarella cheese, shredded

1. In a large heavy skillet, brown the sausage well over moderate heat, breaking up any pieces and drain off the grease. Add the garlic, oregano, basil, salt, tomatoes, and tomato paste, stir well, return to a simmer over low heat, and cook, stirring occasionally, about 30 minutes.

2. Meanwhile, in a large pot of salted boiling water, cook the noodles according to the package directions and drain.

3. Preheat the oven to 375°F. Grease a 3-quart casserole and set aside.

4. In a large mixing bowl, combine the cottage cheese, eggs, parsley, pepper, and Parmesan, stirring till well blended.

Crazy for Casseroles

5. Layer half the noodles over the bottom of the prepared casserole, spread half the cottage cheese mixture over that, layer in half the meat sauce, and sprinkle half the mozzarella evenly over the top. Repeat with the remaining noodles, cottage cheese mixture, meat sauce, and mozzarella and bake till bubbly and slightly browned, 30 to 35 minutes. Let stand about 10 minutes before serving.

MAKES 10 SERVINGS

Sausage and Leek Buffet Casserole

In many respects, I consider this to be the ultimate casserole for a crowd, not only because it requires nothing else but a large tossed salad, good bread, and a sturdy red wine but also because the unbaked casserole minus the bread crumbs and melted butter can be made well in advance and frozen. It also happens to be one of the most delicious casseroles ever conceived, whether prepared with bulk sausage, as directed, or with browned hot or sweet Italian sausages cut into small rounds. Just make sure to serve the casserole piping hot.

1½ pounds bulk pork sausage

12 large leeks (3 to 3½ pounds)

¼ cup (½ stick) butter

2 garlic cloves, minced

1½ cups heavy cream

Large pinch of ground nutmeg

Salt and black pepper to taste

½ cup dry bread crumbs

¼ cup (½ stick) butter, melted

1. In a large heavy skillet, break up the sausage meat with a fork and fry over moderate heat till nicely browned all over. Drain on paper towels and set aside.

2. While the sausage is frying, trim the leeks of all but about 2 inches of the green tops, slice the whites down the middle almost to the root ends, and rinse the layers thoroughly under cold running water. Slice the leeks crosswise at 2-inch intervals.

3. Preheat the oven to 375°F. Butter a shallow 3½-quart casserole and set aside.

4. In a large heavy saucepan, melt the solid butter over moderate heat, add the garlic, and stir for 1 minute. Add the leeks and cook, stirring, till they have softened a bit, about 3 minutes. Add the heavy cream and nutmeg, season with salt and pepper, and cook till the leeks are tender, 10 to 15 minutes.

5. Scrape the mixture into the prepared casserole and spoon the sausage evenly over the top. Sprinkle the bread crumbs over that, drizzle the melted butter over the crumbs, and bake till golden, about 35 minutes.

MAKES 10 TO 12 SERVINGS

Crazy for Casseroles

Creole Ham and Shrimp Jambalaya

1/2 pound sliced lean bacon, cut into 1-inch pieces

1 large onion, finely chopped

2 medium-size green bell peppers, seeded and cut into 1-inch-wide strips

1 garlic clove, minced

2 cups raw long-grain white rice

1 pound smoked ham, cut into strips

One 28-ounce can whole tomatoes, drained and coarsely chopped

1 teaspoon dried thyme, crumbled

Salt and black pepper to taste

3 cups chicken broth

1 1/2 pounds fresh medium-size shrimp, peeled and deveined

1. Preheat the oven to 350°F.

2. In a heavy, flameproof 3- to 3 1/2-quart casserole, fry the bacon over moderate heat till browned but not crisp and drain on paper towels. Add the onion, bell pepper, and garlic to the fat in the casserole and stir till softened, about 5 minutes. Add the rice and stir till the grains become opaque. Add back the bacon, as well as the ham, tomatoes, and thyme, season with salt and pepper, and stir till well blended. Add the broth, bring to a boil, cover the casserole, and place in the oven for 15 minutes.

3. Remove the casserole from the oven, add the shrimp, pushing them down into the rice, and continue to bake till all the broth is absorbed and the rice is tender and still moist, about 15 minutes.

MAKES 10 SERVINGS

One of the great dishes of American gastronomy, jambalaya (the name possibly derives from the Spanish word for ham, *jamón*, a prime ingredient) can be traced back to the Louisiana Territory of the eighteenth century and is both Creole and Cajun in origin. Different styles are made with beef, pork, chicken, shrimp, oysters, crawfish, and numerous other components; the dish can be prepared in a large pot, skillet, or casserole; and Louisianians are so passionate about jambalaya that today they even hold an annual jambalaya cookoff in the Cajun town of Gonzales. This classic version was inspired by one prepared for me by Paul Prudhomme when he was chef at Commander's Palace in New Orleans back in the 1970s. Since the rice must remain moist, add a little more chicken broth if the casserole seems too dry during the final minutes of baking.

Cape Fear Shrimp, Mushroom, and Olive Supper

Some of the sweetest shrimp on the entire East Coast are hauled in around Southport at the mouth of North Carolina's Cape Fear River, and it is in this immediate area just south of Wilmington that I've eaten some of my most memorable seafood casseroles. Coastal Tarheels have been concocting shrimp casseroles such as this one for centuries, most of which are highly seasoned and ideal for big outdoor gatherings around wooden tables under ancient live oaks dripping with Spanish moss. It may cost considerably more, but you can make an even more impressive (and richer) casserole by substituting at least a pound of fresh lump crabmeat for the shrimp. This, however, is one casserole I do not recommend freezing in advance of baking, since it affects the texture of the seafood.

$^1/_2$ cup (1 stick) butter

1 medium-size onion, finely chopped

$^1/_2$ cup all-purpose flour

$2^1/_2$ cups half-and-half

3 large egg yolks, beaten

2 teaspoons Dijon mustard

3 tablespoons dry sherry

2 teaspoons Worcestershire sauce

4 dashes Tabasco sauce

$1^1/_2$ pounds fresh shrimp, peeled, deveined, and coarsely diced

$^1/_4$ pound fresh mushrooms, finely chopped

2 large hard-boiled eggs, diced

1 cup slivered pimento-stuffed green olives

2 tablespoons chopped fresh parsley leaves

Salt and black pepper to taste

1 cup dry bread crumbs

$^1/_2$ cup shredded Swiss cheese

2 tablespoons butter, melted

1. Preheat the oven to 350°F. Butter a 3-quart casserole and set aside.

2. In a large heavy saucepan, melt the butter over moderate heat, add the onion, and stir till softened, about 5 minutes. Sprinkle the flour over the onion and stir 1 minute longer. Gradually add the half-and-half, whisking till thickened. Whisk about 2 tablespoons of hot sauce into the egg yolks, add the yolks and mustard to the sauce, and whisk steadily till smooth. Add the sherry, Worcestershire, and Tabasco and stir till well blended. Add the shrimp, mushrooms, hard-boiled eggs, olives, and parsley, season with salt and pepper, and stir till well blended.

3. Scrape the mixture into the prepared casserole. In a medium-size mixing bowl, combine the bread crumbs, cheese, and melted butter, toss well, spoon the mixture evenly over the top of the casserole, and bake till bubbly and lightly browned, about 30 minutes.

MAKES 10 SERVINGS

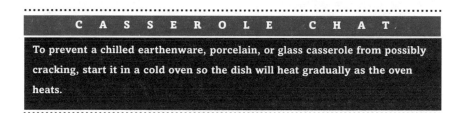

To prevent a chilled earthenware, porcelain, or glass casserole from possibly cracking, start it in a cold oven so the dish will heat gradually as the oven heats.

Casseroles for a Crowd

Classic Tuna Noodle Casserole

Created about a half-century ago by the Campbell Soup Company, tuna noodle casserole is now an American classic with as many detractors as enthusiasts, depending on both the level of snobbism and how well the dish is prepared. Use inferior noodles, canned peas, cheap tuna, and processed cheese, or overbake the casserole, and of course you'll end up with a disaster. On the other hand, if you respect the ingredients and watch the casserole carefully to make sure it remains moist and succulent, there simply is no better party dish. Cream of mushroom soup can also be used, but be warned that trying to substitute something like a light cream sauce for the soup produces results that won't impress many people. Note also that neither salt nor pepper is needed, and, please, no crushed potato chips on top!

8 ounces egg noodles, cooked according to package directions (but not overcooked) and drained

2 cups cooked fresh or frozen green peas, drained

4 large hard-boiled eggs, chopped

$1/4$ cup chopped pimentos

Four 6-ounce cans solid white tuna packed in oil, drained and flaked

Two $10^3/4$-ounce cans Campbell's condensed cream of celery soup

1 cup milk

$1/4$ cup dry bread crumbs

$1/2$ cup shredded sharp cheddar cheese

2 tablespoons butter, melted

1. Preheat the oven to 375°F.

2. Butter a $2^1/2$- to 3-quart casserole, then combine in the casserole the noodles, peas, eggs, pimentos, and tuna and stir till well blended. Add the condensed soup and milk, stir till the mixture is well blended, and bake for 20 minutes.

3. In a small mixing bowl, combine the bread crumbs, cheese, and melted butter, stir till well blended, spoon evenly over the top of the casserole, and continue to bake till lightly browned but not too dry, about 10 minutes.

MAKES 8 TO 10 SERVINGS

Peerless Pimentos

Pimentos can add a very special tang (not to mention color) to numerous casseroles, and because of their superior flavor, I'm very touchy about using genuine bottled pimentos versus ordinary roasted red bell peppers. Contrary to what most people think, the large, red, heart-shaped pimento pepper (indigenous to the Americas and taken back to Spain by Columbus) is *not* the same as its humbler cousin. Today most pimento production and packing is done in the South, and whole, sliced, and diced pimentos are available nationwide in 4- and 7-ounce jars. Although their flavor is distinctive, it is not aggressive, so feel free to experiment liberally with pimentos—especially in poultry, seafood, and vegetable casseroles, and in casserole breads.

Tuna and Spinach Company Bake

This layered casserole is not necessarily any better than the classic tuna-noodle one; it is simply more sophisticated and can be served with great pride at any upscale get-together. I do recommend using fresh spinach here instead of frozen for ideal texture, and while I personally have no use for all the raw and tough grilled fresh tuna that is currently so fashionable, I have no objection at all to substituting about a pound of fresh yellowfin chunks for the canned in this particular casserole. Expert chefs know that fresh tuna is always best when baked, and this is the perfect dish to test the principle if, and only if, you find a beautiful slab of fish.

3 pounds fresh spinach, rinsed well and stems removed

$1/4$ cup ($1/2$ stick) butter

$1/2$ pound fresh mushrooms, sliced

1 medium-size onion, finely chopped

$1/4$ cup all-purpose flour

2 bay leaves, finely crumbled

$1^1/2$ teaspoons salt

$1/2$ teaspoon black pepper

$2^1/2$ cups half-and-half

3 large egg yolks, beaten

Four 6-ounce cans solid white tuna packed in oil, drained

$1/2$ cup dry bread crumbs

2 tablespoons butter, melted

1. Preheat the oven to 350°F. Butter a 3-quart casserole and set aside.

2. Place the spinach in a large pot with about 1 inch of water, bring to a boil, cover, and cook till it wilts, about 8 minutes. Drain and squeeze dry.

3. In a large heavy saucepan, melt the butter over moderate heat, add the mushrooms and onion, and stir till softened. Sprinkle the flour over the top, add the bay leaves, salt, and pepper, and stir for 2 minutes. Add the half-and-half and stir till bubbly. Rapidly stir about 3 tablespoons of the hot sauce into the egg yolks, then add the yolks to the sauce, stirring steadily till the sauce is thickened and smooth. Remove from the heat.

4. Arrange the spinach evenly in the casserole, then layer the tuna evenly over that and pour the sauce over the tuna. In a small mixing bowl, combine the crumbs and butter, stir till well blended, spoon over the top of the casserole, and bake till bubbly and slightly browned, about 30 minutes.

MAKES 10 SERVINGS

Crazy for Casseroles

Sweet Potato and Carrot Casserole

4 large sweet potatoes, peeled and diced

6 medium-size carrots, scraped and diced

$^1/_2$ cup orange juice

1 large egg

$^1/_4$ cup ($^1/_2$ stick) butter, melted

3 tablespoons firmly packed dark brown sugar

$^1/_8$ teaspoon ground nutmeg

2 tablespoons bourbon

Salt and black pepper to taste

$^1/_2$ cup chopped pecans

1. In a large pot, combine the potatoes and carrots with enough water to cover, bring to a boil, reduce the heat to low, cover, and simmer till very tender, about 30 minutes.

2. Preheat the oven to 350°F. Butter a 2$^1/_2$-quart casserole and set aside.

3. Drain the vegetables, transfer to a large mixing bowl, and mash with a potato masher till almost a puree. Add the orange juice, egg, butter, brown sugar, nutmeg, and bourbon, season with salt and pepper, and stir till well blended and smooth. Stir in the pecans, scrape the mixture into the prepared casserole, and bake till slightly browned, about 30 minutes.

MAKES 10 SERVINGS

Why baked sweet potatoes and carrots have such an affinity, I don't know, but there is simply no better casserole with the holiday turkey, goose, or duck than this one. When I serve the rich casserole on a festive buffet, I might well sprinkle about a cup of grated coconut over the top at the last minute. Note: For the right texture, do not puree the vegetables in a food processor.

Company Mixed Vegetable Scramble

How often have you wanted to bake a beautiful glazed ham, leg of lamb, or beef rump for a crowd and debated what vegetables would be most appropriate? My answer is this luscious all-purpose vegetable casserole, which, along with maybe some roasted potatoes and small dinner rolls, is not only to everybody's taste but attractive on the buffet or dinner table. You can substitute virtually any fresh seasonal vegetables, and I even like to feature the casserole as a main dish for about six guests when I have plenty of country ham biscuits or reheated barbecued ribs to go along.

4 cups shelled fresh or thawed frozen green peas

1¹/₂ cups finely chopped celery

1¹/₂ cups scraped and shredded carrots

1¹/₂ cups finely chopped onions

3 large eggs, beaten

3 cups milk

¹/₂ cup all-purpose flour

1¹/₂ teaspoons salt

³/₄ teaspoon black pepper

1¹/₂ cups fine dry bread crumbs

2 cups shredded sharp cheddar cheese

6 tablespoons (³/₄ stick) butter, melted

1. In a large mixing bowl, combine the peas, celery, carrots, and onions and set aside.

2. In a large heavy saucepan, combine the eggs, milk, flour, salt, and pepper and cook over moderate heat, stirring constantly, till the sauce is thickened.

3. Preheat the oven to 350°F.

4. Butter a 3-quart casserole and arrange half the vegetable mixture over the bottom. Sprinkle evenly with ¹/₂ cup of the bread crumbs, 1 cup of the cheese, and half the sauce. Repeat with the remaining vegetables, ¹/₂ cup of the bread crumbs, and the remaining 1 cup cheese and sauce. Sprinkle the remaining ¹/₂ cup bread crumbs over the top, drizzle with the melted butter, and bake till golden brown, about 35 minutes.

MAKES 10 SERVINGS

Vegetable Bakes, Gratins, and Soufflés

Yukon Gold Potato and Goat Cheese Casserole

Yukon Gold potatoes first began to appear in American markets about a decade ago and, since they now seem to be grown virtually everywhere, my only explanation for their catchy name is that they are indeed one of the richest, creamiest, and most buttery potatoes around. They make luscious mashed potatoes and, in casseroles, they absorb milk and cream beautifully. This is one gratin-style casserole that requires no butter, but do baste the potatoes several times and watch them carefully to make sure they stay moist.

2 pounds Yukon Gold potatoes, peeled and thinly sliced

1 garlic clove, minced

Salt and freshly ground black pepper to taste

Ground nutmeg to taste

6 ounces fresh soft goat cheese, crumbled

2 cups half-and-half

1. Preheat the oven to 325°F.

2. Butter a 1½-quart casserole. Layer one-third of the potatoes overlapping across the bottom and sprinkle part of the garlic, salt and pepper, and just a trace of nutmeg over the top. Layer one-third of the cheese over the top, then repeat layering the potatoes and cheese 2 more times, seasoning each layer with garlic, salt and pepper, and traces of nutmeg. Pour the half-and-half around the edges of the casserole.

3. Bake till the top is golden brown, about 1¼ hours, basting several times and not allowing the casserole to get too dry.

MAKES 4 SERVINGS

California Scalloped Potatoes

l cup crumbled dry goat cheese

1 cup shredded Monterey Jack cheese

2 tablespoons all-purpose flour

Salt and black pepper to taste

4 medium-size baking potatoes (about 2 pounds), peeled and very thinly sliced

One 10-ounce can green chiles, drained, peeled, seeded, and finely chopped

$^1/_4$ cup ($^1/_2$ stick) butter, cut into pieces

2 cups milk

1. Preheat the oven to 350°F. Generously butter a 2-quart casserole and set aside.

2. In a medium-size mixing bowl, combine the two cheeses and flour, season with salt and pepper, toss well, and set aside.

3. Layer one-third of the potatoes overlapping across the bottom of the prepared casserole. Sprinkle half the chiles over them, dot with about 1 tablespoon of the butter, and sprinkle one third of the cheese mixture evenly over the top. Repeat the sequence 2 more times with the remaining ingredients, saving the last tablespoon of butter for the top layer and ending with the cheese mixture. Pour the milk around the sides and bake till golden brown, about 1$^1/_4$ hours, basting several times.

MAKES 6 SERVINGS

When it comes to my beloved scalloped potatoes, I was always a purist till the famous San Francisco chef, Jeremiah Tower, introduced me to this sublime California version made with chile peppers and two regional cheeses. I normally bake plain scalloped potatoes very slowly at 300°F to allow them to absorb all the milk or cream; these are cooked for less time at a higher temperature since the cheeses create a different textural effect. Nonetheless, watch them carefully after about an hour to make sure they don't get too dry.

Potato, Wild Mushroom, and Sorrel Gratin

Baked slowly at a relatively low temperature, this is without question one of the most luscious vegetable casseroles in my entire repertoire. The flavor contrast of the mild potatoes, earthy mushrooms, and slightly bitter sorrel is phenomenal, and if you have plenty of time, bake the casserole at 300°F for up to 2 hours for even greater succulence, adding a little more milk or half-and-half if necessary to keep the ingredients moist. Fresh sorrel (which is also wonderful added to salads) is now available almost year round in finer markets, but do remember that the larger leaves can be tough and very bitter. If you can't find sorrel, you might substitute either radicchio or arugula with different results.

2 tablespoons butter

$^1/_2$ pound fresh wild mushrooms (chanterelles, ceps, or shiitakes), stems removed or trimmed and thinly sliced

1 garlic clove, minced

5 large baking potatoes (about 2$^1/_2$ pounds), peeled and thinly sliced

4 ounces tender young fresh sorrel leaves, rinsed and shredded

Salt and freshly ground black pepper to taste

1 cup milk

1 cup half-and-half

3 large eggs

1$^1/_2$ cups freshly grated Parmesan cheese

1. Preheat the oven to 325°F. Butter a 2-quart casserole and set aside.

2. In a medium-size skillet, melt the butter over moderate heat, add the mushrooms and garlic, stir till softened, about 3 minutes, and remove from the heat.

3. Layer half the potatoes overlapping over the bottom of the prepared casserole, spoon the mushrooms evenly over the potatoes, and sprinkle the sorrel over the mushrooms. Layer the remaining potatoes overlapping over the top and season generously with salt and pepper.

4. In a large mixing bowl, whisk together the milk, half-and-half, and eggs till well blended, pour over the casserole, and bake for 1 hour. Sprinkle the cheese evenly over the top and continue to bake till golden brown, about 30 minutes, basting once or twice and not allowing the casserole to get too dry.

MAKES 6 SERVINGS

Crazy for Casseroles

Potato Power

Quite honestly, I don't hesitate a second to use such "boiling" potatoes as round reds, Maine, Eastern, or California whites when making casseroles if they're the best looking potatoes I have on hand. But by far the finest casserole potatoes are russets, the most popular being Idahoes. The russets are starchier, mealier, and drier than most others, which not only allows them to hold their shape well but contributes to the texture of casserole liquids.

Some of the potatoes found in markets today are a disgrace: soft, discolored, sprouting, or with a green tinge, the result of overexposure to light. I reject any potato that is not fresh-looking, firm, well-shaped, and blemish-free, and I suggest you do the same. Nor do I buy potatoes casually in 5- or 10-pound bags just because they're on sale, insisting instead on handpicking each and every spud and rarely purchasing many more than the number I plan to use. Never store extra potatoes (especially russets) in the refrigerator, since the cold will convert the starch into sugar, and to prevent bitter green "sun spots" from forming, remember that potatoes much prefer the dark to light.

As wonderful as potatoes are in so many casseroles, the single down side is that they lose their texture and can become mushy when frozen. What I do with a leftover baked casserole containing potatoes that I want to freeze is to simply pick out whatever potatoes remain, then replace them with a few freshly boiled ones when I eventually reheat the casserole.

Eggplant and Potato Casserole

Although this vegetable casserole will serve eight as a side dish, I usually like to feature is as a main course with a composed meat or poultry salad and toasted garlic bread, sometimes adding a few chopped Greek olives or anchovies with the oregano for more piquancy. Without the mozzarella sprinkled on top, the casserole is also delicious at lunch served at room temperature or cold.

2 small eggplants (about 1½ pounds), peeled and cut lengthwise into ¼-inch-thick slices

Salt to taste

Olive oil for brushing

1½ pounds red potatoes, peeled and cut into ¼-inch-thick slices

1 garlic glove, minced

Freshly ground black pepper to taste

½ teaspoon dried oregano, crumbled

1 pound ripe tomatoes, peeled, seeded, and chopped

1 cup milk

1 large egg

1 cup freshly grated Parmesan cheese

1 cup shredded mozzarella cheese

1. Place the eggplant slices in a colander over a plate, sprinkle with salt, toss, and let drain for 30 minutes.

2. Meanwhile, preheat the oven broiler. Grease a 2-quart casserole and set aside.

3. Rinse the eggplant slices under running water and pat dry with paper towels. Arrange the slices in a single layer on one or two baking sheets, brush lightly with olive oil, and broil for about 4 minutes. Turn the slices over, brush again with oil, broil about 4 minutes, and set aside.

4. Reduce the oven temperature to 350°F.

5. Layer the potatoes overlapping across the bottom of the prepared casserole. Sprinkle the garlic over the top, season with salt and pepper, and layer the eggplant over the potatoes. Sprinkle ¼ teaspoon of the oregano over the eggplant, layer the tomatoes over the top, and sprinkle with the remaining ¼ teaspoon oregano.

6. In a medium-size mixing bowl, combine the milk, egg, and Parmesan, whisk till well blended, and pour over the vegetables. Sprinkle the mozzarella evenly over the top, and bake till bubbly and lightly browned, about 30 minutes.

MAKES 6 SERVINGS

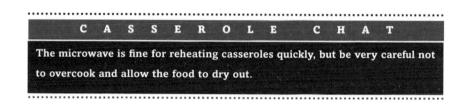

C A S S E R O L E   C H A T

The microwave is fine for reheating casseroles quickly, but be very careful not to overcook and allow the food to dry out.

Caroline's Pumpkin and Eggplant Casserole

Unlike the rest of her oil-rich Dallas family, Caroline Hunt Schoellkopf is so passionate about pumpkin that she not only named her air charter service Pumpkin Air but also produced and published privately a fat cookbook devoted to nothing but pumpkin dishes. This casserole is one of her favorites, and while the version she once served me was topped with dollops of plain yogurt, I prefer sour cream. Sometimes, I also grate a touch of fresh nutmeg into the egg mixture. If you don't want to fool around with preparing fresh pumpkin (which can be a pain), about 4 cups of canned chunks (not puree) are just as good. And if you want to transform this dish into a lip-smacking main-course meal, add about 1½ cups of leftover lamb to the vegetables, adjust the seasonings, and use a 3-quart casserole. Do watch to make sure the casserole doesn't dry out.

2 large eggplants, stemmed

1 teaspoon salt

1 very small pumpkin (3 to 4 pounds)

¼ cup fresh lemon juice

Freshly ground black pepper to taste

Medium-hot paprika to taste

3 tablespoons butter

1 medium-size onion, finely chopped

5 large eggs

½ cup sour cream

1. Cut the eggplants lengthwise into quarters, slice 2 inches thick, and place in a large mixing bowl. Sprinkle the salt over the top, toss well, and let stand about 20 minutes to extract excess liquid. Meanwhile, peel the pumpkin, remove and discard the seeds and membranes, cut the flesh into dice to measure about 3½ cups, and place in a large pot.

2. Transfer the eggplant to a colander, rinse well under cold running water, and add to the pumpkin. Add about 1 inch of water to the pot, bring to a boil, reduce the heat slightly, cover, and steam the vegetables till tender, about 10 minutes.

3. Preheat the oven to 325°F. Grease a 2½-quart casserole. With a slotted spoon, transfer the vegetables to the prepared casserole, sprinkle with 2 tablespoons of the lemon juice, and season with the pepper and paprika.

4. In a small skillet, melt the butter over moderate heat, add the onion, stir for 2 minutes, remove from the heat, and stir in the remaining 2 tablespoons lemon juice.

5. In a medium-size mixing bowl, beat the eggs till frothy, add the onion mixture, and stir. Pour the egg mixture evenly over the vegetables and bake till slightly crusted on top, about 25 minutes. Serve each portion topped with a dollop of the sour cream.

MAKES 6 TO 8 SERVINGS

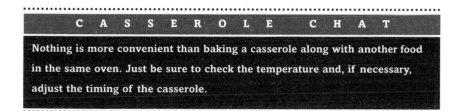

CASSEROLE CHAT

Nothing is more convenient than baking a casserole along with another food in the same oven. Just be sure to check the temperature and, if necessary, adjust the timing of the casserole.

North Dakota Colcannon

It was probably the Swedes who first brought rutabagas to the American West and Midwest, but it was the Scottish settlers of North Dakota who utilized the vegetable to reproduce their native dish called colcannon. A hybrid of the turnip and cabbage, the rutabaga is at its peak in October and November. They usually weigh two pounds or more and should be smooth, but since they're very hard and difficult to peel, be sure to use a heavy knife. For the right texture, do not use a blender or food processor for this dish.

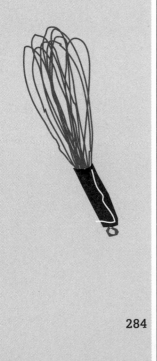

3 medium-size baking potatoes (about 1¹/₂ pounds), peeled and cubed

1 medium-size rutabaga, peeled and cubed

2 cups cored and shredded green cabbage

6 tablespoons (³/₄ stick) butter, softened

¹/₂ cup half-and-half

3 scallions (white part only), finely chopped

Salt and black pepper to taste

1. In a large saucepan, combine the potatoes and rutabaga with enough salted water to cover, bring to a simmer, cook till very tender, about 30 minutes, and drain well. Meanwhile, blanch the cabbage in another saucepan of boiling water for 5 minutes and drain well.

2. Preheat the oven to 350°F. Butter a 2-quart casserole and set aside.

3. Place the drained potatoes and rutabaga in a large heavy mixing bowl, add 4 tablespoons of the butter and the half-and-half, and mash with a potato ricer or heavy fork into a thick puree. Add the cabbage and scallions, season with salt and pepper, and mix till well blended.

4. Scrape the mixture into the prepared casserole and dot the top with the remaining 2 tablespoons butter. Bake till slightly crusted, about 25 minutes.

MAKES 6 SERVINGS

Sticky Sweet Potatoes

6 medium-size sweet potatoes, peeled and cut into thin slices

1 cup water

2 tablespoons dark rum

$^1/_2$ cup granulated sugar

$^1/_2$ cup firmly packed dark brown sugar

$^1/_2$ teaspoon ground cinnamon

$^1/_2$ teaspoon ground cloves

$^1/_4$ cup ($^1/_2$ stick) butter, melted

1. Preheat the oven to 325°F.

2. Butter a 2-quart casserole, arrange the potatoes in it in overlapping layers, and set aside.

3. In a medium-size saucepan, combine the remaining ingredients, bring to a low boil, reduce the heat to low, and stir till well blended and smooth, about 5 minutes. Pour the mixture evenly over the potatoes, cover, and bake, basting from time to time, till the potatoes are tender, about 50 minutes. Allow the casserole to stand at room temperature about 5 minutes before serving.

MAKES 6 SERVINGS

I first encountered these wonderfully gooey potatoes at none other than a bereavement buffet following a Greek funeral in Tarpon Springs, Florida, and have since served them both at Thanksgiving and with . . . pit-cooked pork barbecue. The trick is to allow the potatoes to stand at least 5 or 10 minutes before serving so that a beautiful glaze sets on the top. If you don't have any dark rum in the house, bourbon or even Scotch whisky can be substituted—obviously rendering distinctively different tastes.

Sweet Potato and Coconut Pudding

Yes, this traditional Southern casserole is rich as sin, which is why most hosts and hostesses usually serve it with a baked ham or any plain pork dish. Of course, many truly dedicated Southern cooks use only freshly grated coconut, but given that impracticality for most people, the frozen—not the canned—product is completely acceptable.

2 cups half-and-half

2 large eggs

3/4 cup sugar

2 large sweet potatoes, peeled and grated

1/2 teaspoon ground cinnamon

1/2 teaspoon ground nutmeg

Salt and black pepper to taste

1 cup frozen unsweetened shredded coconut, thawed

1/4 cup (1/2 stick) butter, melted

2 tablespoons bourbon

1/2 cup chopped pecans or hazelnuts

1. Preheat the oven to 350°F. Butter a 1 1/2-quart casserole and set aside.

2. In a large mixing bowl, combine the half-and-half, eggs, and sugar and whisk till well blended. Add the sweet potatoes, cinnamon, nutmeg, salt and pepper, coconut, 2 tablespoons of the butter, and the bourbon and stir till well blended.

3. Scrape the mixture into the prepared casserole. Sprinkle the nuts evenly over the top, drizzle the remaining 2 tablespoons butter evenly over the nuts, and bake till slightly firm, about 1 hour.

MAKES 4 TO 6 SERVINGS

Corn, Onion, and Bell Pepper Soufflé

8 ears fresh corn

1 to 1½ cups milk, as needed

6 tablespoons (¾ stick) butter

1 medium-size onion, finely chopped

½ medium-size green bell pepper, seeded and finely chopped

¼ cup all-purpose flour

Salt and black pepper to taste

8 large eggs, separated

1 cup shredded sharp cheddar or Monterey Jack cheese

1. With a sharp knife, cut the kernels off the corn into a large mixing bowl and set aside. Scrape the milk from the cobs into a glass measuring cup, add enough regular milk to yield 2 cups of liquid, and set aside.

2. Preheat the oven to 375°F. Butter a 2-quart casserole and set aside.

3. In a large heavy saucepan, melt the butter over moderate heat, add the onion and bell pepper, and stir for 2 minutes. Add the flour, season with salt and pepper, and stir 2 minutes longer. Remove the pan from the heat. Slowly whisk in the milk mixture, return to the heat, and whisk till thickened, about 2 minutes. Remove from the heat and whisk in the egg yolks one at a time till well blended and smooth. Add the corn kernels and stir till well blended.

4. In another large mixing bowl, beat the egg whites with an electric mixer till stiff peaks form, then fold into the corn mixture. Scrape the mixture into the prepared casserole, sprinkle the cheese evenly on top, and bake till puffed and golden brown, 30 to 35 minutes.

MAKES 6 SERVINGS

Talk about a beautiful and delicious summer buffet casserole that will have guests gasping! What really gives the dish much of its ambrosial flavor is the sweet milk scraped from the fresh corn cobs, so I do not advise trying to substitute frozen or canned corn. Needless to say, the fresher the corn, the better the casserole will be.

Iowa Corn Pudding

I know that other areas of the country lay claim to growing the world's finest corn (New Jersey, Long Island, South Carolina), but the truth remains that no region can boast the long tradition and know-how of corn production like the state of Iowa. It's believed that the cultivation of corn in Iowa goes back some 2,000 years, and it's for sure that Native Americans had developed many varieties of the grain long before the white man came to the prairies. Today, almost half the state's farmland is planted in corn (some more than seven feet high), and while I've eaten memorable corn pudding all over the East and Midwest, none has ever equaled this sublime version once prepared for my mother and me when we were visiting the Maytag blue cheese farm in Newton, Iowa. If at all possible, do try to use fresh white Silver Queen corn for this pudding.

2 large eggs

3 cups fresh corn kernels

2 teaspoons minced onion

3 tablespoons all-purpose flour

$^{1}/_{2}$ teaspoon salt

2 tablespoons sugar

Cayenne pepper to taste

Ground nutmeg to taste

$^{1}/_{4}$ cup ($^{1}/_{2}$ stick) butter, melted and cooled

$1^{1}/_{2}$ cups half-and-half

1. Preheat the oven to 350°F. Butter a 2-quart casserole and set aside.

2. In a large mixing bowl, beat the eggs with an electric mixer till frothy, then stir in the corn and onion. In a small bowl, combine the flour, salt, sugar, cayenne, and nutmeg and add to the corn mixture, stirring. Add the butter and half-and-half and stir well.

3. Pour the mixture into the prepared casserole, place the dish in a large roasting pan, place the pan in the oven, and pour enough boiling water into the pan to come one-quarter of the way up the sides of the casserole. Bake the pudding for 15 minutes, then stir gently to distribute the corn as evenly as possible and continue to bake till the top is golden brown and a knife inserted into the center comes out clean, about 20 minutes longer.

MAKES 6 SERVINGS

Rhode Island Succotash

One 10-ounce package frozen corn kernels, thawed

One 10-ounce package frozen lima beans, thawed

2 tablespoons chopped fresh chives

1 cup half-and-half

1 teaspoon sugar

1 teaspoon salt

$^1/_8$ teaspoon black pepper

$^1/_8$ teaspoon paprika

1. Preheat the oven to 350°F. Butter a 1$^1/_2$-quart casserole and set aside.

2. In a large mixing bowl, combine the corn, limas, and chives and stir till well blended. Add the half-and-half, sugar, salt, pepper, and paprika and stir till well blended.

3. Scrape the mixture into the prepared casserole, cover, and bake till slightly crusty, about 30 minutes.

MAKES 4 TO 6 SERVINGS

Despite what most Southerners believe, succotash can be traced back to the Narraganset Indians of Rhode Island, who referred to the corn and other ingredients in a stew pot as *sukguttahash*. In the mid-eighteenth century, succotash was indeed little more than corn and lima beans simmered with "top milk" (the cream on the top of whole milk) in a pot, but by the twentieth century, some form of onion had been added to the dish, minced bacon or bacon grease was often used to enhance the flavor, and the concoction was prepared as much in casseroles as in pots. The "modern" version here has been adapted from an old *Good Housekeeping* pamphlet I've had since the late fifties. Do check the casserole after about 20 minutes to make sure it isn't too dry.

Miss Edna's Turnip Casserole

Edna Lewis, one of the most talented cooks of our time, was born in Freetown, Virginia, a town founded by her grandfather shortly after Emancipation. I first met "Miss Edna" when she was cooking at an upscale restaurant in North Carolina, but it was later, when she was in charge of the kitchen at the legendary Gage & Tollner's in Brooklyn, that she taught me lots about turnips and told me about this Thanksgiving casserole. I'm the one who added a little bacon grease to the recipe, and I doubt that Miss Edna would object.

2 pounds turnips, peeled and thinly sliced

2 tablespoons bacon grease

1$\frac{1}{2}$ teaspoons sugar

1 cup chicken broth

1 cup heavy cream

Salt and black pepper to taste

$\frac{3}{4}$ cup dry bread crumbs

1. Preheat the oven to 350°F. Butter a 1$\frac{1}{2}$-quart casserole and set aside.

2. Place the turnips in a large saucepan with enough water to cover and add the bacon grease and sugar. Bring to a boil, reduce the heat to moderate, simmer till tender, about 20 minutes, and remove from the heat.

3. Meanwhile, combine the chicken broth and heavy cream in a medium-size saucepan, bring to a low boil over moderate heat, cook till slightly thickened, and remove from the heat.

4. With a slotted spoon, transfer the turnips to the prepared casserole and pour the cream mixture over the top. Season with salt and pepper, spread the bread crumbs evenly over the top, and bake till golden brown, about 30 minutes. Serve hot.

MAKES 4 TO 6 SERVINGS

Crazy for Casseroles

Glorious Grease

Maybe it's the Southern blood that runs through my veins, but never am I without a coffee can at least a quarter full of strained bacon grease to flavor any number of boiled vegetables, stews, wilted salads, breads, and, indeed, casseroles. Not only is bacon grease a wonderful flavoring agent by itself in many casseroles (see, for example, the distinctive Onion and Bacon Casserole Bread on page 326), but quite often, when I feel a dish needs a bit of extra oomph and mystery, I think nothing of sautéing chopped onions or bell peppers or garlic in a little bacon grease instead of butter or oil. Do note, however, that, like any other fat, bacon grease left unrefrigerated will turn rancid after about a month. If you have lots of bacon grease that you want to conserve for future use, an old trick is to pour it into a saucepan, add a few tablespoons of water, bring to a boil over moderate heat without stirring, let cool, then strain through cheesecloth into a large jar, cover, and refrigerate.

New Hampshire Turnip, Beet, and Hazelnut Soufflé

Most people associate turnips with the South, but the truth is that the root was probably first introduced by English settlers in New Hampshire at the early part of the eighteenth century and used primarily in soups, stews, and casseroles. During Colonial days, I'm sure a casserole such as this one would have been made by simply layering sliced turnips and beets and crushed nuts, but I love the more modern idea of pureeing these earthy ingredients and turning them into an elegant soufflé. Do not substitute butter for the shortening, and don't forget to add the sugar to counteract the bitterness of the turnips.

6 medium-size white turnips, peeled and diced

One 15-ounce can whole beets, drained and diced

2 tablespoons vegetable shortening

$^1/_2$ cup chopped hazelnuts

2 teaspoons sugar

1 teaspoon salt

Black pepper to taste

$^1/_2$ teaspoon all-purpose flour

2 large eggs, separated

1. Place the turnips in a large pot with enough salted water to cover. Bring to a boil, reduce the heat to low, cover, and simmer till very tender, 20 to 30 minutes. Drain off the water, add the beets and shortening to the turnips, and mash with a potato masher till the mixture is smooth. Add the hazelnuts, sugar, salt, pepper, and flour and stir till well blended.

2. Preheat the oven to 350°F. Grease a 2-quart casserole and set aside.

3. In a medium-size mixing bowl, beat the egg whites with an electric mixer till stiff peaks form; set aside. In a small mixing bowl, beat the yolks till light, then gradually stir into the turnip-and-beet mixture and fold in the egg whites.

4. Scrape the mixture into the prepared casserole and bake till puffy, 30 to 35 minutes.

MAKES 6 SERVINGS

Green and Red Onion Casserole

1/4 cup (1/2 stick) butter

6 bunches scallions (white part and some of the green), cut into
1-inch pieces (about 12 cups)

2 medium-size red onions, coarsely chopped

2 garlic cloves, minced

1/4 cup heavy cream

1/2 cup freshly grated Parmesan cheese

Salt and black pepper to taste

1 cup dry bread crumbs

2 tablespoons butter, melted

I like to serve this simple, slightly sweet onion casserole with baked or grilled pork chops or ribs, but, in truth, it's an all-purpose dish that goes well with any relatively uncomplicated main course, including barbecued meats and poultry and a thick steak.

1. Preheat the oven to 350°F. Butter a shallow 2-quart casserole and set aside.

2. In a large heavy saucepan, melt the butter over moderate heat, add the scallions, red onion, and garlic, and stir till fully softened, about 15 minutes. Stir in the heavy cream and cheese till well blended, and season with salt and pepper.

3. Scrape the mixture into the prepared casserole, sprinkle the bread crumbs evenly over the top, drizzle the melted butter over the crumbs, and bake till golden, about 20 minutes.

MAKES 6 SERVINGS

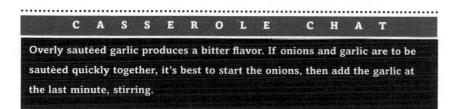

C A S S E R O L E   C H A T

Overly sautéed garlic produces a bitter flavor. If onions and garlic are to be sautéed quickly together, it's best to start the onions, then add the garlic at the last minute, stirring.

Cheesy Vidalia Onion and Rice Casserole

Why, you might ask, are Vidalia onions so much sweeter than ordinary yellow ones, and the answer lies in the low sulfur content of the soil in the small Southeastern town of Vidalia, Georgia, and the surrounding counties. (And, unbeknownst to many, it's the sulfur in most onions that brings on the tears.) Vidalias are harvested once a year in late spring or early summer, and the relative in Macon who gave me this recipe never dreamed of using them even in July. "I don't care what anybody says," she used to huff, "but the sweetness of Vidalias starts to fade about a month after they're dug up." If Cudin' Berta was right, I haven't noticed, and I relish the onion throughout the summer.

1 cup water

$^1/_2$ cup raw long-grain white rice

$^1/_4$ cup ($^1/_2$ stick) butter

4 large Vidalia onions, chopped

1 tablespoon minced fresh parsley leaves

$^3/_4$ cup freshly grated Parmesan cheese

1 cup half-and-half

Salt and black pepper to taste

Paprika to taste

1. Preheat the oven to 350°F. Butter a 1$^1/_2$- to 2-quart casserole and set aside.

2. Bring the water to a boil in a small saucepan, add the rice, and reduce the heat to low. Cover, simmer for 10 minutes, drain, and set aside.

3. In a large heavy skillet, melt the butter over moderate heat, add the onions, and cook, stirring, for 10 minutes or till golden. Remove from the heat, add the rice, parsley, $^1/_2$ cup of the cheese, and the half-and-half, season with salt and pepper, and stir till well blended.

4. Scrape the mixture into the prepared casserole, sprinkle the remaining $^1/_4$ cup cheese evenly over the top, sprinkle with paprika, and bake till golden, about 30 minutes.

MAKES 6 SERVINGS

Carrot and Raisin Casserole

1½ pounds carrots, scraped and cut into thin rounds

¼ cup (½ stick) butter

1 large onion, chopped

2 tablespoons all-purpose flour

2 cups milk

1 teaspoon dry mustard

Pinch of ground nutmeg

Salt and black pepper to taste

1 cup shredded sharp cheddar cheese

1 cup seedless golden raisins

1 cup crumbled soda crackers

1. In a large saucepan, combine the carrots with enough water to cover, bring to a boil, reduce the heat to moderate, cook till just tender, about 6 minutes, and drain.

2. Preheat the oven to 350°F. Butter a 2-quart casserole and set aside.

3. In a large heavy saucepan, melt 2 tablespoons of the butter over moderate heat, add the onion, and stir till softened, about 3 minutes. Sprinkle the flour over the top and stir for 2 minutes. Add the milk, mustard, and nutmeg, season with salt and pepper, stir till thickened, about 3 minutes, and remove from the heat. Add the cheese and stir till melted and the sauce is smooth. Add the carrots and raisins and stir till well blended.

4. Scrape the mixture into the prepared casserole. Sprinkle the crackers evenly over the top, dot with the remaining 2 tablespoons butter, and bake till bubbly, about 25 minutes.

MAKES 6 SERVINGS

Carrot and raisin casseroles have been around for almost a century and complement virtually any meal featuring pork, poultry, or game when made properly. Unfortunately, far too many of these casseroles were abused in the old days by ridiculous, gloppy marshmallow toppings, reason enough for their falling into disrepute. If you don't have soda crackers on hand, substitute dry bread crumbs, biscuit crumbs, or crushed croutons.

Honey Carrots and Sugar Snap Peas

Now readily available in spring and early summer, sugar snap peas make an interesting component in casseroles so long as their delicate flavor is not overwhelmed by other ingredients. When shopping, remember that the peas should be slender and crisp, and to prepare them for cooking, be sure to trim off the stem ends and pull to remove the tough strings.

7 medium-size carrots, scraped and cut into matchsticks

$^1/_2$ pound tiny whole onions, peeled

$^1/_2$ pound sugar snap peas

$^1/_2$ cup hot water

$^1/_4$ cup honey

$^1/_2$ teaspoon salt

$^1/_4$ teaspoon black pepper

$^1/_4$ cup ($^1/_2$ stick) butter, cut into pieces

1. Preheat the oven to 350°F.

2. Butter a 1$^1/_2$-quart casserole and arrange the carrots over the bottom. Layer the onions over the carrots, then layer the sugar snap peas over the onions. In a small mixing bowl, combine the water, honey, salt, and pepper and stir till well blended. Pour the mixture evenly over the vegetables, dot the top of the casserole with the butter, cover, and bake till the vegetables are tender, about 20 minutes. Uncover and continue to bake till lightly browned, about 10 minutes.

MAKES 4 TO 6 SERVINGS

New Mexican Colache

3 tablespoons peanut oil

2 medium-size onions, chopped

1 garlic clove, minced

4 medium-size yellow squash (about $1^1/_2$ pounds), cut into $^1/_4$-inch-thick rounds

1 pound fresh green beans, ends trimmed and cut in half

1 small jalapeño, seeded and finely chopped

3 medium-size ripe tomatoes, peeled and chopped

$^1/_2$ cup chicken broth

Salt and black pepper to taste

1 cup fresh or frozen corn kernels

$^1/_2$ cup shredded Monterey Jack cheese

1. Preheat the oven to 350°F. Grease a 2-quart casserole and set aside.

2. In a large heavy pot, heat the oil over moderate heat, add the onions and garlic, and stir till golden, about 4 minutes. Add the squash, green beans, and jalapeño and stir 2 minutes longer. Add the tomatoes and broth, season with salt and pepper, bring to a low simmer, and cook for 10 minutes Add the corn and stir well.

3. Scrape the mixture into the prepared casserole, sprinkle the cheese evenly over the top, and bake till golden brown, about 30 minutes.

MAKES 6 SERVINGS

Colache, found all around the Southwest in homes and modest restaurants, is often prepared as a thick stew, but the casserole version served at The Shed restaurant in Sante Fe has to be the best I've ever eaten. Just watch the baking carefully after about 25 minutes to make sure the casserole doesn't get too dry. It can be served either as a side dish to barbecued ribs or any roasted meat or as a main course with something like cured-ham biscuits or small grilled sausages.

Fennel and Belgian Endive Gratin

While fennel has been prized in Europe since the Middle Ages, it's only in the last few years that the delicious licorice-tasting vegetable has found a limited audience in the U.S. I love fennel braised, stuffed into baked fish, added to salads, or simply eaten raw with a tangy dip, but never does the bulb display its distinctive savor so much as when combined with slightly bitter Belgian endives, sprinkled with genuine Parmesan cheese, and baked slowly in a casserole. You can boil and layer the vegetables separately, of course, but I personally like them mixed together. Be sure to add the sugar to tame the endives and, when shopping for fresh fennel, refuse any bulb that has wilted feathery tops.

4 fennel bulbs

4 heads Belgian endives

1 tablespoon sugar

Salt and black pepper to taste

$^1/_4$ cup ($^1/_2$ stick) butter, cut into small bits

1 cup chicken broth

$^1/_2$ cup freshly grated Parmesan cheese

1. Trim off and discard the feathery tops of the fennel, peel away and discard the heavy outer leaves, cut the hearts into small chunks, and place in a large saucepan. Pull off and discard any discolored leaves of the endives, cut the heads into thin rounds, and add to the fennel. Add enough water to cover, bring to a low boil, cover, cook till the vegetables are just tender, 5 to 7 minutes, and drain.

2. Preheat the oven to 325°F.

3. Butter a 2-quart casserole, then layer the fennel and endives across the bottom, sprinkle the sugar and salt and pepper over the top, and dot with the butter. Pour the broth around the edges, sprinkle the cheese evenly over the top, and bake till golden brown, about 40 minutes.

MAKES 6 SERVINGS

Acorn Squash and Brazil Nut Casserole

2 large acorn squashes

¹/₂ cup (1 stick) butter, cut into pieces

2 large eggs, beaten

¹/₂ teaspoon ground cinnamon

¹/₂ teaspoon ground nutmeg

¹/₄ cup half-and-half

1 cup firmly packed light brown sugar

¹/₄ cup shaved Brazil nuts (often found only in specialty food shops)

Salt and black pepper to taste

1. Preheat the oven to 350°F. Grease a 2¹/₂-quart casserole and set aside.

2. Place the whole squashes on a large heavy baking sheet and bake till tender when stuck with a fork, 1¹/₂ to 2 hours. When cool enough to handle, cut the squashes into quarters, remove the seeds and skins, place the flesh in a large mixing bowl, and mash well with a potato masher or heavy fork. Add the butter, eggs, cinnamon, and nutmeg, beat the mixture with an electric mixer till well blended and smooth and scrape into the prepared casserole.

3. Increase the oven temperature to 375°F.

4. In a small mixing bowl, combine the half-and-half, brown sugar and nuts, season with salt and pepper, stir till well blended, pour over the squash mixture, and bake till golden brown, about 35 minutes.

MAKES 6 TO 8 SERVINGS

There are two ways to make this or any other winter squash casserole with totally different results. Either counteract the blandness of the squash with spices, brown sugar, and very fatty Brazil nuts (as I've done here) or add a minced clove of garlic plus about half a cup of grated Parmesan to the mashed squash, eggs, and butter mixture, forget about the half-and-half and nuts, and sprinkle more Parmesan over the top before baking till golden. In both cases, the unbaked casserole (or two small casseroles) freezes beautifully and can be thawed in almost no time when ready to bake.

Montana Cabbage and Leek Casserole

Although ordinary green cabbage was introduced to the New England and Middle Atlantic areas by the original English settlers, it was the German and Russian immigrants in the Mountain states who cultivated not only the green but also red and Savoy-style cabbages used to reproduce numerous soups, stews, and casseroles from their homelands. This particular casserole does require a bit of work, but what I love about it is that it's not only the ideal accompaniment to pork and game dishes but, with a few lusty sausages layered between the cabbage and leeks, can be transformed into a wholesome main course. If leeks are unavailable, two sliced Spanish onions could be substituted, but do try to use genuine Swiss Emmenthaler cheese and Parmigiano-Reggiano in this casserole.

One 2-pound head green cabbage

3 medium-size leeks (white part and some of the green), washed well

6 tablespoons (³/₄ stick) butter

2 tablespoons all-purpose flour

2 cups milk

1¹/₂ cups shredded Swiss cheese

Salt and black pepper to taste

1 medium-size onion, finely chopped

1 garlic clove, minced

¹/₂ cup dry white wine

¹/₂ teaspoon ground allspice

¹/₂ teaspoon ground cloves

¹/₄ cup freshly grated Parmesan cheese

1. Pull off and discard any discolored leaves from the cabbage, cut away and discard the core, cut the cabbage into quarters, and cut the quarters into thin slices. Place the slices in a large saucepan with enough salted water to cover, bring to a boil, cook for 2 minutes, and drain.

2. Cut the leeks crosswise into 2-inch pieces, place in a large saucepan with enough salted water to cover, bring to a boil, cook for 10 minutes, and drain.

3. Rinse and dry one of the saucepans, melt 2 tablespoons of the butter over moderate heat, add the flour, and whisk for 1 minute. Add the milk, whisking, remove from the heat, add the Swiss cheese, season with salt and pepper, and stir till the cheese is melted and the sauce is smooth. Set aside.

4. Preheat the oven to 350°F. Butter a 2-quart casserole and set aside.

Crazy for Casseroles

5. In a large heavy skillet, melt the remaining 4 tablespoons butter over moderate heat, add the onion and garlic, and stir for 2 minutes. Add the drained cabbage, wine, allspice, and cloves, season with salt and pepper, and cook till the liquid evaporates. Add half the cheese sauce and stir till well blended.

6. Layer the cabbage in the prepared casserole, layer the leeks over the cabbage, and pour the remaining cheese sauce evenly over the top. Sprinkle the Parmesan evenly over the top and bake till nicely browned, 30 to 35 minutes.

MAKES 6 SERVINGS

CASSEROLE CHAT

Many casseroles can be baked frozen, but the cooking time will be longer. Check with an instant-read thermometer, which should register about 160°F when the casserole is fully cooked.

Flossie's Butternut Squash Orange Bake

Southern ladies exchange as many casserole recipes as gossipy stories, and no dish does my own mother treasure more than this spicy one created by her closest childhood friend. The casserole couldn't be easier to prepare and goes well with virtually all roasted meats and poultry. Do try to find a good "thick-cut" English marmalade with plenty of tangy peel.

1 large butternut squash (about 3 pounds)

$1/4$ cup ($1/2$ stick) butter

$1/2$ cup fresh orange juice

$1/4$ cup firmly packed light brown sugar

$1/2$ teaspoon salt

$1/4$ teaspoon ground cinnamon

$1/8$ teaspoon ground ginger

$1/8$ teaspoon ground cloves

Orange marmalade

1. Peel and halve the squash, discard the seeds, and cut into chunks. Place the chunks in a large saucepan with enough salted water to cover, bring to a boil, reduce the heat to moderate, cover, and cook till fork-tender, about 20 minutes.

2. Preheat the oven to 350°F. Butter a 2-quart casserole and set aside.

3. Drain the squash, place in a large mixing bowl, and mash well with a potato masher till smooth. Add the butter and mix well until melted. Add the orange juice, brown sugar, salt, cinnamon, ginger, and cloves and mix well.

4. Scrape the mixture into the prepared casserole, spread a thin layer of marmalade over the top, and bake till nicely glazed, about 30 minutes.

MAKES 6 SERVINGS

Broccoli Casserole Supreme

1 large head broccoli, stems removed

One 10 3/4-ounce can Campbell's condensed cream of mushroom soup

1 cup mayonnaise

1/2 cup (1 stick) butter, softened

2 large eggs, beaten

1 small onion, finely chopped

1 teaspoon salt

Black pepper to taste

1 1/2 cups shredded sharp cheddar cheese

2 cups finely crushed Ritz crackers

1. Place the broccoli in a large saucepan with 1 inch of water, bring to a boil, cover, and steam the broccoli for 5 minutes. Drain and chop coarsely.

2. Preheat the oven to 350°F. Butter a 2-quart casserole and set aside.

3. In a large mixing bowl, combine the broccoli, condensed soup, mayonnaise, butter, eggs, onion, and salt, season with pepper, and mix till well blended. Add 1 cup of the cheese and mix well.

4. Scrape the mixture into the prepared casserole. In a medium-size mixing bowl, combine and blend the remaining 1/2 cup cheese and the crackers, sprinkle evenly over the top of the casserole, and bake till a straw inserted into the middle comes out clean, 30 to 40 minutes. Let stand about 20 minutes before serving.

MAKES 6 TO 8 SERVINGS

I've tried over and over to make this classic broccoli casserole with a fresh mushroom cream sauce instead of the canned soup, and it just doesn't work as well. Don't ask me why, but if ever a case can be made for the ever-questionable virtues of sometimes cooking with canned soups, this casserole is it. And it is great for all sorts of occasions: as a side dish on the dinner table, on a stylish buffet, even as a main-course luncheon dish served with small ham biscuits or cold fried chicken drumettes. Do let the casserole stand a while to mellow before serving.

No-Nonsense Spinach Casserole

The secret to this simple casserole is the seasoning, so be sure to taste the stirred mixture before baking, perhaps adjusting the cheese, garlic, and nutmeg. The casserole also makes an ideal buffet dish for a crowd, in which case the recipe should be doubled and a larger casserole dish used.

Two 10-ounce packages frozen chopped spinach

1 cup sour cream

$1/2$ cup freshly grated Parmesan cheese

1 garlic clove, minced

$1/8$ teaspoon ground nutmeg

Salt and black pepper to taste

$1/2$ cup dry bread crumbs

2 tablespoons butter, cut into pieces

1. Place the spinach in a large pot, add enough water to just cover, and bring to a boil. Reduce the heat to moderate, cover, cook till the spinach is tender, about 8 minutes, and drain in a colander, pressing down with the back of a spoon to get out as much water as possible.

2. Preheat the oven to 350°F. Grease a $1^{1}/_{2}$-quart casserole and set aside.

3. In a large mixing bowl, combine the drained spinach, sour cream, cheese, garlic, and nutmeg, season with salt and pepper, and stir till well blended.

4. Scrape the mixture into the prepared casserole, sprinkle the bread crumbs evenly over the top, dot the bread crumbs with the butter, and bake till bubbly and golden brown, about 30 minutes. Serve piping hot.

MAKES 4 TO 6 SERVINGS

Brussels Sprouts and Chestnut Bake

2 tablespoons butter

1 tablespoon all-purpose flour

1 tablespoon Dijon mustard

³/₄ cup chicken broth

1 teaspoon fresh lemon juice

Salt and black pepper to taste

Two 10-ounce packages frozen Brussels sprouts, cooked according to package directions and drained

1 cup frozen pearl onions, thawed

1 cup coarsely chopped canned chestnuts

1. Preheat the oven to 350°F. Butter a 2-quart casserole and set aside.

2. In a large saucepan, melt the butter over moderate heat, add the flour, stir for 1 minute, add the mustard, and stir till well blended. Gradually add the broth and cook, stirring, till slightly thickened, add the lemon juice, and season with salt and pepper. Add the Brussels sprouts, onions, and chestnuts and stir till well blended.

3. Scrape the mixture into the prepared casserole and bake till slightly golden, about 25 minutes.

MAKES 6 SERVINGS

Brussels sprouts and chestnuts are one of the great food marriages and never so much so as in this simple casserole that begs to be served at a stylish buffet dinner. Frozen Brussels sprouts are almost as good as fresh, but if, in late fall, you find some healthy-looking stalks at a farmers' market, measure out about 2¹/₂ pints of sprouts, remove any discolored leaves and cut off the stem ends, and simmer them in chicken broth about 8 minutes before using in the casserole.

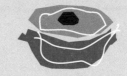

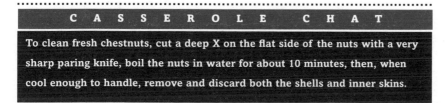

CASSEROLE CHAT

To clean fresh chestnuts, cut a deep X on the flat side of the nuts with a very sharp paring knife, boil the nuts in water for about 10 minutes, then, when cool enough to handle, remove and discard both the shells and inner skins.

Mixed Vegetable Casserole

Although this versatile casserole can be made with various frozen vegetables in addition to the necessary celery and onions, it's almost a shame not to utilize fresh vegetables when they're in season—especially at the height of summer. Fresh lima beans, diced yellow squash, corn kernels, and broccoli or cauliflower florets also make delightful components, so feel free to experiment and adjust according to your taste.

3 cups fresh shelled or frozen green peas

1 cup finely chopped celery

1 cup scraped and shredded carrots

1 cup finely chopped onions

2 large eggs, beaten

2^1/$_2$ cups milk

3 tablespoons all-purpose flour

1 teaspoon salt

^{1}/$_2$ teaspoon black pepper

1^1/$_2$ cups fine dry bread crumbs

2 cups shredded sharp cheddar cheese

5 tablespoons butter, melted

1. In a large mixing bowl, combine the peas, celery, carrots, and onions and set aside.

2. In a medium-size saucepan, combine the eggs, milk, flour, salt, and pepper, slowly heat over moderate heat, and cook, stirring constantly, till the sauce is thickened. Set aside.

3. Preheat the oven to 350°F.

4. Butter a 2^1/$_2$-quart casserole and arrange half the vegetable mixture over the bottom. Top with ^{1}/$_2$ cup of the bread crumbs, 1 cup of the cheese, and half the sauce. Repeat with the remaining vegetables, ^{1}/$_2$ cup of the bread crumbs, and the remaining cheese and sauce. Sprinkle the remaining ^{1}/$_2$ cup bread crumbs over the top, drizzle with the melted butter, and bake till golden brown, about 35 minutes.

MAKES 6 TO 8 SERVINGS

California Chickpea, Cheese, and Chile Pepper Casserole

One 1-pound, 3-ounce can chickpeas, drained

1 medium-size onion, chopped

¼ teaspoon dried thyme, crumbled

¼ teaspoon dried oregano, crumbled

Salt and black pepper to taste

4 ounces canned whole mild green chiles, drained and cut into thin strips

½ pound Monterey Jack cheese, shredded

1 cup chicken broth

1 cup sour cream

1. Preheat the oven to 325°F.

2. Butter a 2-quart casserole and spread about one-third of the chickpeas over the bottom. Sprinkle half the onion over the peas, sprinkle half of each herb over the onion, and season with salt and pepper. Layer half the chiles and one-third of the cheese over the top. Repeat the process, then top with the remaining chickpeas and cheese.

3. In a medium-size mixing bowl, combine the broth and sour cream, stir till well blended, pour over top of the casserole, and bake till bubbly, about 30 minutes.

MAKES 6 SERVINGS

Chickpeas, also called garbanzos, are grown mostly around Tracy, California, where a dry bean festival is held every August. Nutty in flavor, chickpeas are delicious not only in any number of soups, stews, and salads but in spicy Mexican-style casseroles such as this one enhanced with a couple of herbs. If I have time, I prefer to soak dried peas (1 pound) overnight and substitute a little of the soaking water for part of the chicken broth, but there's nothing wrong with the canned ones so long as you drain them well.

Ham Bone Three-Bean Casserole

Our Colonial and pioneering ancestors learned at early dates not only numerous ways to utilize meat bones in cooking, but the many advantages of simmering beans with all sorts of flavor-rendering ingredients. In many respects, this is the quintessential American casserole, a sumptuous blending of three different beans, heady malt vinegar, molasses, tangy sage, and a meaty ham bone, all baked slowly for almost six hours. It's a casserole to be made on a cold winter afternoon, taken out of the oven to mellow just as guests arrive, and, if necessary, reheated before being served with a tart salad, maybe fresh cornbread or crusty rolls, and either a sturdy red wine or beer. Just make sure that you leave plenty of meat on the leftover bone, which can either be left in the casserole or removed before serving.

$^1/_2$ pound dried white navy beans, rinsed and picked over

$^1/_2$ pound dried red kidney beans, rinsed and picked over

$^1/_2$ pound dried small black beans, rinsed and picked over

4 medium-size onions, thinly sliced

3 celery ribs, finely chopped

2 garlic cloves, minced

2 to 3 cups chicken broth, as needed

$^1/_2$ cup malt vinegar

$^1/_4$ cup molasses

1 tablespoon dried sage, crumbled

2 teaspoons salt

$^1/_2$ teaspoon black pepper

1 large, meaty ham bone

1. Combine the three beans in a large mixing bowl with enough cold water to cover generously and let soak overnight.

2. Pick over the beans for loose husks, then place the beans and their soaking liquid in a large pot, adding more water to cover by 1 inch. Bring to a boil, reduce the heat to low, and simmer for 30 minutes. Drain, reserving the liquid, and place the beans in a large mixing bowl. Add the onions, celery, and garlic and toss till well blended. Measure the reserved liquid, add enough chicken broth to make 3 cups, pour over the beans, and stir well.

3. Preheat the oven to 350°F.

4. In a small mixing bowl, combine the vinegar, molasses, sage, salt, and pepper, stir till well blended, and pour over the beans.

5. Place the ham bone in a 5-quart casserole, scrape the bean mixture over the bone, cover, and bake for 45 minutes. Reduce the oven tem-

perature to 300°F and continue to bake, covered, for 3 hours. Uncover and continue to bake till only about 1½ cups of liquid remain, about 2 hours. Let the casserole rest at room temperature about 30 minutes before serving.

MAKES 6 TO 8 SERVINGS

C A S S E R O L E   C H A T

Partially cooked casseroles intended to be fully baked later on should be tightly covered and cooled to refrigerator temperature (below 45°F) to prevent bacterial growth and possible spoilage.

Homestead Lima Bean and Bacon Casserole

First cultivated in Lima, Peru, lima beans were grown and eaten by the natives in North America long before the arrival of European settlers and were also a favorite dried staple of pioneers during the days of western expansion in the U.S. This particular casserole might well have been cooked in a more rudimentary manner on any number of chuck wagons crossing the Plains (give or take a few modern ingredients), and the basic technique is as simple today as 150 years ago. During the summer, I make this casserole with fresh limas when I can find them, but I must say that the frozen beans today are almost as good.

Two 10-ounce packages frozen lima beans, cooked according to package directions, drained, and cooking liquid reserved

1 tablespoon butter

1 tablespoon all-purpose flour

1 tablespoon firmly packed light brown sugar

2 teaspoons dry mustard

2 teaspoons fresh lemon juice

Salt and black pepper to taste

$^1/_2$ cup dry bread crumbs

2 tablespoons butter, melted

$^1/_2$ cup shredded sharp cheddar cheese

6 strips lean bacon

1. Preheat the oven to 350°F.

2. Butter a 1$^1/_2$-quart casserole and layer the drained lima beans over the bottom.

3. In a small heavy saucepan, melt the butter over moderate heat, add the flour, and whisk for 1 minute. Slowly add $^1/_2$ cup of the reserved cooking liquid from the beans, whisking till thickened and smooth. Add the brown sugar, mustard, and lemon juice, season with salt and pepper, stir till well blended, and pour over the limas.

4. In a small mixing bowl, combine the bread crumbs, melted butter, and cheese, stir till well blended, and spoon the mixture evenly over the limas. Arrange the bacon over the top and bake till it is crisp, about 30 minutes.

MAKES 4 TO 6 SERVINGS

Locke-Ober's Boston Baked Beans

2 cup dried pea beans, rinsed and picked over

$^3/_4$ pound salt pork, thinly sliced

$^1/_2$ cup molasses

2 teaspoons dry mustard

$^1/_2$ pound sliced lean bacon, chopped

1 small onion, finely chopped

1 teaspoon instant coffee

1. In a large pot, combine the beans with enough cold water to cover and let soak overnight. Drain the beans and cover with fresh water. Bring to a simmer over moderate heat, cover, cook for 1 hour, and drain, reserving the cooking water.

2. Preheat the oven to 300°F.

3. Layer one-third of the salt pork over the bottom of a 1$^1/_2$-quart earthenware bean pot or casserole, layer the drained beans over the top, and layer the remaining salt pork over the beans. Add the molasses, mustard, bacon, onion, and $^1/_2$ cup of the reserved bean water, mix gently so as not to break up the beans, cover, and bake for 6 hours, adding a little more bean water every hour and stirring gently to keep the beans moist.

4. During the last hour of baking, stir in the instant coffee and bake till crusty on top.

MAKES 6 SERVINGS

C A S S E R O L E   C H A T

Fine domestic clay-pot casseroles are especially good for slow, even baking, but to temper the clay, they should first be soaked in water per the manufacturer's directions. Usually casseroles prepared in clay pots should start out in a cold oven.

The earliest Puritan settlers of Massachusetts appropriated beans from the natives, and since no cooking was allowed on Sundays, beans were baked slowly overnight on Saturdays. Eventually, Boston baked beans evolved as an accompaniment to fish cakes and brown bread for the traditional Saturday night dinner, and possibly the best I ever tasted were (and, I hope, still are) served at the city's most venerable restaurant, Locke-Ober. What makes the beans so distinctive is the subtle addition of instant coffee.

Fancy Baked Beans with Apricots

For years, I considered it utter heresy to make any baked beans with canned products, but when a former student of mine from Kansas City served these "fancy" ones of his mother's doctored with sausage and apricots, I had a sudden change of heart. Yes, when it comes to ideal texture there's still nothing like dried beans that are soaked overnight, then slowly simmered, but when time is valuable and you need an extra buffet dish that will impress, these beans fit the bill beautifully.

½ pound bulk pork sausage

Two 1-pound cans baked beans (best quality available)

One 15-ounce can apricot halves, drained and all but 6 coarsely chopped

⅓ cup firmly packed dark brown sugar, plus more for stuffing

1 teaspoon dry mustard

2 tablespoons butter, cut into pieces

1. In a medium-size skillet, fry the sausage over moderate heat till cooked thoroughly, breaking it up into small pieces with a fork. Remove from the skillet using a slotted spoon, drain on paper towels, and transfer to a large mixing bowl.

2. Preheat the oven to 350°F. Butter a 2-quart casserole and set aside.

3. Add the baked beans to the sausage, then the chopped apricots, reserving the 6 halves. Add the brown sugar and mustard and stir till the mixture is well blended.

4. Scrape the mixture into the prepared casserole, press the reserved 6 apricot halves, cut side up, across the top, and stuff each half lightly with brown sugar. Dot the apricot halves with the butter and bake till bubbly, about 20 minutes.

MAKES 6 TO 8 SERVINGS

Nutty Apple and Cranberry Casserole

3 Granny Smith apples, cored, left unpeeled, and cut into dice

2 cups fresh or thawed frozen cranberries

1¹/₂ cups granulated sugar

1 cup rolled oats (not quick-cooking kind)

¹/₂ cup firmly packed dark brown sugar

¹/₃ cup all-purpose flour

¹/₂ cup chopped walnuts

¹/₂ cup (1 stick) butter, cut into pieces

1. Preheat the oven to 350°F. Butter a 2¹/₂-quart casserole and set aside.

2. In a large mixing bowl, combine the apples, cranberries, and granulated sugar, toss well, and layer over the bottom of the prepared casserole. In the same bowl, combine the oats, brown sugar, flour, and walnuts, toss well, and spoon evenly over the fruit.

3. Dot the top with the butter, cover the casserole, and bake for 45 minutes. Uncover and continue to bake till slightly crusty, 10 to 15 minutes. Serve hot.

MAKES 6 TO 8 SERVINGS

Technically, of course, this is not a vegetable casserole, but so what? Not all fruits must be used only for dessert casseroles, and this one, created by my beloved mentor from Virginia and New York restaurateur, Pearl Byrd Foster, is utterly delectable served with pork, baked ham, and roast turkey or duck. The oats give the casserole a delightful crunch.

Casserole Breads

Spiced Oatmeal-Raisin Batter Bread

The Upper Midwest of the U.S. is the world's leading producer of oats, and while the vast majority of the crop is turned into animal feed, the rest is puffed into breakfast cereal, rolled into oatmeal, or ground into flour. Rolled oats are not only very nutritious but also a delicious component of all sorts of baked breads, and if you think you've always loved oatmeal-raisin cookies, wait till you taste this simple batter bread made in a casserole. Just make sure that the milk used to soak the oats is hot enough to soften them completely.

1 cup rolled oats (not quick-cooking kind)

1 cup hot milk

2 large eggs, beaten

6 tablespoons (3/4 stick) butter, melted

1/4 cup firmly packed light brown sugar

1/2 cup seedless dark raisins

2 to 2 1/2 cups all-purpose flour, as needed

2 teaspoons baking powder

1/2 teaspoon salt

1/4 teaspoon ground cinnamon

1. Preheat the oven to 350°F. Butter a deep 1 1/2-quart casserole and set aside.

2. In a large mixing bowl, combine the oats and milk, stir, and let stand till softened, about 10 minutes. Add the eggs, butter, brown sugar, and raisins and stir till well blended. Sift 2 cups of the flour, the baking powder, salt, and cinnamon directly into the oat mixture and stir till well blended and smooth, adding more flour as necessary for a firm consistency.

3. Scrape the batter into the prepared casserole and bake till a straw inserted into the center comes out clean, about 1 hour. Let the bread cool slightly, then transfer to a wire rack to cool completely. To serve, cut into slices.

MAKES 1 LOAF; 6 SERVINGS

Banana-Hazelnut Casserole Bread

1/2 cup vegetable shortening

1 cup sugar

2 large eggs

1 1/2 cups mashed ripe bananas (about 4 medium-size bananas)

1 teaspoon pure vanilla extract

2 cups all-purpose flour

1 teaspoon salt

1/2 teaspoon baking soda

1 cup chopped hazelnuts

1. Preheat the oven to 350°F. Grease a deep round or oval 2-quart casserole and set aside.

2. In a large mixing bowl, cream the shortening and sugar together, add the eggs, and beat till well blended. Add the bananas and vanilla and stir till well blended.

3. In a medium-size mixing bowl, sift together the flour, salt, and baking soda, add to the banana mixture, and stir till well blended and smooth. Add the hazelnuts and stir well.

4. Scrape the batter into the prepared casserole and bake till a straw inserted in the center comes out clean, about 1 hour. Let the bread cool, then wrap in aluminum foil and refrigerate overnight before slicing.

MAKES 1 LOAF; 6 SERVINGS

Here is the perfect solution for those overripe bananas you left too long on the counter and were about to toss out. Since the bread bakes out relatively soft, it is a good idea to prepare it a day in advance and let it firm up in the fridge before bringing it back to room temperature and slicing.

Vermont Walnut Casserole Bread with Honey Glaze

I first tasted this delicious casserole bread at an inn in Middlebury, Vermont, that still had an old brick oven in the kitchen. It was prepared in a deep, cast-iron vessel, and I'd like to think the bread's earliest antecedents were the crude colonial loaves made most likely with corn flour, buttermilk, molasses or honey, and maybe beechnuts or hickory nuts, then baked in an open fireplace. Until well into the nineteenth century, molasses and maple syrup were the most popular sweeteners since sugar was so expensive. If you've never baked nut bread made with a little molasses, this is a good time to start.

2 cups whole wheat flour

1 cup all-purpose flour

2 tablespoons sugar

2 teaspoons baking soda

1 teaspoon salt

1/4 teaspoon ground nutmeg

2 cups buttermilk

1/2 cup molasses

1 cup chopped walnuts

2 tablespoons butter, melted

1 tablespoon honey

1. Preheat the oven to 350°F. Grease a deep round or oval 2-quart casserole and set aside.

2. In a large mixing bowl, combine the two flours, sugar, baking soda, salt, and nutmeg and stir till well blended. In a medium-size mixing bowl, combine the buttermilk and molasses and stir till well blended. Pour the buttermilk mixture into the flour mixture, add the walnuts, and stir till well blended and smooth.

3. Scrape the batter into the prepared casserole. In a small bowl, combine the melted butter and honey, stir well, drizzle over the batter, and bake till golden brown, about 45 minutes. Let the bread cool slightly, then transfer to a wire rack to cool completely. To serve, cut the bread into wedges.

MAKES 1 LOAF; 6 SERVINGS

CASSEROLE CHAT

To balance the excess acid and reduce the amount of carbon dioxide generated by buttermilk used in a casserole, always add a little baking soda (an alkali).

Holiday Fruit and Nut Casserole Bread

1 orange

2 tablespoons butter, softened

Boiling water as needed

1 cup fresh cranberries, picked over and rinsed

1 cup cracked walnuts

1 large egg, beaten

2 cups all-purpose flour

$2/3$ cup sugar

1 teaspoon baking powder

$1/2$ teaspoon baking soda

$1/2$ teaspoon salt

1. Preheat the oven to 350°F. Butter a deep $1^1/2$-quart casserole and set aside.

2. Cut two 3-inch-long strips of peel from the orange (without including the white pith underneath) and cut each strip into small pieces. Cut the orange in half, remove the seeds, and squeeze the juice into a measuring cup. Add the butter, then add enough boiling water to measure 1 cup. Pour the orange juice mixture into a blender or food processor, add the orange peel, cranberries, and walnuts and process briefly, till the cranberries and nuts are coarsely chopped. Pour the mixture into a large mixing bowl, add the egg, and stir till well blended.

3. Sift the flour, sugar, baking powder, baking soda, and salt directly into the wet mixture and stir till well blended and smooth. Scrape the batter into the prepared casserole and bake till a straw inserted into the center comes out clean, about 1 hour. Let the bread cool slightly, then transfer to a wire rack to cool completely. To serve, cut into slices.

MAKES 1 LOAF; 4 TO 6 SERVINGS

There's some evidence that the early Native Americans of New England used cranberries not only in their pemmican cakes but in certain crude cornbreads cooked in pots. Whether the legend is true or false, it's for sure that the all-American cranberry cultivated in bogs in the Northeast and Northwest is a fascinating ingredient in all sorts of holiday breads, and I like to believe that this particularly delectable one made in a casserole provides at least an indirect link with the cooking of our original natives. If possible, I suggest you make several loaves since they make beautiful gifts.

Manhattan Irish Soda Bread

In rural Ireland, where peat is still burned in many indoor fireplaces, soda bread is not only made with just whole wheat flour and no fat but often cooked over coals in a suspended iron pot. An Irish-American friend of mine in Manhattan may corrupt tradition by using part white flour and half a stick of butter in his soda bread, but he does honor his roots by preparing his bread in a casserole instead of adopting the more modern method of baking it free-form on a cookie sheet. This is a dense loaf that could be sliced thinly for either teatime or delicate sandwiches.

2 cups all-purpose flour, plus more for dusting

2 cups whole wheat flour

2 teaspoons baking soda

2 teaspoons salt

$^1/_4$ cup ($^1/_2$ stick) cold butter, cut into small pieces

2 cups buttermilk

$^1/_2$ cup seedless dark raisins

1. Preheat the oven to 375°F. Butter a deep round or oval 2-quart casserole and set aside.

2. In a large mixing bowl, combine the two flours, baking soda, and salt and stir till well blended. Add the butter and, using your fingertips, squeeze the flour and butter together till the texture resembles coarse meal. Add the buttermilk and raisins and stir with a wooden spoon till well blended.

3. Transfer the dough to a lightly floured work surface, knead till smooth, 5 to 7 minutes, then form into a round loaf large enough to fit easily in the prepared casserole and place the loaf in the casserole. With a sharp knife, cut a 4-inch cross about $^1/_4$ inch deep in the top of the dough, dust lightly with the white flour, and bake till crusty brown and hollow-sounding when thumped, about 45 minutes. Let cool slightly, in the casserole, then transfer to a wire rack to cool completely. To serve, cut into thin wedges.

MAKES 1 LOAF; 6 SERVINGS

Crazy for Casseroles

Steamed Boston Brown Bread

½ cup whole wheat flour

½ cup rye flour

½ cup yellow cornmeal

½ teaspoon baking powder

½ teaspoon baking soda

½ teaspoon salt

1 cup milk

½ cup molasses, warmed

1. Preheat the oven to 325°F. Butter generously the inside of a clean 13-ounce coffee can and set aside.

2. In a large mixing bowl, combine the two flours, cornmeal, baking powder, baking soda, and salt and stir well. Add the milk and molasses and beat with a wooden spoon till well blended and smooth.

3. Scrape the batter into the prepared coffee can, cover the top with a piece of aluminum foil, and tie securely with string to make it airtight. Place the can in a baking pan filled with enough boiling water to come halfway up the sides, place the pan in the oven, and let steam for 2½ hours, adding more boiling water if needed. Remove the cover and test the bread with a skewer, which should come out clean. Return just the can to the oven for about 5 minutes to allow the bread to dry slightly, then let cool about 1 hour before unmolding. Slice the bread with a length of heavy string.

MAKES 1 LOAF; 4 TO 6 SERVINGS

Okay, so a coffee can must be the most primitive-style casserole imaginable, but that is the vessel that has been used for generations to bake this famous bread found all over New England and traditionally served with the region's baked beans. There's good evidence that the bread was being widely made in pudding molds by seventeenth-century colonists, its popularity most likely due to the scarcity of yeast. Exactly when the first one-pound coffee can was used to give the bread its now-familiar round shape is anybody's guess, and today we can only be thankful that the commercial swindlers who've downsized most canned coffees from 16 to 13 ounces at least haven't changed the size of the cans themselves. Since this historic bread contains very little gluten, it is a little heavy and should be sliced as thinly as possible—preferably with a piece of heavy string. For even more interesting flavor, you can also add about a half cup of seedless raisins or dried currants—as, no doubt, our ancestors did occasionally.

Flour Info

Casserole cookery rarely calls for any flour other than all-purpose white, which is a blend of enriched hard and soft wheats. For biscuit crusts, I do always have a good supply of superior Southern soft-wheat flour like White Lily or Red Band (increasingly available in fine food shops), and for certain casserole breads, I like to keep small quantities of rye, whole wheat, cracked wheat, and bran flours on hand. Since any flour (especially the naturally milled varieties found in health food stores) can attract bugs and go rancid, I either wrap mine tightly in *double* plastic bags or store it in tightly sealed jars in the refrigerator.

Casserole Cornbread

1 quart milk

3 large eggs

1½ cups yellow cornmeal

2 teaspoons baking powder

2 teaspoons sugar

1 teaspoon salt

¼ teaspoon black pepper

3 tablespoons peanut oil

1. Preheat the oven to 350°F. Grease a 2-quart casserole and set aside.

2. In a large mixing bowl, whisk together the milk and eggs till well blended. In another large mixing bowl, combine the cornmeal, baking powder, sugar, salt, and pepper and stir till well blended. Add the egg mixture and oil to the cornmeal mixture and stir till well blended and smooth.

3. Scrape the batter into the prepared casserole and bake till golden, 40 to 45 minutes. Let the cornbread cool slightly, then cut into squares.

MAKES 6 SERVINGS

This cornbread can just as easily and successfully be made in a large, well-greased cast-iron skillet as in a casserole, but it won't look half as nice if you plan to serve it on a buffet. This particular casserole cornbread hails from the Midwest, but if you happen to be serving it to Southerners, I suggest you leave out the sugar.

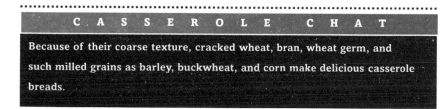

CASSEROLE CHAT

Because of their coarse texture, cracked wheat, bran, wheat germ, and such milled grains as barley, buckwheat, and corn make delicious casserole breads.

Fearrington House Country Ham Spoonbread

In the South, there are as many ways of making spoonbread (so called because, when baked only to a soft consistency, the custardy dish is served with a spoon) as biscuits, and one of the most original is this firm casserole version with country ham served at the Fearrington House restaurant outside Chapel Hill, North Carolina. For the right tang and consistency, buttermilk must be used, and if you want your squares to be light, don't substitute butter or margarine for the shortening. For even finer texture, use white instead of yellow cornmeal.

1 cup boiling water

1 1/4 cups yellow cornmeal

1 tablespoon sugar

2 large eggs, beaten

Black pepper to taste

1/2 teaspoon baking soda

1 cup buttermilk

1 1/2 tablespoons vegetable shortening, melted

1 cup minced cured country ham

1. Preheat the oven to 400°F. Grease a 2- to 2 1/2-quart casserole and set aside.

2. In a large mixing bowl, pour the boiling water over the cornmeal, stir, cover, and let cool. Add the sugar and eggs, season with pepper, and stir till well blended.

3. In a small mixing bowl, dissolve the baking soda in the buttermilk, stir, then beat into the cornmeal mixture along with the shortening and ham till smooth.

4. Scrape the mixture into the prepared casserole and bake till firm, about 35 minutes. Serve hot, cut into squares.

MAKES 6 TO 8 SERVINGS

Cheesy Potato Casserole Bread

1 envelope active dry yeast

1 cup warm milk

1/3 cup vegetable shortening, at room temperature

1 large egg

1 teaspoon salt

1/2 teaspoon black pepper

3 cups all-purpose flour

1 cup mashed potatoes, at room temperature

1/2 cup shredded extra-sharp cheddar cheese

1/2 cup freshly grated Parmesan cheese

1. Grease a deep round or oval 2-quart casserole and set aside.

2. In a large mixing bowl, sprinkle the yeast over the milk and let dissolve. Add the shortening, egg, salt, pepper, and 1 cup of the flour and beat till smooth, about 2 minutes. Stir in the remaining 2 cups flour, the potatoes, and cheddar till well blended, scrape the dough into the prepared casserole, cover with plastic wrap, and let rise in a warm area till doubled in bulk, about 40 minutes.

3. Preheat the oven to 375°F.

4. Sprinkle the Parmesan evenly over the top of the dough and bake till golden brown, about 45 minutes. Transfer the bread to a wire rack to cool, then cut into slices.

MAKES 1 LOAF; 6 SERVINGS

There are many ways to use up leftover mashed potatoes, but for me the easiest and most practical is to incorporate them into this classic casserole yeast bread that requires only one rising of the batter. Feel free to experiment with any number of firm, assertive cheeses, and by all means add a few herbs, dried seeds, or chopped nuts as our ancestors did if you prefer more complex flavor.

Liz's Onion and Bacon Casserole Bread

Liz Clark's cooking school in Keokuk, Iowa, is one of the best in the country, and this delectable casserole bread she teaches students how to make hails back to the days when her mother always kept a coffee can of bacon grease on hand to make fried eggs, wilted lettuce salads, and all sorts of country breads. If, like Liz, you prefer to use a heavy-duty mixer that has a dough hook, simply proof the yeast with the sugar and first 1½ cups of flour in the machine's bowl, then proceed to mix the dough till smooth and ready to knead.

1 envelope active dry yeast

1½ cups warm water

2 tablespoons sugar

2 teaspoons salt

4 to 5 cups unbleached bread flour, as needed

Bacon grease

1 medium-size onion, finely diced

Cornmeal for coating casserole

1. In a large mixing bowl, sprinkle the yeast over ½ cup of the water and let dissolve. Add the sugar, salt, the remaining 1 cup water, and 1½ cups of the flour and beat with an electric mixer till smooth, about 2 minutes.

2. In a small skillet, heat about 1 tablespoon bacon grease over moderate heat, add the onion, and stir till softened. Remove from the heat.

3. Add 2½ cups of the flour, 2 tablespoons of bacon grease, and the onion to the dough in the mixing bowl and stir till well blended, adding more flour as necessary to make a soft dough. Transfer the dough to a floured work surface, knead till spongy, about 5 minutes, and form into a ball. Place the ball in a greased bowl, cover with plastic wrap, and let rise in a warm area till doubled in bulk, about 40 minutes.

4. Preheat the oven to 400°F. Coat the inside surfaces of a deep round or oval 2½-quart casserole with bacon grease and sprinkle the surfaces with cornmeal to coat completely.

5. Transfer the risen dough to the prepared casserole, cover, and let rise again for about 20 minutes. Place the casserole on the center rack of the oven and bake till the bread sounds hollow when thumped, about 40 minutes. Brush the top with bacon grease, then transfer to a wire rack to cool. Serve the bread warm or at room temperature in wedges or slices.

MAKES 1 LOAF; 6 SERVINGS

Crazy for Casseroles

Onion-Sesame Casserole Bread

1 envelope active dry yeast

$^{1}/_{2}$ cup warm water

$^{1}/_{2}$ cup warm milk

$^{3}/_{4}$ cup ($1^{1}/_{2}$ sticks) butter, cut into pieces and softened

2 large eggs

1 teaspoon salt

3 cups all-purpose flour

1 small onion, finely chopped

2 tablespoons butter, melted

3 tablespoons sesame seeds

1. In a large mixing bowl, sprinkle the yeast over the water and let dissolve. Add the milk, butter, eggs, salt, and 1 cup of the flour and beat till smooth. Add the remaining 2 cups flour and the onion and stir till well blended and smooth. Cover the bowl with plastic wrap and let the dough rise in a warm area till doubled in bulk, about 1 hour.

2. Butter a deep round or oval 2-quart casserole. Stir the dough well, scrape into the prepared casserole, cover, and let rise again till doubled in bulk, about 40 minutes. Preheat the oven to 375°F.

3. Brush the top of the dough with the melted butter, sprinkle the sesame seeds over the top, and bake till golden, 35 to 40 minutes. Transfer the bread to a rack to cool completely, then cut into wedges.

MAKES 1 LOAF; 6 TO 8 SERVINGS

C A S S E R O L E   C H A T

To test whether packaged yeast is still active after the expiration date on the envelope, combine the yeast with $^{1}/_{2}$ cup lukewarm water and 1 teaspoon sugar or honey in a bowl and wait 10 minutes. If the mixture becomes bubbly and frothy, the yeast is still good.

This slightly crunchy but light casserole bread is utterly addictive, and when I gave the recipe to one friend, he even used the bread for hamburgers. If you want a more subtle flavor, substitute about half a cup of finely chopped scallions or fresh chives for the onion.

Dilly Casserole Bread

A true American classic was born when, in the early 1960s, a Nebraska cook entered her dilly casserole bread in the Pillsbury baking contest and took home first prize. Since then, every variation of the recipe imaginable has appeared in cookbooks and magazines all over the country, but this is basically the original method and, in my opinion, still the best. The dough definitely needs two risings, so don't cheat if you want sublime bread.

1 envelope active dry yeast

¹/₄ cup warm water

1 cup creamy-style cottage cheese

¹/₄ cup (¹/₂ stick) butter or margarine

2 tablespoons sugar

2 teaspoons dill seeds

1 teaspoon salt

¹/₄ teaspoon baking soda

1 large egg

2¹/₂ cups all-purpose flour

1. In a large mixing bowl, sprinkle the yeast over the water and let dissolve.

2. Meanwhile, combine the cottage cheese and butter in a small heavy saucepan, stir over low heat till warmed, and add to the yeast mixture. Add the sugar, dill seeds, salt, baking soda, and egg and beat with an electric mixer till well blended. Using a wooden spoon, gradually add the flour and mix to form a stiff dough. Cover with plastic wrap and let rise in a warm area till doubled in bulk, about 1 hour.

3. Butter a deep round or oval 2-quart casserole. Stir the dough well, scrape into the prepared casserole, cover, and let rise again till doubled in bulk, about 40 minutes.

4. Preheat the oven to 375°F.

5. When the dough has risen, bake till golden brown and hollow-sounding when thumped, 35 to 40 minutes. Transfer the bread to a wire rack to cool completely, then cut into slices.

MAKES 1 LOAF; 6 TO 8 SERVINGS

Multigrain Casserole Bread

1¹/₂ cups warm milk

1 cup warm water

1 envelope active dry yeast

3 tablespoons pure maple syrup

3 tablespoons vegetable shortening, at room temperature

2 teaspoons salt

1¹/₂ cups cracked wheat flour

1 cup rolled oats (not the quick-cooking kind)

¹/₂ cup rye flour

2 cups all-purpose flour, plus more if needed

1. In a large mixing bowl, combine the milk, water, yeast, maple syrup, and shortening, stir till the yeast has dissolved, and let sit till bubbly and frothy, about 5 minutes. Add the salt, cracked wheat flour, ¹/₂ cup of the oats, and the rye flour and beat with an electric mixer till smooth. Gradually add the all-purpose flour and beat till the dough is smooth and stiff, adding a little more all-purpose flour if necessary. Cover with plastic wrap and let rise in a warm area till doubled in bulk, about 1 hour.

2. Grease a deep round or oval 2¹/₂-quart casserole and sprinkle the remaining ¹/₂ cup oats evenly over the bottom and along the sides. Stir the dough, transfer to the prepared casserole, cover, and let rise again till doubled in bulk, about 45 minutes.

3. Preheat the oven to 350°F.

4. When the dough has risen, bake till golden brown and hollow-sounding when thumped, 45 to 50 minutes. Let the bread cool slightly, then transfer to a wire rack to cool completely. To serve, cut into slices.

MAKES 1 LARGE LOAF; 6 TO 8 SERVINGS

The reason you don't need to use equal amounts or more all-purpose flour for this beautifully crusted yeast bread is because there's sufficient gluten produced by the cracked wheat flour to assure a good framework. If you are forced to substitute whole wheat flour for the cracked wheat flour, use only 1 cup and increase the all-purpose flour to 2¹/₂ cups. You can also substitute molasses for the maple syrup.

Bran-Walnut Casserole Bread

Because of its coarse texture, bran flour makes sublime breads, especially when they are leavened with lots of yeast and sufficient eggs. Bran flour is usually available in specialty food shops, but if you have trouble finding it, you can substitute 1½ cups of whole wheat flour and 1½ cups of unprocessed bran with very good results. Like any batter yeast bread, this large loaf is best when allowed to cool slowly and, if practical, I like to serve it slightly warm.

1 cup warm milk

1 cup warm water

2 envelopes active dry yeast

¹/₂ cup vegetable shortening, at room temperature

¹/₂ cup honey

2 teaspoons salt

3 large eggs, beaten

3 cups all-purpose flour

2 cups bran flour

¹/₂ cup finely crushed walnuts

2 tablespoons butter, melted

1. In a large mixing bowl, combine the milk, water, yeast, shortening, honey, and salt, stir till the yeast has dissolved, and let proof about 5 minutes. Add the eggs and stir till well blended.

2. In a large mixing bowl, combine the two flours, then with an electric mixer gradually beat the flours into the yeast mixture till the batter is smooth. Add the walnuts and stir till well blended. Cover with plastic wrap and let rise in a warm area till doubled in bulk, about 1 hour.

3. Grease a deep round or oval 2½-quart casserole. Stir the dough, transfer to the prepared casserole, cover, and let rise again till doubled in bulk, about 45 minutes.

4. Preheat the oven to 350°F.

5. With a sharp knife, cut a 4-inch cross about ¼ inch deep in the top of the dough and bake till golden brown and hollow-sounding when tapped, about 45 minutes. Drizzle the butter over the top, let cool slightly, then transfer to a wire rack. Serve slightly warm in slices or wedges.

MAKES 1 LARGE LOAF; 8 SERVINGS

Crazy for Casseroles

Casserole Cheese Bread

2 envelopes active dry yeast

2 cups warm water

1 tablespoon sugar

2 tablespoons salt

2 tablespoons butter, softened

$1/2$ cup finely shredded extra-sharp cheddar cheese

$1/2$ cup freshly grated Parmesan cheese

2 tablespoons finely chopped fresh oregano leaves or $1^1/2$ teaspoons dried

$4^1/2$ cups all-purpose flour

1. In a large mixing bowl, sprinkle the yeast over the warm water and let dissolve completely. Add the sugar, salt, butter, both cheeses, oregano, and 3 cups of the flour and beat with an electric mixer at low speed till well blended. Increase the speed to medium and beat till smooth, about 2 minutes. Scrape the batter off the beaters back into the bowl and, using a wooden spoon, beat in the remaining $1^1/2$ cups flour till the batter is smooth. Cover with a sheet of waxed paper and a clean kitchen towel and let rise in a warm area till doubled in bulk, about 45 minutes.

2. Preheat the oven to 375°F. Grease a $2^1/2$-quart casserole and set aside.

3. With a wooden spoon, beat the batter in the bowl vigorously for 30 seconds, scrape it into the prepared casserole, and bake till lightly browned, about 1 hour. Transfer the bread to a wire rack to cool completely, then cut into wedges.

MAKES 1 LARGE LOAF; 8 SERVINGS

Dating back at least to the nineteenth century, this beguiling cheese bread was traditionally made strictly by hand and baked in a casserole not only in the South but all along the East Coast and in the first Midwestern states. As a result, the texture was very firm, almost coarse, as I discovered when I made a loaf without using an electric mixer. This modern version is relatively light, slightly mysterious, and utterly delicious, the only rules being that it must have the oregano (or a similar herb) to give it truly distinctive flavor and be baked one full hour for ideal texture. The bread is right for virtually any occasion, but also try toasting it for breakfast.

Sally Lunn Casserole Bread

Legend has it that this slightly sweet bread was created over two centuries ago in Bath, England, by some lady named Sally Lunn, who sold it on the streets. Like biscuits, the bread evolved in the American South more as a savory yeast bread than a tea cake, and at some point in the twentieth century, it was baked as often in an attractive casserole as in a tube pan. When the tradition of beating the dough with a wooden spoon exactly 100 times began remains a mystery, but this is the standard technique for dealing with a dough that, by nature, can be very stiff. Not even a heavy-duty electric mixer with a dough hook equals plenty of elbow grease in producing the right texture of dough necessary for a perfect loaf. Think about baking this casserole alongside another main-course meat or poultry casserole, and unless you're nuts about sweet breads (I'm not), you might leave out the sugar altogether.

2 envelopes active dry yeast

$^1/_2$ cup warm water

1 cup hot milk

4 cups sifted all-purpose flour

3 large eggs, beaten

$^1/_2$ cup (1 stick) butter, melted

2 tablespoons sugar (optional)

1 teaspoon salt

1. Butter and flour a deep round or oval 2$^1/_2$-quart casserole and set aside.

2. In a large mixing bowl, sprinkle the yeast over the water and let dissolve completely. Add the milk and 2 cups of the flour and beat with a wooden spoon or electric mixer till smooth. Add the eggs, butter, sugar, if using, salt, and the remaining 2 cups flour, beat vigorously with a wooden spoon till smooth, cover with plastic wrap, and let rise in a warm area till doubled in bulk, 45 to 55 minutes.

3. Beat the dough again with a wooden spoon for 100 strokes, transfer to the prepared casserole, cover, and let rise again till doubled in bulk, 35 to 40 minutes.

4. Preheat the oven to 350°F.

5. When the dough has risen, bake till browned and hollow-sounding when thumped, 35 to 40 minutes. Turn the bread out of the casserole, cut into wedges, and serve hot with butter.

MAKES 1 LARGE LOAF; 8 SERVINGS

Casserole Cobblers, Crisps, Crunches, and Delights

Hot Brandied Fruit Casserole

There's hardly a single church, charity league, or junior league cookbook in America that doesn't include at least one recipe for hot brandied fruit, the reason being that the casserole couldn't be easier to prepare and is just as appropriate for a brunch buffet as a formal dinner table. Any variety of canned fruits can be used, and if you want to be really nostalgic in the tradition of the 1940s and '50s, arrange a few maraschino cherries over the top of the casserole before baking. Sherry, rum, or bourbon can be used in place of the brandy, but, of course, the flavor will be altogether different.

One 16-ounce can pear halves, drained

One 16-ounce can peach halves, drained

One 16-ounce can apricot halves, drained

One 16-ounce can pineapple chunks, drained

$1/2$ cup (1 stick) butter

$1/4$ cup granulated sugar

$1/4$ cup firmly packed light brown sugar

2 tablespoons cornstarch

1 cup brandy (preferably Cognac)

1. Preheat the oven to 350°F.

2. Butter a 2- to $2^1/2$-quart casserole and arrange the fruits in alternating layers, ending with the pineapple.

3. In a medium-size heavy saucepan, melt the butter over low heat, add the two sugars, cornstarch, and brandy, and stir slowly but steadily till the mixture is thickened and smooth, about 10 minutes. Pour the mixture evenly over the fruit and bake till bubbly and slightly glazed on top, about 30 minutes. Serve hot or warm.

MAKES 6 TO 8 SERVINGS

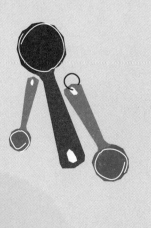

Pennsylvania Dutch Spiced Rhubarb Casserole

2 pounds fresh rhubarb stalks, washed, trimmed, and cut into 1-inch pieces

2 tablespoons water

1^1/$_2$ cups sugar

^{1}/$_4$ teaspoon ground cinnamon

^{1}/$_8$ teaspoon ground nutmeg

^{1}/$_8$ teaspoon ground cloves

3 tablespoons orange juice

1. Preheat the oven to 350°F.

2. Butter a 2-quart casserole, add the rhubarb in an even layer, and sprinkle the water over the top. Sprinkle the sugar evenly over, then sprinkle with the cinnamon, nutmeg, cloves, and orange juice.

3. Cover the casserole and bake for 15 minutes. Stir gently, baste the rhubarb with the syrup, cover, and bake till the rhubarb is tender but not mushy, about 15 minutes. Let cool slightly before serving.

MAKES 6 SERVINGS

Why the Pennsylvania Dutch seem to relish rhubarb more than most Americans is anybody's guess, but the truth is that the plant is so important to their culinary traditions that they often refer to it simply as "the pie plant." No doubt rhubarb pie is indeed the most popular dessert, but cooks who don't want to fool with making a pie crust simply bake the stalks with lots of spices in a casserole and serve it warm or cold with their homemade butter cookies. Be sure to trim off both the leaves and bases of the stalks and remember that the roots of rhubarb are poisonous.

Southern Strawberry-Rhubarb Cobbler

The sublime combination of strawberries and rhubarb in baked desserts goes back to the mid-nineteenth century, and while strawberry-rhubarb pie is a classic American creation served throughout the country, only in the South will you find this sumptuous cobbler casserole made with a biscuit crust. Remember that field rhubarb, available (like fresh strawberries) in late spring and early summer, is redder and much more flavorful than the hothouse variety, and never forget that the roots and leaves of this plant are poisonous and must be trimmed off completely.

1 pound fresh rhubarb stalks, washed, trimmed, and cut into 1-inch pieces

1 pint fresh ripe strawberries, rinsed, hulled, and cut in half

2 cups sugar

1 teaspoon grated lemon peel

1/2 teaspoon ground cinnamon

2 tablespoons fresh lemon juice

3 tablespoons butter, cut into small pieces

1 cup all-purpose flour, plus more if needed

2 teaspoons baking powder

2 large eggs, beaten

1 cup milk

1 teaspoon pure vanilla extract

Vanilla ice cream

1. Butter a 2-quart casserole, add the rhubarb in an even layer, then layer the strawberries evenly over the rhubarb.

2. In a small mixing bowl, combine 1 cup of the sugar, the lemon peel, and cinnamon, mix well, and sprinkle the mixture evenly over the strawberries. Sprinkle the lemon juice over the top, dot with the butter, and set the casserole aside.

3. Preheat the oven to 350°F.

4. Sift the flour and baking powder together in a large mixing bowl, add the remaining 1 cup sugar, the eggs, milk, and vanilla and stir with a wooden spoon, adding a little more flour if necessary to produce a loose but not wet batter.

5. Scrape the batter evenly over the top of the casserole and bake till golden brown, 40 to 45 minutes. Serve hot or lukewarm with ice cream.

MAKES 6 SERVINGS

Crazy for Casseroles

California Mango, Prune, and Raisin Surprise

¹/₂ cup grated fresh coconut or canned sweetened flaked coconut

2 cups pitted and halved prunes

2 cups peeled, pitted, and sliced ripe mangoes

¹/₂ cup seedless golden raisins

¹/₄ cup firmly packed light brown sugar

1¹/₂ cups orange juice

1 teaspoon ground ginger

1. To toast the coconut, preheat the oven to 300°F, spread the coconut out on a shallow, ungreased baking pan and toast, stirring often, till golden, about 35 minutes. Set aside. Increase the oven temperature to 350°F.

2. Butter a 1¹/₂-quart casserole, layer the prunes, mango slices, and raisins alternately in the casserole, and sprinkle the brown sugar evenly over the top.

3. In a 2-cup measuring cup, stir the orange juice and ginger together till well blended, pour over the top of the casserole, and bake till bubbly and slightly glazed, 40 to 45 minutes. Sprinkle the toasted coconut evenly over the top and serve the fruit hot with a slotted spoon.

MAKES 4 TO 6 SERVINGS

The California prune industry was begun in the mid-nineteenth century when a French immigrant in the Santa Clara Valley south of San Francisco grafted the first French prune-plum cuttings to the root stock of native wild plum trees and came up with perfect dried plums. Bake these prunes with mangoes and raisins, top the fruit with toasted coconut, and you have not only the simplest but one of the most unusual dessert casseroles imaginable. And if you want to be even more adventurous, play around with the same recipe using sliced peaches, pears, and apples.

Rice and Apricot Dessert Casserole

Since what you want for this subtle dessert is a smooth apricot puree, I don't recommend using either a blender or food processor, both of which tend to produce a stringy mush. The casserole can be served either warm or chilled, and I like to pass a bowl of heavy cream to be spooned over each portion.

$^1/_2$ pound dried apricots

2$^1/_2$ cups milk

$^1/_2$ cup raw long-grain rice

$^1/_2$ teaspoon salt

$^1/_2$ teaspoon ground nutmeg

$^3/_4$ cup half-and-half

2 large eggs

$^1/_2$ cup sugar

2 teaspoons grated lemon peel

1 teaspoon pure vanilla extract

1. In a large heavy saucepan, combine the apricots with enough water to cover, bring to a simmer, cover, and cook over low heat till tender, about 45 minutes. Drain, then force the apricots through a sieve or food mill into a bowl and set the puree aside.

2. In another large heavy saucepan, heat the milk over moderate heat just till bubbles form around the edges. Add the rice, salt, and nutmeg, stir, reduce the heat to low, cover, and cook till most of the milk is absorbed and the rice is tender, 20 to 25 minutes.

3. Preheat the oven to 350°F. Butter a 1$^1/_2$-quart casserole and set aside.

4. In a large mixing bowl, whisk together the half-and-half, eggs, sugar, lemon peel, and vanilla till frothy. Vigorously whisk about 3 tablespoons of the hot rice into the egg mixture, then add the remaining rice plus the apricot puree to the egg mixture and stir till well blended.

5. Scrape the mixture into the prepared casserole and bake till golden, 45 to 50 minutes. Serve either warm or chilled.

MAKES 6 SERVINGS

Spicy Pumpkin and Hazelnut Dessert Casserole

One 16-ounce can pumpkin puree

1 cup firmly packed light brown sugar

1 teaspoon salt

1 teaspoon ground cinnamon

$^1/_2$ teaspoon ground nutmeg

$^1/_4$ teaspoon ground cloves

2 cups half-and-half

3 large eggs

1 cup chopped hazelnuts

2 tablespoons butter, melted

Whipped cream

1. Preheat the oven to 350°F. Butter a 1½-quart casserole and set aside.

2. Scrape the pumpkin into a large mixing bowl and set aside. In a small mixing bowl, combine the brown sugar, salt, and spices and mix well. Add to the pumpkin and stir till well blended.

3. In a medium-size mixing bowl, whisk together the half-and-half and eggs till frothy, add to the pumpkin mixture, and stir till well blended and smooth.

4. Scrape the mixture into the prepared casserole, sprinkle the hazelnuts evenly over the top, drizzle the butter over the nuts, and bake till a knife inserted into the center comes out almost clean, 50 to 55 minutes. Let the casserole cool, then spoon whipped cream in a decorative manner over the top and serve.

MAKES 6 SERVINGS

Pumpkins were one of the first fruits introduced by Native Americans to the early colonists and legend has it that some type of pumpkin pie was served at the Pilgrims' second Thanksgiving in 1623. Of course, I can't prove my theory, but given the fact that initial efforts to grow wheat failed in the New World, and that corn flour was used almost exclusively for all baked goods, my guess is that the first pumpkin dessert was much like this simple casserole. In any case, the casserole, with its crunchy, nutty topping, is a nice change from traditional pumpkin pie, and it can be given even more character by adding a few tablespoons of rum or bourbon to the pumpkin mixture.

Nutty Matters

There's virtually no limit to the use of various nuts in casseroles, both as a primary ingredient and a component in all sorts of toppings. Since nuts add not only texture but distinctive flavor to any casserole, I'm pretty particular about the ones I buy, the prices I pay, and the way they're stored for optimum quality. While nuts in the shell (1 pound of unshelled nuts equals ½ pound shelled) are the least expensive and have the advantage of lasting many months without going rancid, they are a pain to prepare. Consequently, I generally buy shelled, unblanched, whole walnuts, almonds, filberts, hazelnuts, pistachios, and pine nuts in vacuum-packed bags at reputable food shops. I order fat Virginia peanuts from The Original Nut House in Wakefield, Virginia. And when it comes to pecans (probably the most popular—and perishable—nut in casserole cookery), I settle for nothing less than the whole, savory beauties available directly by mail from Atwell Pecan Company in Wrens, Georgia.

No matter where or how you obtain shelled nuts, remember that all turn rancid in almost no time if not packaged or stored properly. (When I sniff or taste packaged nuts and detect rancidity, I think nothing of returning them for a full refund.) Some people risk keeping nuts for weeks in the refrigerator; I immediately store all of mine in airtight plastic bags in the freezer and use them as I need them.

To toast pecans, walnuts, almonds, peanuts, pine nuts, and cashews, spread the nuts on a baking sheet and bake at 325°F, stirring once, till slightly darker, 10 to 15 minutes. To toast hazelnuts, bake them 15 to 20 minutes, then place in a towel and rub to remove the skins. To roast peanuts, spread the nuts on a baking sheet with melted butter to taste, bake at 325°F, stirring occasionally, for 25 minutes; drain on paper towels.

Indiana Persimmon Casserole

1 cup boiling water

2 large ripe persimmons, stemmed, seeded, peeled, and cut into small chunks

$^3/_4$ cup firmly packed light brown sugar

2 large eggs, beaten

$^3/_4$ cup all-purpose flour

$^1/_2$ teaspoon baking powder

$^1/_2$ teaspoon baking soda

$^1/_4$ teaspoon salt

1 teaspoon ground cinnamon

$^1/_4$ teaspoon ground nutmeg

$^1/_4$ teaspoon ground ginger

$1^1/_2$ cups half-and-half

3 tablespoons butter, melted

Whipped cream

1. Preheat the oven to 325°F. Butter a $1^1/_2$-quart casserole and set aside.

2. In a medium-size mixing bowl, pour the boiling water over the persimmons, stir for about 2 minutes, and drain. Run the persimmons through a food mill, or process very quickly in a food processor, to produce 1 cup of pulp. In a large mixing bowl, combine the pulp, brown sugar, and eggs and beat with a fork till well blended.

3. In a small mixing bowl, combine the flour, baking powder, baking soda, salt, and spices and stir alternately with the half-and-half into the persimmon mixture. Add the butter and stir till well blended and smooth.

4. Scrape the mixture into the prepared casserole and bake till firm, about $1^1/_4$ hours. Serve warm topped with whipped cream.

MAKES 6 SERVINGS

Early explorers and colonists loved American wild persimmons and compared them to apricots; natives used the fruit to make bread and beer; and by the mid-nineteenth century, farmers in Indiana had already made a veritable industry of the fat, ripe persimmons harvested after the first frost. Today, they still hold an annual fall persimmon festival near Border, Indiana, at which home cooks serve every type of persimmon pie, pudding, and casserole imaginable, and throughout much of the Midwest, a persimmon casserole is as much a part of the Thanksgiving tradition as turkey and dressing. When shopping, do make sure that the persimmons are fully ripe, plump, and firm-tender (unripe fruit picked before the first frost are terribly acidic and almost inedible).

Midwestern Wild Plum Jelly Rice Pudding

Leave it to my Iowa casserole enthusiast Liz Clark to come up with this highly original version of rice pudding utilizing jelly made from the region's wild plums. Yes, the jelly is rare, but no rarer than the beach plum jelly that I put up every September in East Hampton and have used with great success in this recipe. Wild plum jelly can sometimes be found at farm stands or in farmers' markets, but if you have no luck, substitute red or black currant jelly.

3 cups water

$^1/_2$ teaspoon salt

$1^1/_2$ cups raw long-grain rice

One 12-ounce can evaporated milk

5 large eggs

2 cups granulated sugar

2 teaspoons pure vanilla extract

$1^1/_2$ teaspoons ground cinnamon

$^1/_2$ teaspoon ground nutmeg

$^1/_4$ cup ($^1/_2$ stick) butter, melted

1 cup wild plum jelly

$^1/_2$ cup firmly packed light brown sugar

Heavy cream

1. Combine the water and salt in a large heavy saucepan and bring to a boil. Add the rice, return to a boil, reduce the heat to low, cover, and cook till all the water is absorbed and the rice is tender, about 20 minutes. Let cool.

2. In a large mixing bowl, whisk together the evaporated milk and eggs till well blended, add the rice, granulated sugar, vanilla, 1 teaspoon of the cinnamon, the nutmeg, and butter and stir till well blended.

3. Preheat the oven to 350°F.

4. Butter a 2-quart casserole and spoon the rice mixture evenly into the casserole. Spoon the jelly evenly over the top, place the casserole in a roasting pan, and add enough boiling water to the pan to come 1 inch up the sides of the casserole. Bake till the pudding is set, about 30 minutes.

5. In a small mixing bowl, combine the brown sugar and remaining ½ teaspoon cinnamon, sprinkle evenly over the top of the casserole, and bake till a knife inserted into the center comes out clean, about 30 minutes longer. Serve warm with a pitcher of heavy cream.

MAKES 6 TO 8 SERVINGS

Steaded Lemon and Date Pudding

Here's another enticing pudding that calls for one of your most attractive casseroles. I love dates flavored with lemon, but you could also use seedless raisins, dried currants, and even chopped candied fruits, and substitute orange juice and orange peel for the lemon—in which case, the amount of sugar should be reduced. Do notice that, unlike bread pudding, this pudding must be baked in a water bath for the right delicate texture. The dessert almost begs to be served at a Christmas dinner or on a festive holiday buffet.

$^1/_4$ cup vegetable shortening

$^1/_4$ cup ($^1/_2$ stick) butter, softened

$^1/_2$ cup sugar

2 large eggs

$^1/_4$ cup fresh lemon juice

1 tablespoon grated lemon peel

$1^1/_2$ cups all-purpose flour

2 teaspoons baking powder

$^3/_4$ cup milk

$^1/_2$ cup pitted and finely chopped dates

1. Preheat the oven to 350°F. Butter a $1^1/_2$-quart casserole and set aside.

2. In a large mixing bowl, cream the shortening, butter, and sugar with an electric mixer till light, then add the eggs one at a time, beating till well blended. Add the lemon juice and peel and beat till well blended. Sift the flour and baking powder directly into the mixture and stir it in, then gradually add the milk, beating steadily as it is added. Add the dates and stir till well blended.

3. Scrape the mixture into the prepared casserole. Place the casserole in a large baking pan, pour enough boiling water into the pan to come 1 inch up the sides of the casserole, and bake till firm and slightly browned, 50 to 55 minutes. Serve warm or at room temperature.

MAKES 6 SERVINGS

Florida Key Lime Pudding

¹/₄ cup (¹/₂ stick) butter, softened

¹/₂ cup sugar

2 large eggs, separated

Juice and grated peel of 3 large limes (or 4 to 5 Key limes)

¹/₂ cup all-purpose flour

¹/₂ teaspoon baking powder

¹/₂ teaspoon salt

1¹/₄ cups milk

1. Preheat the oven to 325°F. Butter a 1¹/₂-quart casserole and set aside.

2. In a large mixing bowl, cream the butter and sugar together with an electric mixer till smooth, add the egg yolks, and beat till fluffy. Add the lime juice and beat till well blended. With a wooden spoon, fold in the flour, baking powder, and salt till well blended, then add the milk and lime peel and stir till the batter is smooth. Wash and dry the electric mixer blades.

3. In a medium-size mixing bowl, beat the egg whites with the electric mixer till stiff peaks form, then fold them into the lime batter. Scrape the mixture into the prepared casserole and bake till puffy and golden, about 45 minutes.

MAKES 4 TO 6 SERVINGS

Anybody who's traveled to Key West and around southern Florida has most likely tasted the region's indigenous Key lime pie, but few would have had the opportunity to sample this elegant casserole pudding (almost a soufflé) I was once served at a private boating club in Miami. True Key limes are rarely available outside the Florida Keys and Miami, but while their very tart flavor is no doubt unique, there's certainly nothing wrong with using ordinary Persian limes. The puffy pudding is indeed quite tart, so feel free to adjust the amount of sugar according to your taste. And this is another time to use the most beautiful ceramic casserole in your collection.

North Fork Peach Crisp with Lemon Cream Topping

Although the large summer peaches of New Jersey and Long Island are never quite as sweet as the smaller Georgia Elbertas, I can't imagine a better peach crisp than this one with a tangy lemon cream topping prepared one weekend by a housewife near Mattituck, Long Island, for a small picnic overlooking Peconic Bay. If your fresh peaches seem excessively juicy and almost watery, combine them only with the lemon juice and sprinkle with a dusting of flour before mixing and placing them in the casserole. This crisp is also delicious made with fresh Bosc or Seckel pears.

1 cup all-purpose flour

$^1/_2$ cup granulated sugar

$^1/_2$ cup firmly packed light brown sugar

$^1/_2$ teaspoon salt

$^1/_2$ teaspoon ground cinnamon

$^1/_2$ cup (1 stick) cold butter, cut into pieces

4 cups peeled, pitted, and sliced ripe peaches

1 tablespoon fresh lemon juice

2 tablespoons water

$^1/_2$ cup heavy cream

$^1/_2$ teaspoon grated lemon peel

2 teaspoons sifted confectioners' sugar

1. Preheat the oven to 350°F. Butter a 2-quart casserole and set aside.

2. In a large mixing bowl, combine the flour, two sugars, salt, cinnamon, and butter and work the butter into the dry mixture with your fingertips till it resembles coarse meal.

3. In another large mixing bowl, combine the peaches, lemon juice, and water, stir till well blended, and spoon the mixture into the prepared casserole. Sprinkle the flour mixture evenly over the peaches, cover with aluminum foil, and bake for 15 minutes. Remove the foil and continue to bake till the top is golden and crisp, 35 to 45 minutes.

4. To make the topping, beat the cream in a medium-size mixing bowl with an electric mixer till soft peaks form, then fold in the lemon peel and confectioners' sugar.

5. Serve the crisp warm or at room temperature with the lemon cream topping.

MAKES 6 SERVINGS

Peach, Raspberry, and Almond Brown Betty

$^1/_2$ cup slivered almonds

2 tablespoons butter, melted

1$^1/_2$ cups stale angel food cake, pound cake, or spongecake crumbs

$^1/_4$ cup granulated sugar

$^1/_4$ cup firmly packed light brown sugar

1 teaspoon ground cinnamon

$^1/_4$ teaspoon ground nutmeg

Pinch of salt

4 medium-size ripe peaches, peeled, pitted, and cut into thin wedges

1 pint fresh raspberries, picked over and rinsed

$^1/_3$ cup water

$^1/_4$ cup ($^1/_2$ stick) cold butter, cut into small pieces

Vanilla ice cream

1. Preheat the oven to 350°F. Butter a shallow 1$^1/_2$-quart casserole.

2. On a baking sheet, toss the almonds with the melted butter, toast till golden in the oven, about 10 minutes, and set aside.

3. Meanwhile, combine the cake crumbs, two sugars, spices, and salt in a medium-size mixing bowl, toss to blend well, and set aside.

4. Scatter a few tablespoons of the crumb mixture over the bottom of the prepared casserole and layer half the peaches and raspberries on top. Pour the water over the fruit, scatter about half the almonds and half the remaining crumbs over the top, and dot with half the cold butter pieces. Layer the remaining fruit over the top, scatter the remaining almonds and crumbs over the fruit, dot with the remaining butter, and bake till the casserole is bubbly and browned on top, 40 to 45 minutes. Serve warm with scoops of ice cream.

MAKES 6 SERVINGS

Contrary to popular belief, brown bettys can be made with many fruits other than apples, this elegant dessert casserole being just one example. Although soft bread crumbs can be substituted for the cake crumbs, the result will not be quite as sumptuous. If I don't have some sort of leftover cake sitting about, I might even buy a small, cheap, commercial pound cake just to have the right crumbs for this dessert. Three to four cups of frozen sliced peaches and about two cups of frozen raspberries can be substituted for the fresh, but if you do this, delete the one-third cup of water.

Raspberry and Blueberry Crunch

Wild raspberries are mentioned in documents as a staple for the Massachusetts Bay colonists, and later on, Captain James Cook wrote about the fat blueberries used by settlers in all sorts of desserts. Debate rages today about which region produces the finest raspberries, and I'm not about to argue whether the low-bush blueberries of Maine are superior to the high-bush berries of New Jersey, North Carolina, and Washington State. What I will say is that I simply can't imagine a more delectable berry dessert than this simple casserole with a crunchy topping that is utterly irresistible. It's best warm enough for vanilla ice cream to melt all over the top, but I also don't hesitate to eat it cold on a hot summer day.

2 pints fresh raspberries, picked over and rinsed

2 pints fresh blueberries, picked over and rinsed

3/4 cup granulated sugar

1 1/2 cups all-purpose flour

1 cup firmly packed light brown sugar

1/2 teaspoon salt

3/4 cup (1 1/2 sticks) cold butter, cut into pieces

Vanilla ice cream or whipped cream

1. Preheat the oven to 350°F. Butter a 2-quart casserole and set aside.

2. In a large mixing bowl, combine the raspberries, blueberries, and granulated sugar, toss well, and transfer to the prepared casserole.

3. In another large mixing bowl, combine the flour, brown sugar, and salt and stir till well blended. Add the butter to the flour mixture and work the butter into the flour with your fingertips till the mixture resembles coarse meal. Sprinkle the mixture evenly over the berries and bake till bubbly and golden, 45 to 50 minutes. Allow to cool slightly, then serve with vanilla ice cream or whipped cream spooned over each portion.

MAKES 6 SERVINGS

Cape Cod Cranberry-Apple Casserole Cobbler

3 1/2 cups fresh or thawed frozen cranberries, picked over and rinsed

1 cup sweetened cranberry juice

2 medium-size cooking apples (such as Granny Smith)

1 tablespoon finely chopped orange peel

1 cup all-purpose flour, plus more if needed

2 teaspoons baking powder

1 cup sugar

2 large eggs, beaten

1 cup milk

1 teaspoon pure vanilla extract

1 teaspoon grated lemon peel

Whipped cream or vanilla ice cream

1. In a large, heavy, nonreactive saucepan, combine the cranberries and cranberry juice, bring to a boil, reduce the heat to low, and simmer till the cranberries pop, about 10 minutes.

2. Meanwhile, core, peel, and cut the apples into 1/2-inch-thick slices (about 2 cups). Add them to the cranberries along with the orange peel, return the heat to a simmer, and cook about another 10 minutes.

3. Preheat the oven to 375°F. Grease a 2-quart casserole and set aside.

4. Sift the flour and baking powder together in a large mixing bowl, then add the sugar, eggs, milk, vanilla, and lemon peel and stir with a wooden spoon till well blended, adding a little more flour if necessary to produce a loose but not wet batter.

5. Pour the apple mixture into the prepared casserole, scrape the batter evenly over the top, and bake till golden brown, 35 to 40 minutes. Serve hot or at room temperature with whipped cream or ice cream on top.

MAKES 6 SERVINGS

Although the cranberry bogs of New Jersey, Wisconsin, and Oregon constitute a major industry for these states, without doubt the plumpest and most flavorful cranberries in America are those cultivated around Cape Cod, Massachusetts. Combine these luscious berries with the region's equally superior Baldwin apples in a casserole cobbler as did a lady I used to visit in East Sandwich and even Southerners would be put to shame. This cobbler is ideal for either Thanksgiving or Christmas, and at other times of the year you might make it with fresh raspberries and blackberries, pears and apricots, or mangoes and oranges. Cranberries are widely available during the cold months, but be warned that even the frozen ones virtually disappear from most markets by March.

Apple and Raisin Brown Betty

The origins of the name brown betty are lost in history, but, most likely, they extend back to rural England long before the dish itself was popularized in America in the mid-nineteenth century as a clever and delicious way to use up stale bread. Don't worry if the casserole looks initially over-crowded; the apples will cook down fairly quickly. For variations, cooking pears or about ten fresh apricots can be substituted for the apples—so long as they're not too soft.

6 large Granny Smith or Rome apples

3 tablespoons fresh lemon juice

2 cups coarse stale bread crumbs

$^1/_2$ cup (1 stick) butter, melted

$^1/_2$ cup granulated sugar

$^1/_2$ cup firmly packed light brown sugar

1 teaspoon ground cinnamon

Grated peel of $^1/_2$ orange

1 cup seedless dark raisins

$^1/_2$ cup boiling water

Heavy cream

1. Preheat the oven to 350°F. Butter a 2$^1/_2$-quart casserole and set aside.

2. Peel and core the apples, slice thinly, sprinkle with 1 tablespoon of the lemon juice, and set aside.

3. Place the bread crumbs in a medium-size mixing bowl. In a small mixing bowl, combine the butter and remaining 2 tablespoons lemon juice, stir till well blended, pour over the bread crumbs, and mix well. In another small mixing bowl, combine the two sugars, cinnamon, and orange peel and mix well.

4. Arrange a layer of apples over the bottom of the prepared casserole, sprinkle part of the raisins over the apples, spoon about one third of the bread crumb mixture over the top, and sprinkle part of the sugar mixture over the crumbs. Repeat till all the ingredients are used up, but before adding the final layer of crumbs, pour the boiling water over the top, then add the remaining crumbs and sugar mixture.

5. Cover the casserole with aluminum foil and bake till the apples are soft, about 30 minutes. Uncover and continue to bake till the top is browned and crumbly, about 10 minutes. Serve warm with cream spooned over the top of each portion.

MAKES 8 SERVINGS

New England Indian Pudding

One of America's oldest desserts, Indian pudding was called "Indian meal" by the early colonists and was most surely prepared originally in iron casseroles over an open fire. Eventually in Puritan New England, it evolved as a dessert to be cooked along with baked beans on Saturday night, and even today, no authentic New England weekend boiled dinner is complete without a good Indian pudding smothered with freshly whipped cream.

4 cups milk

$^1/_3$ cup yellow cornmeal

$^1/_4$ cup ($^1/_2$ stick) butter

$^1/_2$ cup pure maple syrup

$^1/_4$ cup molasses

$^1/_2$ teaspoon ground cinnamon

$^1/_2$ teaspoon ground nutmeg

$^1/_8$ teaspoon salt

$^1/_3$ cup seedless golden raisins

$^1/_3$ cup cored and finely diced apple

2 large eggs, beaten

Vanilla ice cream or whipped cream

1. Preheat the oven to 325°F. Butter a 1$^1/_2$-quart casserole and set aside.

2. In a large heavy saucepan, bring the milk almost to a boil, then add the cornmeal in a steady stream, whisking constantly. Reduce the heat to moderate and continue to cook till the mixture thickens. Add the butter, maple syrup, molasses, cinnamon, nutmeg, and salt, stir till well blended, remove from the heat, and fold in the raisins and apples. Add the eggs and stir till well blended.

3. Scrape the mixture into the prepared casserole and bake till firm, about 1 hour. Serve at room temperature with ice cream or whipped cream.

MAKES 6 SERVINGS

Oregon Two-Bread Pudding

3 large eggs

1 cup sugar

3 tablespoons butter, melted

1 teaspoon pure vanilla extract

$^1/_2$ teaspoon ground cinnamon

$^1/_2$ teaspoon ground nutmeg

2 cups milk

$^1/_2$ cup seedless golden raisins

2 to 3 cups stale white bread cubes

2 cups stale whole wheat bread cubes

Whipped cream

1. Preheat the oven to 325°F. Butter a 1$^1/_2$-quart casserole and set aside.

2. In a large mixing bowl, beat the eggs till very frothy, add the sugar, butter, vanilla, cinnamon, and nutmeg, and beat till well blended. Add the milk, beat till well blended, then stir in the raisins.

3. In a medium-size mixing bowl, combine the bread cubes, then layer them in the prepared casserole. Pour the egg mixture over the top, toss till the bread is well soaked, and let stand for 1 hour, patting the bread down into the liquid from time to time.

4. Place the casserole in the oven and bake till the pudding is set, about 30 minutes. Increase the oven temperature to 375°F and continue to bake till puffed and nicely browned, about 30 minutes. Serve warm with whipped cream.

MAKES 6 SERVINGS

I assume that bread pudding was introduced to the Oregon Territory in the late eighteenth century by British fur traders from Canada. Whatever the origins, I'm sure that the dessert was a staple in certain Northwest homes by the late nineteenth century since none other than James Beard used to tell me about the spicy two- and three-bread puddings with currants or raisins his English mother prepared in one of her colorfully glazed casseroles—served with either a custard or lemon sauce. Today, bread pudding is relished as much in Louisiana (where it's often served with a bourbon sauce) and Massachusetts as in Oregon, made either with slices of day-old buttered bread or, as here, bread cubes drenched in a spicy custard sauce. Personally, I like my bread pudding topped with nothing more than a few fluffs of whipped cream.

Double Chocolate and Nut Delight

Today, some food snobs love nothing more than to blindly ridicule the entire casserole craze that overtook the country back in the 1940s and '50s. No doubt some terrible culinary abuses did occur during that carefree era, but when you find truly delectable creations like this chocolate wonder included in a 1954 casserole booklet, it only confirms the opinion that there were just as many serious cooks around then as now. What happens here is that the pudding separates into a rich but feathery cake with a creamy sauce below, produced partly by the use of unenriched cake flour milled from soft wheat. It's an exquisite dessert that can enhance even the most formal dinner.

1¼ cups cake flour

1 cup granulated sugar

2 teaspoons baking powder

¼ teaspoon salt

One 1-ounce square unsweetened (baking) chocolate

2 tablespoons butter

½ cup milk

1 teaspoon pure vanilla extract

½ cup chopped pecans or walnuts

½ cup firmly packed light brown sugar

2 tablespoons unsweetened cocoa powder

1 cup boiling water

Whipped cream

1. Preheat the oven to 350°F. Butter a shallow 2-quart casserole.

2. In a large mixing bowl, sift together the flour, ¾ cup of the granulated sugar, baking powder, and salt and set aside.

3. In a small heavy saucepan, combine the chocolate and butter over very low heat and stir till the chocolate melts and the mixture is smooth. Add the milk and vanilla and stir till well blended and smooth. Add the chocolate mixture to the dry ingredients and stir till thoroughly blended. Add the nuts and stir till evenly distributed. Scrape the mixture into the prepared casserole.

4. In a small mixing bowl, combine the remaining ¼ cup granulated sugar, the brown sugar, and cocoa and sprinkle the mixture evenly over the batter in the casserole. Slowly pour the water around the edges and bake till cake is firm, 45 to 50 minutes. Serve warm with whipped cream.

MAKES 8 SERVINGS

Crazy for Casseroles

Index

ABOUT THE AUTHOR

For more than thirty years James Villas has enjoyed a career as one of the best known and most respected authorities on American cuisine. He was the food and wine editor of *Town & Country* for 27 years, as well as the author of hundreds of articles appearing in magazines such as *Gourmet*, *Bon Appétit*, and *Esquire*. Villas has written numerous cookbooks, three of which he co-authored with his mother, Martha Pearl Villas, and one memoir.

Villas grew up in North Carolina and earned his doctoral degree from the University of North Carolina. He also attended the University of Grenoble in France as a Fulbright Scholar. Among his many awards he won the James Beard Journalism Award in 2000; he was also a James Beard Book Award nominee in 1995 for his book *My Mother's Southern Kitchen*. He has been listed in Who's Who in American Food and Wine, and his books *My Mother's Southern Desserts* and *My Mother's Southern Entertaining* have been included in *Food & Wine's Best of the Best* series. Villas lives in New York City and East Hampton, New York.